W9-BVY-490

# Java EE Development with Eclipse

Develop Java EE applications with Eclipse and commonly used technologies and frameworks

**Deepak Vohra**

*dongwaters2@gmail*
*1!A1M*

*oracle d.e gmail*
*1392 I*

[PACKT] open source*

PUBLISHING    community experience distilled

BIRMINGHAM - MUMBAI

# Java EE Development with Eclipse

Copyright © 2012 Packt Publishing

All rights reserved. No part of this book may be reproduced, stored in a retrieval system, or transmitted in any form or by any means, without the prior written permission of the publisher, except in the case of brief quotations embedded in critical articles or reviews.

Every effort has been made in the preparation of this book to ensure the accuracy of the information presented. However, the information contained in this book is sold without warranty, either express or implied. Neither the author, nor Packt Publishing, and its dealers and distributors will be held liable for any damages caused or alleged to be caused directly or indirectly by this book.

Packt Publishing has endeavored to provide trademark information about all of the companies and products mentioned in this book by the appropriate use of capitals. However, Packt Publishing cannot guarantee the accuracy of this information.

First published: December 2012

Production Reference: 1131212

Published by Packt Publishing Ltd.
Livery Place
35 Livery Street
Birmingham B3 2PB, UK.

ISBN 978-1-78216-096-0

www.packtpub.com

Cover Image by Asher Wishkerman (wishkerman@hotmail.com)

# Credits

**Author**
Deepak Vohra

**Reviewers**
Filippo Bosi
Frank Nimphius
Federico Tomassetti
Phil Wilkins

**Acquisition Editors**
Mary Nadar
Dhwani Devater

**Lead Technical Editors**
Sweny M. Sukumaran
Neeshma Ramakrishnan

**Technical Editors**
Sharvari Baet
Devdutt Kulkarni

**Project Coordinator**
Amey Sawant

**Proofreader**
Maria Gould

**Indexer**
Tejal R. Soni

**Production Coordinator**
Conidon Miranda

**Cover Work**
Conidon Miranda

# About the Author

**Deepak Vohra** is a consultant and a principal member of the NuBean.com
software company. Deepak is a Sun Certified Java Programmer and Web
Component Developer, and has worked in the fields of XML and Java programming
and J2EE for over five years. Deepak is the co-author of the Apress book, *Pro XML
Development with Java Technology,* and was the technical reviewer for the O'Reilly
book, *WebLogic: The Definitive Guide.* Deepak was also the technical reviewer for the
Course Technology PTR book, *Ruby Programming for the Absolute Beginner,* and the
technical editor for the Manning Publications book, *Prototype and Scriptaculous in
Action.* Deepak is also the author of the Packt Publishing books, *JDBC 4.0 and Oracle
JDeveloper for J2EE Development, Processing XML documents with Oracle JDeveloper 11g,
EJB 3.0 Database Persistence with Oracle Fusion Middleware 11g,* and *Java 7 JAX-WS
Web Services.*

# About the Reviewers

**Filippo Bosi** (Twitter @filippobosi) is currently employed at Imola Informatica (www.imolinfo.it), an Italian consulting company where he works as Senior Advisor, managing important projects for banking and insurance companies.

He has been working for more than 25 years in the computer programming field. He started his career as a freelance consultant and writer for some Italian computer magazines, while at the same time offering freelance consultancies in the first years that banking and insurance companies were starting to move away from mainframes in order to implement their business.

In the last four years, he's been involved in redesigning from scratch the entire information system of a banking institution in an SOA fashion, in studying ways to apply Semantic Web technologies to address Enterprise Architecture and Knowledge Management problems for some Italian large banking and insurance companies, and an European project (Cloud4SOA – www.cloud4soa.eu) that attempts, through the use of semantics, to address the portability of applications and data between different PaaS providers.

He is currently interested in Agile and Lean Management (applied), design of SOA Architectures, Enterprise Architecture, Cloud Computing, and Semantic Web.

He can be contacted at fbosi@imolinfo.it.

**Frank Nimphius** is a Senior Principal Product Manager in the Oracle Application Development Tools group at Oracle Corporation, specializing in Oracle JDeveloper and the Oracle Application Development Framework (ADF).

In his current position, Frank represents and evangelizes the Oracle JDeveloper and Oracle ADF product worldwide as a speaker at user group and technology conferences, as well as in various publications. Frank runs the ADF Code Corner website, the *OTN Forum Harvest* blog, and is the co-author of the *Oracle Fusion Developer Guide* book published in 2009 by McGraw Hill.

**Federico Tomassetti** is a software engineer and a PhD student in computer engineering. He is interested mainly in model-driven development and domain specific languages. He has experience as a technical writer, teacher, and consultant about these technologies.

He is studying at the Politecnico di Torino. He spent a semester in the Universität Karlsruhe and one at Fortiss, an Institut of the Technische Universität München.

**Phil Wilkins** has spent nearly 25 years in the software industry working with both multinationals and software startups. He started out as a developer and has worked his way up through technical and development management roles. The last 12 years have been primarily in Java based environments. He now works as an architect with an enterprise wide technical remit within the IT group for a global optical healthcare manufacturer and retailer.

Outside of his work commitments, he has contributed his technical capabilities to supporting others in a wide range of activities from the development of community websites to providing input and support to people authoring books, and developing software ideas and businesses.

When not immersed in work and technology, he spends his down time pursing his passion for music and time with his wife and two boys.

I'd like to take this opportunity to thank my wife Catherine and our two sons Christopher and Aaron for their tolerance for the innumerable hours that I spent in front of a computer contributing to both my employer and the many other IT related activities that I've supported over the years.

# www.PacktPub.com

## Support files, eBooks, discount offers and more

You might want to visit www.PacktPub.com for support files and downloads related to your book.

Did you know that Packt offers eBook versions of every book published, with PDF and ePub files available? You can upgrade to the eBook version at www.PacktPub.com and as a print book customer, you are entitled to a discount on the eBook copy. Get in touch with us at service@packtpub.com for more details.

At www.PacktPub.com, you can also read a collection of free technical articles, sign up for a range of free newsletters and receive exclusive discounts and offers on Packt books and eBooks.

PACKTLiB®

http://PacktLib.PacktPub.com

Do you need instant solutions to your IT questions? PacktLib is Packt's online digital book library. Here, you can access, read and search across Packt's entire library of books.

## Why Subscribe?

- Fully searchable across every book published by Packt
- Copy and paste, print and bookmark content
- On demand and accessible via web browser

## Free Access for Packt account holders

If you have an account with Packt at www.PacktPub.com, you can use this to access PacktLib today and view nine entirely free books. Simply use your login credentials for immediate access.

## Instant Updates on New Packt Books

- Get notified! Find out when new books are published by following @PacktEnterprise on Twitter, or the *Packt Enterprise* Facebook page..

# Table of Contents

# Preface

Java Platform, Enterprise Edition (Java EE) 6 is the industry standard for enterprise Java computing. Eclipse IDE for Java EE developers is the most commonly used Java IDE for Java EE development. Eclipse IDE for Java EE developers supports Java EE 5 completely and also supports several features from Java EE 6.

The Oracle WebLogic Server product line is the industry's most comprehensive platform for developing, deploying, and integrating enterprise applications. Oracle Enterprise Pack for Eclipse provides a set of plugins (project facets) for Eclipse development with WebLogic Server.

While a number of books are available on Eclipse IDE for Java Developers, none or very few are available on Eclipse IDE for Java EE Developers. In this book, we shall discuss Java EE development in Eclipse IDE for Java EE developers. While it is not feasible to cover all of the more than 30 technologies in the Java EE stack (`http://www.oracle.com/technetwork/java/javaee/tech/index.html`), we shall discuss the most commonly used Java EE technologies, especially the ones Eclipse IDE for Java EE developers (or Oracle Enterprise Pack for Eclipse) provides Project for Facets. Oracle Enterprise Pack for Eclipse is just an enhancement of Eclipse IDE for Java EE developers with integrated support for Oracle WebLogic Server.

The objective of the book is to discuss how a developer would develop Java EE applications using commonly used Java EE technologies and frameworks in Eclipse IDE for Java EE developers. The book covers all aspects of application development including:

- Setting the environment for an application
- Using the Eclipse IDE wizards and the Component Palette
- Running a sample application

# What this book covers

*Chapter 1, EJB 3.0 Database Persistence* discusses creating an EJB project using the EJB 3.0 Module project facet. To create an entity bean, we add the JPA project facet. Subsequently, we generate entity beans from Oracle database tables. We create a session bean facade for the entity beans; wrapping an entity bean in a session bean facade is a best practice. We create a JSP client for the EJB application. We package and deploy the EJB application to Oracle WebLogic Server using an Ant build script and run the test client on the WebLogic Server.

*Chapter 2, O/X Mapping with JAXB 2.x* discusses the Object/XML (O/X) bi-directional mapping provided by the JAXB framework. We discuss the advantages of JAXB 2.x over JAXB 1.0. We create a JAXB web project using the JAXB project facet. We use the EclipseLink 2.4 persistence provider. We create an XML Schema and generate JAXB classes from the XML Schema using JAXB schema compilation. Subsequently, we marshall an XML document from a Java **Document Object Model (DOM)** document object, and also unmarshall an XML document using the compiled Java classes. We map an annotated Java class to an XML document using the annotations API. We also demonstrate the support for mapping Java classes to an XML Schema.

*Chapter 3, Developing a Web Project for JasperReports* demonstrates the use of the Oracle Enterprise Pack for Eclipse's integrated support for Oracle WebLogic Server to deploy and run any web application that requires an application server. First, we configure an Oracle database data source in WebLogic Server. We create and deploy a web application for JasperReports to the WebLogic Server, and subsequently run the web application to create PDF and Excel reports.

*Chapter 4, Creating a JSF Data Table* discusses how to use the JavaServer Faces project facet to create a JSF data table. First, we create a web project. Subsequently, we create a managed bean, create a JSF page, add a JSF data table to the JSF page, and run the JSF web application on the integrated WebLogic Server to create a JSF data table.

*Chapter 5, Templating with Facelets* discusses templating with Facelets. **Templating** is the use of a common "template", which is just an XHTML page, in Facelets' composition pages. Templating makes use of Facelets' header and footer pages for describing the common sections of Facelets' composition pages. WebLogic Server includes a shared library for JSF 2.0, which we configure first. We create a web project for Facelets, and create a managed bean to create a JSF data table. We add the 2.0 version of the JavaServer Faces project facet to the web project. For templating, we add a Facelets Template in which we configure the default sections of a Facelets composition page, a header, a content section, and a footer. We add Facelets composition pages for an SQL query input and a JSF Data Table output. We add the implicit navigation, a new feature in JSF 2.0. We run the Facelets application to demonstrate templating by including the same header and footer images in the input and output pages.

*Chapter 6, Creating Apache Trinidad User Interfaces* discusses the Trinidad project facet. Trinidad was formerly Oracle ADF Faces and provides a set of user interface components. First, we create a web project and add the Trinidad project facet to it. Subsequently, we create JSPs to create and find a catalog entry in Oracle database. We add Trinidad components to the JSP pages. We run the Trinidad application in the integrated WebLogic Server.

*Chapter 7, Creating an AJAX Application* discusses how to develop an AJAX application to send an asynchronous request to the server and receive a response from the server. The JavaScript project facet is enabled by default in a web project. The AJAX application is used to create a catalog entry in Oracle database by first validating the catalog ID using AJAX. The application is packaged, deployed, and run on the WebLogic Server.

*Chapter 8, Creating a JAX-WS Web Service* discusses how to use the Java API for XML web services (JAX-WS) to create a web service. First, we create a web service project, which has the Oracle WebLogic web service project facet associated with it. We test the web service on the server and generate a WSDL, which we test in the web explorer. We create a client class for the web service and package, then deploy and test the web service on the WebLogic Server.

*Chapter 9, RESTful Web Services Using the JAX-RS API* discusses RESTful web services using **Java API for RESTful web services (JAX-RS)**, which are specified in the JSR 311 specification. We use the JAX-RS project facet for the RESTful web service. We create a Resource class, which is exposed as a URI path using the @PATH annotation. Subsequently, we create a Jersey Client API to test the web service.

*Chapter 10, Spring* discusses how to create a Spring framework application using the Spring project facet. We discuss method interception with a method interceptor and a Spring client. We also discuss Aspect Oriented Programming (AOP) in combination with JSF. We discuss creating a Spring bean, a bean definition file, and an AOP JavaBean.

# What you need for this book

The book is based on Eclipse IDE for Java EE Developers version 3.7. We use the Oracle Enterprise Pack for Eclipse packaged Eclipse IDE with integrated support for Oracle WebLogic Server 12*c*, which may be downloaded from `http://www.oracle.com/technetwork/middleware/ias/downloads/wls-main-097127.html`. We have used the Oracle Database Express Edition 11g Release 2, which can be downloaded from `http://www.oracle.com/technetwork/products/express-edition/overview/index.html`.

Some other chapter specific software such as JasperReports is also required. We have used the Windows version, but if you have Linux installed the book may still be used (though the source code and samples have not been tested with Linux). Slight modifications may be required with the Linux Install; for example, the directory paths on Linux would be different than the Windows directory paths used in the book. You need to install J2SE 5.0 or later.

# Who this book is for

The target audience of the book is Java EE application developers who want to learn about the practical use of Eclipse IDE for application development. This book is suitable for professional Java EE developers. The book is also suitable for an intermediate/advanced level course in Java EE development. The target audience is expected to have prior, albeit beginner's, knowledge about Java EE, Enterprise JavaBeans (EJB) 3.0, entity and session EJBs, JavaServer Faces (JSF), ADF Faces, AJAX, web services, and Spring framework. The book also requires some familiarity with WebLogic Server and Eclipse IDE.

# Conventions

In this book, you will find a number of styles of text that distinguish between different kinds of information. Here are some examples of these styles, and an explanation of their meaning.

Code words in text are shown as follows: "The `catalog.xsd` Schema gets parsed and compiled."

A block of code is set as follows:

```xml
<?xml version="1.0" encoding="UTF-8"?>
<xsd:schema xmlns:xsd="http://www.w3.org/2001/XMLSchema"
    targetNamespace="http://www.example.org/catalog"
  xmlns:catalog="http://www.example.org/catalog"
    elementFormDefault="qualified">
    <xsd:element name="catalog" type="catalog:catalogType" />
    <xsd:element name="catalogid" type="xsd:int" />
    <xsd:complexType name="catalogType"> [default]
```

When we wish to draw your attention to a particular part of a code block, the relevant lines or items are set in bold:

```xml
<?xml version="1.0" encoding="UTF-8"?>
<xsd:schema xmlns:xsd="http://www.w3.org/2001/XMLSchema"
    targetNamespace="http://www.example.org/catalog"
  xmlns:catalog="http://www.example.org/catalog"
    elementFormDefault="qualified">
    <xsd:element name="catalog" type="catalog:catalogType" />
```

**New terms** and **important words** are shown in bold. Words that you see on the screen, in menus or dialog boxes for example, appear in the text like this: "clicking the **Next** button moves you to the next screen".

 Warnings or important notes appear in a box like this.

 Tips and tricks appear like this.

# Reader feedback

Feedback from our readers is always welcome. Let us know what you think about this book—what you liked or may have disliked. Reader feedback is important for us to develop titles that you really get the most out of.

To send us general feedback, simply send an e-mail to feedback@packtpub.com, and mention the book title through the subject of your message.

If there is a topic that you have expertise in and you are interested in either writing or contributing to a book, see our author guide on www.packtpub.com/authors.

# Customer support

Now that you are the proud owner of a Packt book, we have a number of things to help you to get the most from your purchase.

# Downloading the example code

You can download the example code files for all Packt books you have purchased from your account at http://www.packtpub.com. If you purchased this book elsewhere, you can visit http://www.packtpub.com/support and register to have the files e-mailed directly to you.

# Errata

Although we have taken every care to ensure the accuracy of our content, mistakes do happen. If you find a mistake in one of our books—maybe a mistake in the text or the code—we would be grateful if you would report this to us. By doing so, you can save other readers from frustration and help us improve subsequent versions of this book. If you find any errata, please report them by visiting http://www.packtpub.com/support, selecting your book, clicking on the **errata submission form** link, and entering the details of your errata. Once your errata are verified, your submission will be accepted and the errata will be uploaded to our website, or added to any list of existing errata, under the Errata section of that title.

# Piracy

Piracy of copyright material on the Internet is an ongoing problem across all media. At Packt, we take the protection of our copyright and licenses very seriously. If you come across any illegal copies of our works, in any form, on the Internet, please provide us with the location address or website name immediately so that we can pursue a remedy.

Please contact us at copyright@packtpub.com with a link to the suspected pirated material.

We appreciate your help in protecting our authors, and our ability to bring you valuable content.

# Questions

You can contact us at questions@packtpub.com if you are having a problem with any aspect of the book, and we will do our best to address it.

# Copyright Credits

Some of the contents of this book were originally published by Oracle Technology Network and http://home.java.net/. They are republished with the permission of Oracle Corporation.

# 1
# EJB 3.0 Database Persistence

EJB's **entity beans** are the most common technology for database persistence. Developing entity EJBs requires a Java IDE, an application server, and a relational database. Eclipse 3.7 provides wizards for developing entity beans and session facades. In this chapter, we shall develop EJB 3.0 entity beans including session facades. We shall deploy the EJB application to WebLogic Server 12*c* (12.1.1) and test database persistence with the Oracle database 11g XE.
In this chapter, we shall learn the following:

- Configuring a data source in **WebLogic Server (WLS)** with the Oracle database
- Creating tables in the Oracle database
- Creating an **Enterprise JavaBeans (EJB)** project
- Adding the **Java Persistence API (JPA)** project facet
- Generating entity beans from database tables
- Creating a session bean facade
- Creating the `application.xml` file
- Creating a test client
- Packaging and deploying the entity bean application
- Testing the **JavaServer Pages** (JSP) client

# Configuring a data source

In this section we shall configure a data source in Oracle WebLogic Server 12*c*. First, download and install the Oracle WebLogic Server from `http://www.oracle.com/technetwork/middleware/ias/downloads/wls-main-097127.html`. Configure the **base_domain** structure in the **WebLogic Server** console. We need to create a data source so that when we deploy and run the application in the server, the application has access to the database. Log in to the **WebLogic Server Administration Console** server for the **base_domain** domain using the URL `http://localhost:7001/Console`. In the **base_domain** domain structure, expand the **Services** tab and select the **Data Sources** node. In the **Data Sources** table, click on **New** and select **Generic Data Source** as shown in the following screenshot:

In **Create a New JDBC Data Source**, specify a data source name and **JNDI Name** (for example, **jdbc/OracleDS**) for the data source. The database shall be accessed using **JNDI Name** lookup in the *Creating a session bean facade* section. Select **Database Type** as **Oracle** and click on **Next** as shown in the following screenshot:

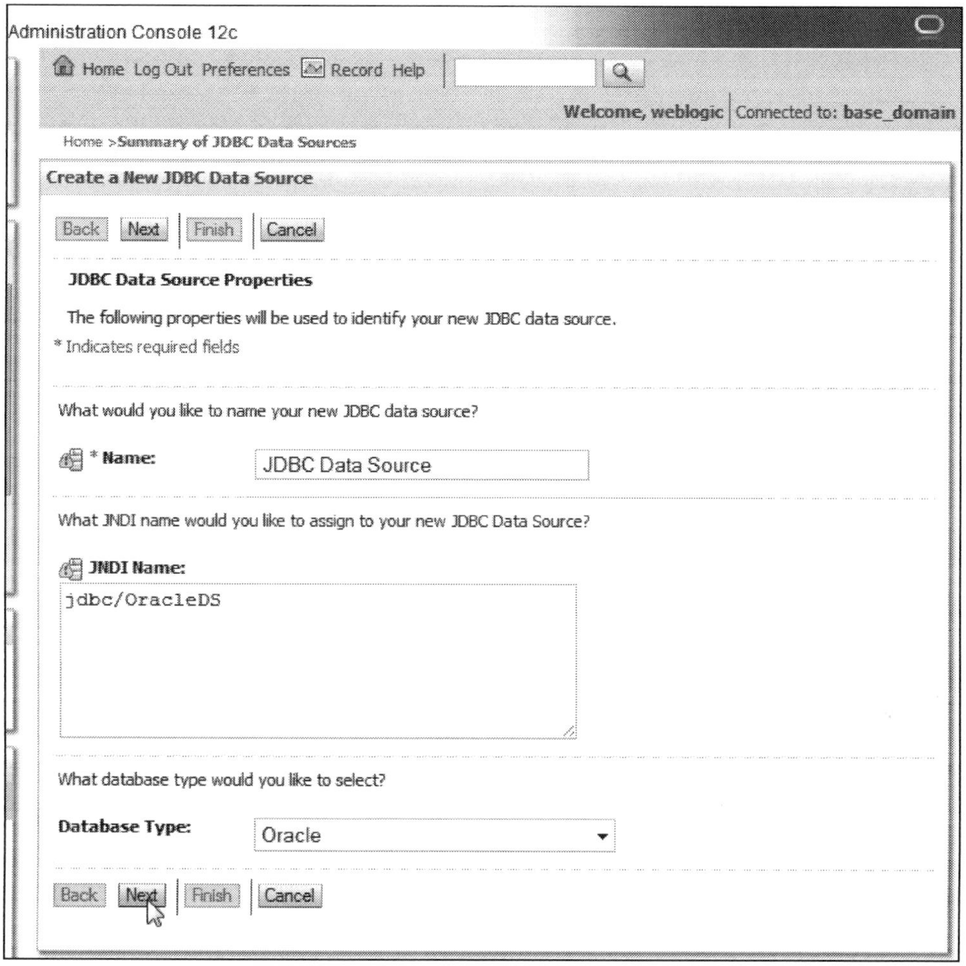

In **JDBC Data Source Properties**, select **Database Driver** as **Oracle's Driver (Thin XA)**. Another JDBC driver may also be selected based on requirements. Refer to the *Selection of the JDBC Driver* document available at `http://docs.oracle.com/cd/E14072_01/java.112/e10590/keyprog.htm#i1005587` for selecting a suitable JDBC driver. Click on **Next** as shown in the following screenshot:

By default, an XA JDBC driver supports global transactions and uses the *Two-Phase Commit* global transaction protocol. **Global transactions** are recommended for EJBs using container managed transactions for relation between the JDBC driver (XA or non-XA) transactionality and EJB container managed transactions. Click on **Next** as shown in the following screenshot. (for more information on global transactions, refer `http://docs.oracle.com/cd/E23943_01/web.1111/e13737/transactions.htm`):

Administration Console 12c

🏠 Home  Log Out  Preferences  📈 Record  Help    [                ] [🔍]

**Welcome, weblogic** | Connected to: **base_domain**

Home >**Summary of JDBC Data Sources**

**Create a New JDBC Data Source**

[ Back ]  [ Next ]  [ Finish ]  [ Cancel ]

**Transaction Options**

You have selected an XA JDBC driver to use to create database connection in your new data source. The data source will support global transactions and use the 'Two-Phase Commit' global transaction protocol. No other transaction configuration options are available.

[ Back ]  [ Next ]  [ Finish ]  [ Cancel ]

Specify **Database Name** as XE, **Host Name** as localhost, **Port** as 1521, **Database User Name** and **Password** as OE, and click on **Next** as shown in the following screenshot:

Administration Console 12c

🏠 Home  Log Out  Preferences  📈 Record  Help    [                ] [🔍]

**Welcome, weblogic** | Connected to: **base_domain**

Home >**Summary of JDBC Data Sources**

**Create a New JDBC Data Source**

[ Back ]  [ Next ]  [ Finish ]  [ Cancel ]

**Connection Properties**

Define Connection Properties.

What is the name of the database you would like to connect to?
**Database Name:** [ XE ]

What is the name or IP address of the database server?
**Host Name:** [ localhost ]

What is the port on the database server used to connect to the database?
**Port:** [ 1521 ]

What database account user name do you want to use to create database connections?
**Database User Name:** [ OE ]

What is the database account password to use to create database connections?
**Password:** [ •• ]

**Confirm Password:** [ •• ]

The **Driver Class Name** textbox and connection **URL** textbox get configured. Click on the **Test Configuration** button to test the database connection. If a connection gets established the message **Connection test succeeded.** gets displayed. Click on **Next** as shown in the following screenshot:

In **Select targets**, select the **AdminServer** option and click on **Finish**. A data source gets added to the data sources table. The data source configuration may be modified by clicking on the data source link as shown in the following screenshot:

# Creating tables in the Oracle database

We need to create database tables for database persistence. Create database tables CATALOG, EDITION, SECTION, and ARTICLE with the following SQL script; the script can be run from the SQL command line:

```
CREATE TABLE CATALOG (id INTEGER PRIMARY KEY NOT NULL,
journal VARCHAR(100));
CREATE TABLE EDITION (id INTEGER PRIMARY KEY NOT NULL,
edition VARCHAR(100));
CREATE TABLE SECTION (id VARCHAR(100) PRIMARY KEY NOT NULL,
sectionName VARCHAR(100));
CREATE TABLE ARTICLE(id INTEGER PRIMARY KEY NOT NULL,
title VARCHAR(100));
```

As Oracle database does not support the autoincrement of primary keys, we need to create sequences for autoincrementing, one for each table. Create sequences CATALOG_SEQ, EDITION_SEQ, SECTION_SEQ, and ARTICLE_SEQ with the following SQL script.

```
CREATE SEQUENCE CATALOG_SEQ MINVALUE 1 START WITH 1 INCREMENT BY 1
NOCACHE;
CREATE SEQUENCE EDITION_SEQ MINVALUE 1 START WITH 1 INCREMENT BY 1
NOCACHE;
CREATE SEQUENCE SECTION_SEQ MINVALUE 1 START WITH 1 INCREMENT BY 1
NOCACHE;
CREATE SEQUENCE ARTICLE_SEQ MINVALUE 1 START WITH 1 INCREMENT BY 1
NOCACHE;
```

We also need to create join tables between tables. Create join tables using the following SQL script:

```
CREATE TABLE  CATALOGEDITIONS(catalogId INTEGER, editionId INTEGER);
CREATE TABLE EditionCatalog(editionId INTEGER, catalogId INTEGER);
CREATE TABLE EditionSections (editionId INTEGER, sectionId INTEGER);
CREATE TABLE SectionEdition (sectionId INTEGER, editionId INTEGER);
CREATE TABLE SectionArticles(sectionId INTEGER, articleId INTEGER);
CREATE TABLE ArticleSection(articleId INTEGER, sectionId INTEGER);
```

# Creating an EJB project

Now, we shall create an EJB project to create entity beans.

In Eclipse, go to **File** | **New** | **Other** to create an EJB project. In the **New** wizard, select **EJB Project** from the **EJB** folder and click on **Next** as shown in the following screenshot:

Specify a **Project name** and click on **New Runtime** to configure a target runtime for **Oracle WebLogic Server 12c** if not already configured, as shown in the following screenshot:

In **New Server Runtime Environment**, select the **Oracle WebLogic Server 12c (12.1.1)** server, tick **Create a new local server** checkbox, and then click on **Next** as shown in the following screenshot:

Select the **WebLogic home** directory, and the **Java home** directory also gets specified. Click on **Next** as shown in the following screenshot:

Select **Server Type** as **Local** and then select **Domain Directory** as `C:\Oracle\Middleware\user_project\domains\base_domain`. Click on **Finish** as shown in the screenshot:

The **Target runtime** server gets configured. Select **EJB module version** as **3.1**. Select the default **Configuration** and click on **Next** as shown in the following screenshot:

Select the default Java configuration for **Source folders on build path** as **ejbModule** and **Default output folder** as `build/classes`, and click on **Next** as shown in the following screenshot:

Select the default EJB module configuration and click on **Finish**. An EJB project gets created. The EJB project does not contain any EJBs, which we shall add in subsequent sections.

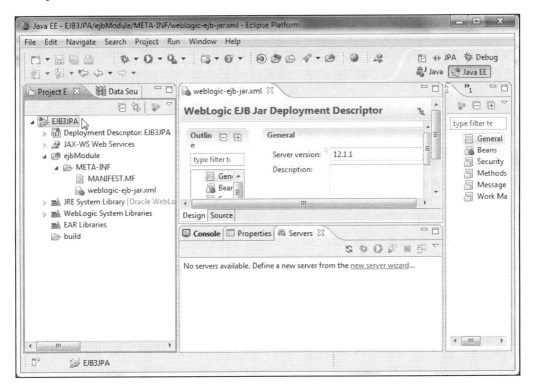

Right-click on the project node in the **Project Explorer** tab and select **Project Properties**. Select **Project Facets** in the **Properties** window. The EJB project should have the **EJB Module** project facet enabled as shown in the following screenshot:

Session beans require an EJB project and entity beans require the JPA project facet for database persistence. We have created an EJB project but this EJB project does not have the **JPA** project facet enabled by default. In the next section, we shall add the **JPA** facet to the EJB project.

# Adding the JPA facet

We require the JPA project facet to create entity beans. We could have created a
JPA project to start with, but to create a session bean facade we first created an EJB
project; session beans require an EJB project by default. To add the JPA project facet,
right-click on the project in **Project Explorer** and select **Properties**. Select the **Project
Facets** node and select the **JPA 1.0** project facet. Click on the **Further configuration
available** link as shown in the screenshot:

In **JPA Facet**, select **Platform** as **Generic 1.0**. Select **JPA implementation** as **Oracle
TopLink 11g R1**. We also need a database connection for JPA. To configure a new
**Connection**, click on the **Add connection** link as shown in the following screenshot:

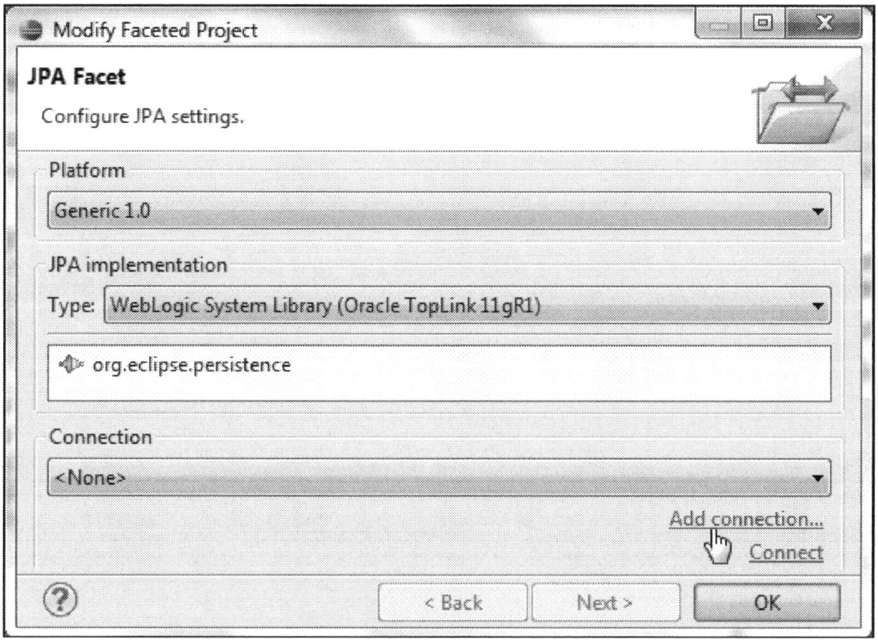

In **Connection Profile**, select the **Oracle Database Connection** profile, specify a connection **Name** and click on **Next** as shown in the following screenshot:

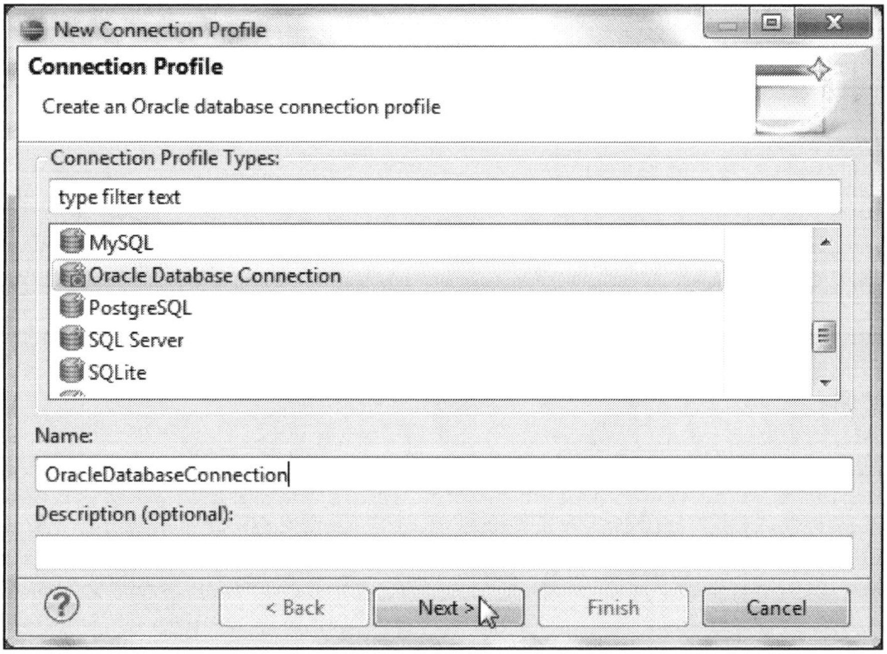

In the **Specify a Driver and Connection Details** window, select the driver as **Oracle Database 10g Driver**. Specify **SID** as XE, **Host** as localhost, **Port number** as 1521, **User name** as OE, and **Password** as OE. The **Connection URL** gets specified. Now, click on **Test Connection** as shown in the following screenshot:

A **Ping succeeded** message indicates that the connection got established. Click on **Next** and then click on **Finish** in **Summary**. A **Connection** for the **JPA Facet** gets configured. Click on **OK** as shown in the following screenshot:

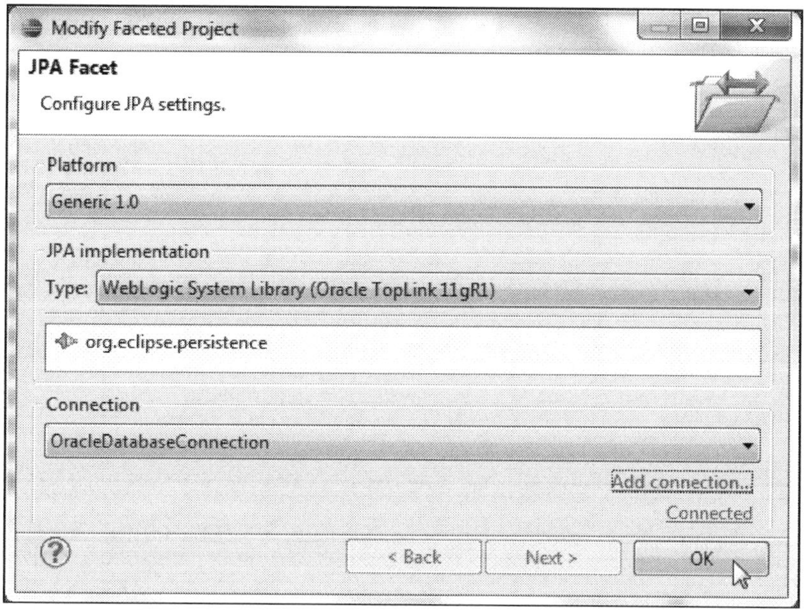

The connection profile we have configured is for the JPA project facet, not to run client applications to entity beans. The data source we configured in the WebLogic server with JNDI **jdbc/OracleDS** is for running client applications to entity beans. Click on **Apply** in **Properties** to install the **JPA** facet as shown in the following screenshot:

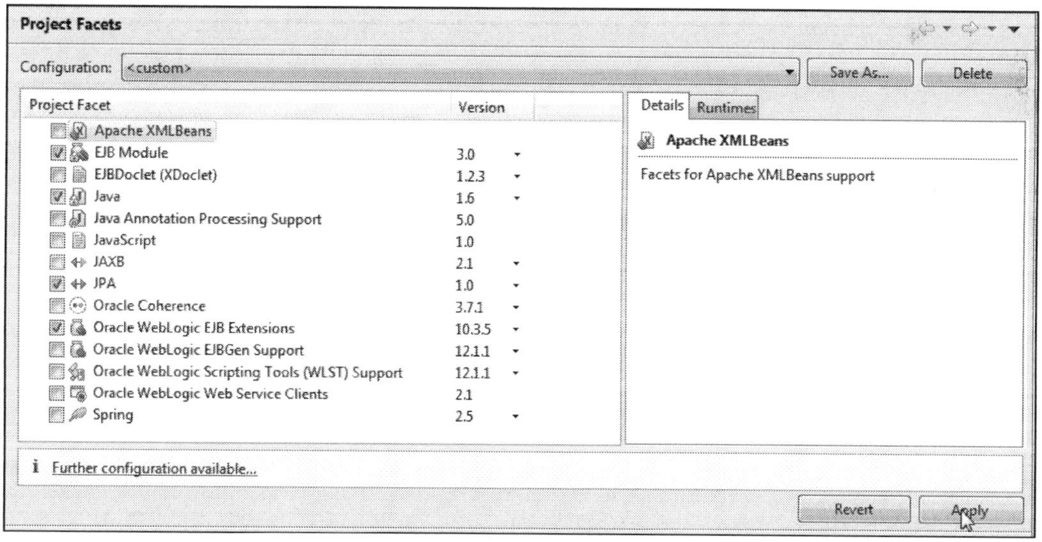

A node for **JPA Content** gets added to the EJB project. A **persistence.xml** configuration file gets added.

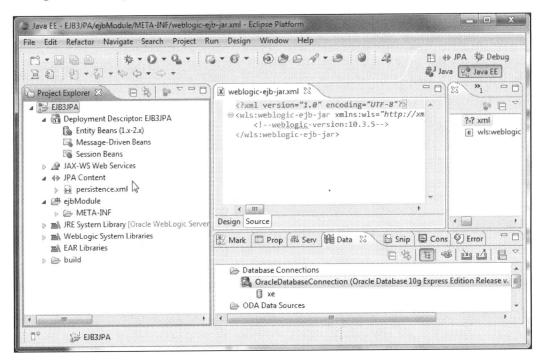

# Creating entity beans from tables

In this section, we shall create entities from database tables we created earlier. Select the project node in **Project Explorer** and go to **File | New | Other**. In the **New** wizard window, select **JPA Entites from Tables** from the **JPA** folder as shown in the following screenshot. Click on **Next**. Alternatively, you can right-click on the project node in **Project Explorer** and select **Generate Entities from Tables** from **JPA Tools**.

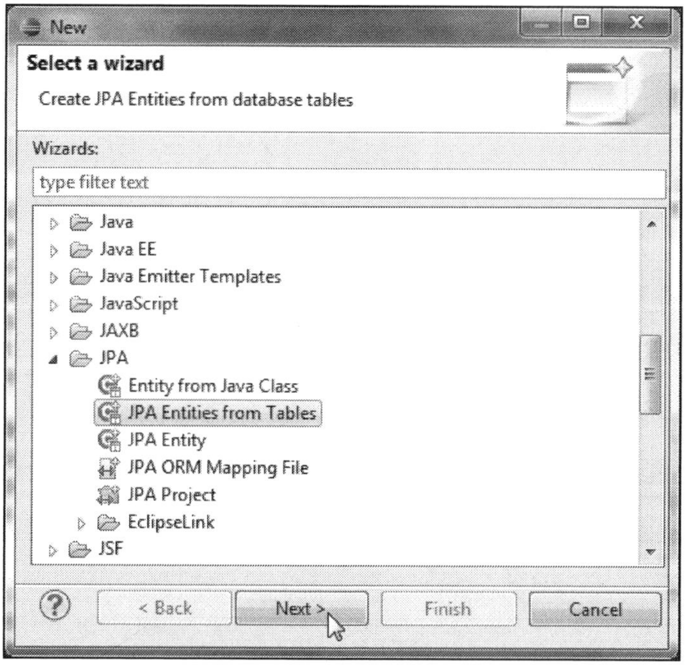

In **Select Tables**, select the database connection configured when adding the JPA project facet. Select the **OE** Schema. Select the **CATALOG, EDITION, SECTION**, and **ARTICLE** tables. Select the checkbox **Update class list in persistence.xml** and click on **Next** as shown in the following screenshot:

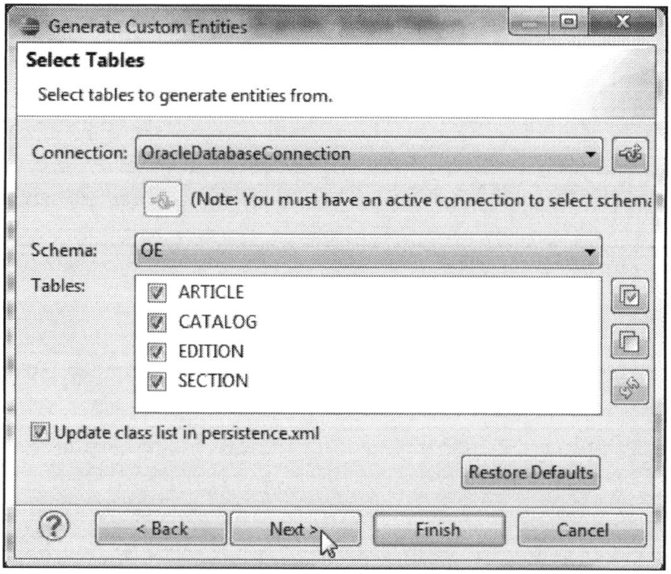

# Defining entity relationships

The entities to be generated have relationships between them. The Catalog entity has a one-to-many relationship with the Edition entity. The Edition entity has a one-to-many relationship with the Section entity and the Section entity has a further one-to-many relationship with the Article entity. In **Table Associations**, we shall define the associations between the tables. Click on the + button to create an association as shown in the following screenshot:

In **Association Tables**, select the tables to create an association between them. We will need to create an association for each of the relationships. Click on the button for the **Table 1** field as shown in the following screenshot:

Select the **CATALOG** table and click on **OK**, as shown in the following screenshot:

Similarly, select **EDITION** as **Table 2**. The **Association kind** is **Simple association** by default, which is what we need. Now, click on **Next** as shown in the following screenshot:

Specify the join columns between the **CATALOG** and **EDITION** tables as **ID** using the **Add** button and click on **Next** as shown in the following screenshot:

As the `Catalog` entity has a one-to-many relation with the `Edition` entity, in **Association Cardinality** select **One to many** and click on **Finish** as shown in the following screenshot:

The table association between the **CATALOG** and **EDITION** tables gets defined and the table join also gets defined.

# Setting cascade

We need to set the cascade value for the association. **Cascading** is used to cascade database table operations to related tables. Select the button adjacent to the **Cascade** field for the **catalog** property as shown in the following screenshot:

Cascade specifies the operations that must be cascaded to the target of the association. The join table is defined on the owning side of the association and cascade operations may be initiated from the owning side. In a one-to-many relationship, the many side is always the owning side of the relationship, which makes the **Edition** the owning side. But, in a bi-directional relationship operations may be initiated from the non-owning side by specifying a join table on the non-owning side also. The **mappedBy** element is only specified on the non-owning side. In the **Edition** entity, select the **Cascade** operations to be **persist**, **merge**, and **refresh**. The **remove** option is not included as we don't want to delete the one-side entity if a many-side entity is deleted as other many-side entities may still be present. Click on **OK** as shown in the following screenshot:

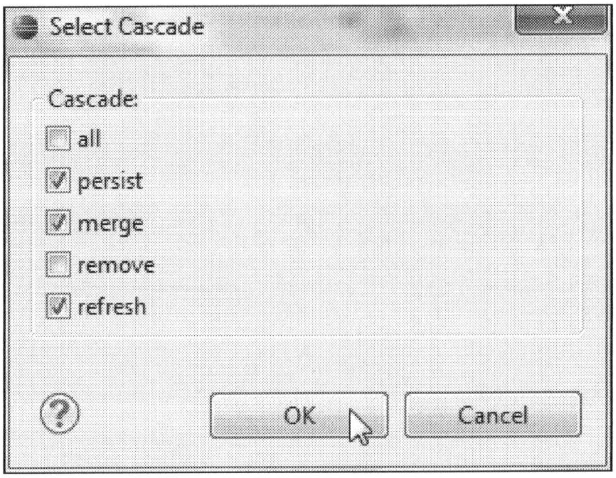

Similarly, select the **Cascade** button for the **Catalog** entity as shown in the following screenshot:

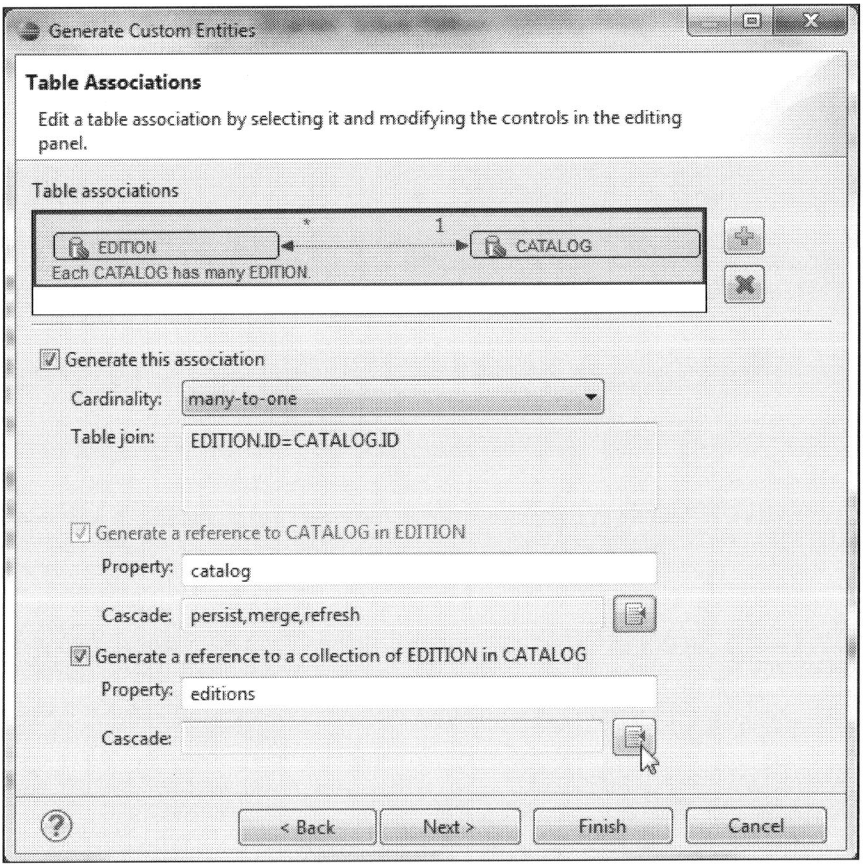

Set the **Cascade** element to **all** as we want to delete all `Edition` entities if the associated `Catalog` entity is deleted as shown in the following screenshot:

The **Cascade** values get specified. Similarly, define associations between the **EDITION** and **SECTION**, and **SECTION** and **ARTICLE** tables. After the associations are defined, click on **Next** as shown in the following screenshot:

# Generating default entities

In this section, we shall customize the default entity generation. The aspects of entities that may be customized are the **Table Mapping** (primary key generator, sequence name, entity access, association fetch, and collection properties type) and Java class. **EclipseLink** creates entity identifiers (primary keys) using one of the strategies specified in the JPA specification; sequence objects, identity columns, tables, or provider specified strategy. Oracle database supports sequences, therefore we shall use **sequence** as the **Key generator**. Specify a sequence generator with **Sequence name** to be the pattern $table_seq. The $table variable shall be replaced by the table name. Specify **Entity access** as **Property**, and **Associations fetch** as **Eager**. With **Eager** fetching the associated entities are immediately fetched when an entity is retrieved. Select **Collection properties type** as **java.util.List**. Specify the **Source Folder** path and **Package** for the entities and click on **Next**.

The provision to customize individual entities is provided, but we don't need to customize individual entities as we already customized the default entity generation which applies to all the entities. Now, click on **Finish** as shown in the following screenshot:

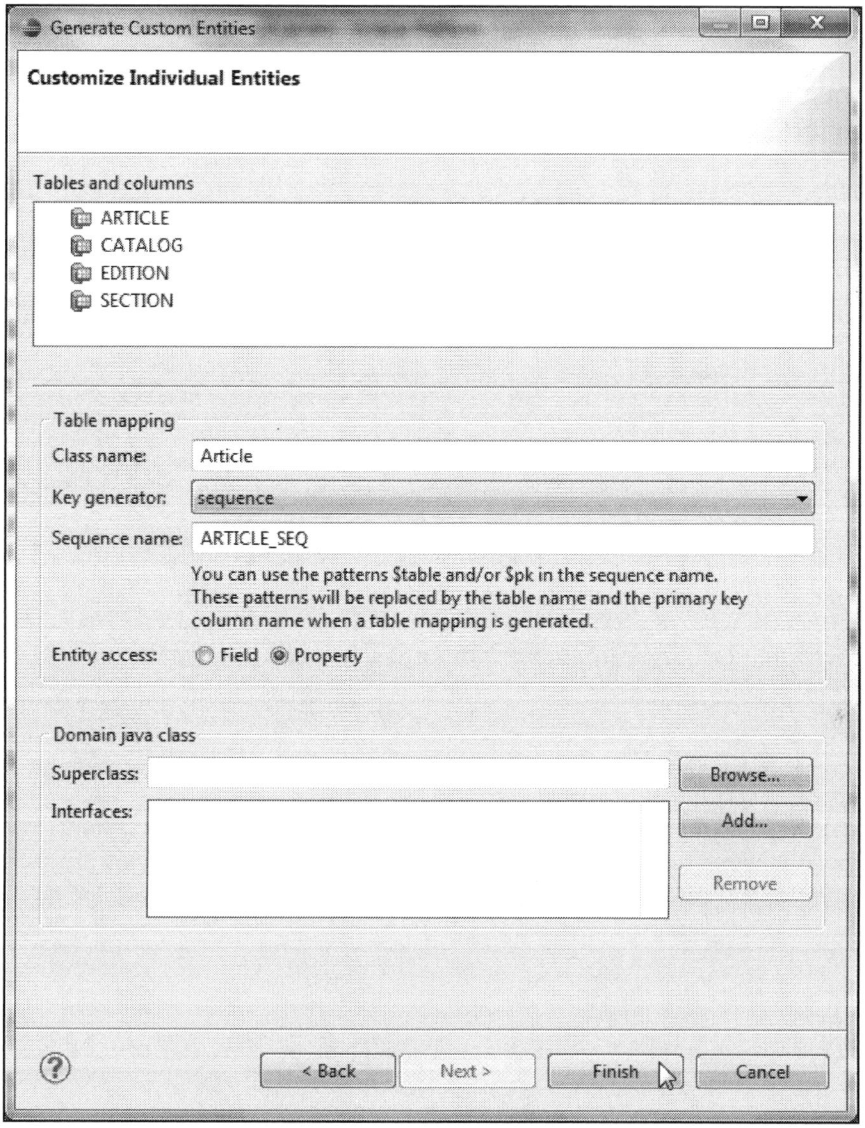

The entities **Catalog, Edition, Section**, and **Article** get created as shown in the following screenshot:

A JPA diagram that shows the relationships between the different entities may also be created. Right-click on **perstistence.xml** and select **Open Diagram** as shown in the following screenshot:

Click on each of the entities in the **Project Explorer** tab and drag the entities to the **JPA Diagram** tab. The relationships diagram between the entities gets displayed as shown in the following screenshot:

The entities are generated automatically by the JPA project facet and may need some customization, such as adding named queries. Next, we construct the entities, and add additional configuration for the entity relationships. We shall discuss the subsequent sections including the entity code automatically generated. If some of the subsequent additions are already in the entities, those code additions do not have to be re-added.

# Creating the Catalog entity

The Catalog entity is the persistent class for the CATALOG database table. The class is annotated with the @Entity annotation that specifies the class to be an entity bean named queries findCatalogAll, which selects all Catalog entities, and findCatalogByJournal, which selects a Catalog entity by Journal, are specified using the @NamedQueries and @NamedQuery annotations.

```
@Entity
@NamedQueries({
    @NamedQuery(name="findCatalogAll", query="SELECT c FROM Catalog
c"),
    @NamedQuery(name="findCatalogByJournal",
        query="SELECT c FROM Catalog c WHERE c.journal = :journal")
})
```

The entity class implements the Serializable interface to serialize a cache enabled entity bean to a cache when persisted to a database. To associate a version number with a serializable class by serialization runtime, specify a serialVersionUID variable.

```
private static final long serialVersionUID = 1L;
```

The Catalog entity includes variables id (primary key), journal of type String, and editions for the Edition entities associated with a Catalog entity.

```
private int id;
private String journal;
private List<Edition> editions;
```

**Downloading the example code**

You can download the example code files for all Packt books you have purchased from your account at http://www.packtpub.com. If you purchased this book elsewhere, you can visit http://www.packtpub.com/support and register to have the files e-mailed directly to you.

The @Id annotation specifies the identifier property. The @Column annotation specifies the column name associated with the property. The nullable element is set to false as the primary key is not nullable. As we selected the primary key generator to be of the type sequence, the @SequenceGenerator annotation is specified with a sequence name. The generation strategy is specified with the @GeneratedValue annotation. The getter and setter methods for the identifier property are also specified.

```
@Id
@Column(name="ID", nullable=false)
@SequenceGenerator(name="CATALOG_ID_GENERATOR", sequenceName="CATALOG_
SEQ",allocationSize=1)
@GeneratedValue(strategy=GenerationType.SEQUENCE, generator="CATALOG_
ID_GENERATOR")
  public int getId() {
    return this.id;
  }
  public void setId(int id) {
    this.id = id;
  }
```

Similarly, specify getter and setter methods for the `journal` property. The `@OneToMany` annotation specifies the bi-directional many-to-one association to `Edition`. The `mappedBy` element is specified on the non-owning side of the relationship, which is the `Catalog` entity. The `cascade` element is set to ALL as we discussed earlier. The `fetch` element is set to EAGER. A join table is included on the non-owning side to initiate cascade operations using the `@JoinTable` annotation. The join columns are specified using the `@JoinColumn` annotation. The getter and setter methods for the `Edition` collection are also specified.

```
@OneToMany(mappedBy="catalog", cascade={CascadeType.ALL},
fetch=FetchType.EAGER)
  @JoinTable(name="CATALOGEDITIONS",
    joinColumns=
        @JoinColumn(name="catalogId", referencedColumnName="ID"),
      inverseJoinColumns=
      @JoinColumn(name="editionId", referencedColumnName="ID")
      )
public List<Edition> getEditions() {
    return this.editions;
  }
public void setEditions(List<Edition> editions) {
    this.editions = editions;
  }
```

Methods `addEdition` and `removeEdition` are also included to add and remove `Edition` entities. For a more detailed discussion on entity beans refer to the *EJB 3.0 Database Persistence with Oracle Fusion Middleware 11g* book.

# The Catalog entity class

The Catalog entity class is listed as follows:

```java
package ejb3;

import java.io.Serializable;
import javax.persistence.*;
import java.util.List;
/**
 * The persistent class for the CATALOG database table.
 *
 */
@Entity
@NamedQueries({
    @NamedQuery(name="findCatalogAll", query="SELECT c FROM Catalog
c"),
    @NamedQuery(name="findCatalogByJournal",
        query="SELECT c FROM Catalog c WHERE c.journal = :journal")
  })
public class Catalog implements Serializable {
  private static final long serialVersionUID = 1L;
  private int id;
  private String journal;
  private List<Edition> editions;

    public Catalog() {
    }
  @Id
  @Column(name="ID", nullable=false)
  @SequenceGenerator(name="CATALOG_ID_GENERATOR",
sequenceName="CATALOG_SEQ",allocationSize=1)
  @GeneratedValue(strategy=GenerationType.SEQUENCE,
generator="CATALOG_ID_GENERATOR")
  public int getId() {
    return this.id;
  }

  public void setId(int id) {
    this.id = id;
  }

  public String getJournal() {
```

```
      return this.journal;
   }

   public void setJournal(String journal) {
      this.journal = journal;
   }

   //bi-directional many-to-one association to Edition
   @OneToMany(mappedBy="catalog", cascade={CascadeType.ALL},
fetch=FetchType.EAGER)
   @JoinTable(name="CATALOGEDITIONS",
      joinColumns=
         @JoinColumn(name="catalogId", referencedColumnName="ID"),
      inverseJoinColumns=
      @JoinColumn(name="editionId", referencedColumnName="ID")
      )
   public List<Edition> getEditions() {
      return this.editions;
   }

   public void setEditions(List<Edition> editions) {
      this.editions = editions;
   }
   public void addEdition(Edition edition) {
      this.getEditions().add(edition);
   }

   public void removeEdition(Edition edition) {
      this.getEditions().remove(edition);
   }
}
```

# Creating the Edition entity

The Edition entity includes the named queries findEditionAll and
findEditionBySection. The class specifies variables serialVersionUID, id,
edition, catalog, and sections. As in the Catalog entity, id is the identifier
property. The bi-directional many-to-one association to the Catalog relationship
is specified using the @ManyToOne annotation. The Edition entity is the owning
side of the relationship. A bi-directional many-to-one association to Section is
also specified. Add and remove methods for the Catalog and Section entities
are also specified. The discussion that applies to the Catalog entity also applies
to the other entities, and has been omitted here for the other entities.

# The Edition entity class

The `Edition` entity is listed as follows:

```java
package ejb3;

import java.io.Serializable;
import javax.persistence.*;

import java.util.List;
/**
 * The persistent class for the EDITION database table.
 *
 */
@Entity
@NamedQueries( { @NamedQuery(name = "findEditionAll",
        query = "SELECT e FROM Edition e")
,
@NamedQuery(name = "findEditionByEdition", query = "SELECT e from
Edition e WHERE e.edition = :edition")
} )
public class Edition implements Serializable {
  private static final long serialVersionUID = 1L;
  private int id;
  private String edition;
  private Catalog catalog;
  private List<Section> sections;

    public Edition() {
    }

  @Id
  @Column(name="ID", nullable=false)
  @SequenceGenerator(name="EDITION_ID_GENERATOR",
sequenceName="EDITION_SEQ",allocationSize=1)
  @GeneratedValue(strategy=GenerationType.SEQUENCE,
generator="EDITION_ID_GENERATOR")
  public int getId() {
    return this.id;
  }
  public void setId(int id) {
    this.id = id;
  }
  //bi-directional many-to-one association to Catalog
  @ManyToOne(cascade={CascadeType.PERSIST, CascadeType.MERGE,
CascadeType.REFRESH})
```

```java
  @JoinTable(name = "EditionCatalog",
              joinColumns = { @JoinColumn(name = "editionId",referenc
edColumnName = "ID")
              } ,
inverseJoinColumns = { @JoinColumn(name = "catalogId",
referencedColumnName ="ID")})
  public Catalog getCatalog() {
    return this.catalog;
  }
  public void setCatalog(Catalog catalog) {
    this.catalog = catalog;
  }


  //bi-directional many-to-one association to Section
  @OneToMany(mappedBy="edition", cascade={CascadeType.ALL},
fetch=FetchType.EAGER)
  @JoinTable(name = "EditionSections",
              joinColumns = { @JoinColumn(name = "editionId",
                                          referencedColumnName =
"ID")
              } ,
        inverseJoinColumns = { @JoinColumn(name = "sectionId",
referencedColumnName =
                                          "ID")
              } )
  public List<Section> getSections() {
    return this.sections;
  }
  public void setSections(List<Section> sections) {
    this.sections = sections;
  }
  public void addSection(Section section) {
      this.getSections().add(section);
      section.setEdition(this);
    }
  public String getEdition() {
      return edition;
    }
    public void setEdition(String edition) {
        this.edition = edition;
    }
    public void removeSection(Section section) {
        this.getSections().remove(section);
    }
}
```

# Creating the Section entity

The Section entity has the named queries findSectionAll and
findSectionBySectionName, and the properties id, sectionname, articles, and
edition. A bi-directional many-to-one association to Article and a bi-directional
many-to-one association to Edition are specified. Add and remove methods for
the Edition and Article entities are also specified.

## The Section entity class

The Section entity is listed as follows:

```
package ejb3;

import java.io.Serializable;
import javax.persistence.*;
import java.util.List;


/**
 * The persistent class for the SECTION database table.
 *
 */
@Entity
@NamedQueries({
    @NamedQuery(name="findSectionAll", query="SELECT s FROM Section
s"),
    @NamedQuery(
      name="findSectionBySectionName", query="SELECT s from Section s
WHERE s.sectionname = :section")
  })
public class Section implements Serializable {
  private static final long serialVersionUID = 1L;
  private int id;
  private String sectionname;
  private List<Article> articles;
  private Edition edition;

    public Section() {
    }
  @Id
  @Column(name="ID", nullable=false)
  @SequenceGenerator(name="SECTION_ID_GENERATOR",
sequenceName="SECTION_SEQ",allocationSize=1)
```

```
  @GeneratedValue(strategy=GenerationType.SEQUENCE,
generator="SECTION_ID_GENERATOR")
  public int getId() {
    return this.id;
  }
  public void setId(int id) {
    this.id = id;
  }
  public String getSectionname() {
    return this.sectionname;
  }

  public void setSectionname(String sectionname) {
    this.sectionname = sectionname;
  }
  //bi-directional many-to-one association to Article
  @OneToMany(mappedBy="section", cascade={CascadeType.ALL},
fetch=FetchType.EAGER)
  @JoinTable(name = "SectionArticles",
          joinColumns = {
              @JoinColumn(name="sectionId",
referencedColumnName="ID")},
              inverseJoinColumns = { @JoinColumn(name="articleId",
referencedColumnName="ID")})
  public List<Article> getArticles() {
    return this.articles;
  }
  public void setArticles(List<Article> articles) {
    this.articles = articles;
  }
  //bi-directional many-to-one association to Edition
  @ManyToOne(cascade={CascadeType.PERSIST, CascadeType.MERGE,
CascadeType.REFRESH})
  @JoinTable(name = "SectionEdition",
              joinColumns = { @JoinColumn(name = "sectionId",
                                          referencedColumnName =
"ID")
                } ,
        inverseJoinColumns = { @JoinColumn(name = "editionId",
referencedColumnName =
                                          "ID")
                } )

  public Edition getEdition() {
```

```
    return this.edition;
  }
  public void setEdition(Edition edition) {
    this.edition = edition;
  }
  public void addArticle(Article article) {
      this.getArticles().add(article);
      article.setSection(this);
  }
  public void removeArticle(Article article) {
      this.getArticles().remove(article);
  }
}
```

# Creating the Article entity

The `Article` entity has a named query `findArticleAll`, and the properties `id`, `title`, and `section`. A bi-directional many-to-one association to `Section` is also defined.

## The Article entity class

The `Article` entity is listed as follows:

```
package ejb3;

import java.io.Serializable;
import javax.persistence.*;
/**
 * The persistent class for the ARTICLE database table.
 *
 */
@Entity
@NamedQueries({
    @NamedQuery(name="findArticleAll", query="SELECT a FROM Article
a"),
    @NamedQuery(
      name="findArticleByTitle", query="SELECT a from Article a WHERE
a.title = :title")
  })
public class Article implements Serializable {
  private static final long serialVersionUID = 1L;
  private int id;
  private String title;
  private Section section;
```

```
    public Article() {
    }

  @Id
  @Column(name="ID", nullable=false)
  @SequenceGenerator(name="ARTICLE_ID_GENERATOR",
sequenceName="ARTICLE_SEQ",allocationSize=1)
  @GeneratedValue(strategy=GenerationType.SEQUENCE,
generator="ARTICLE_ID_GENERATOR")
  public int getId() {
    return this.id;
  }

  public void setId(int id) {
    this.id = id;
  }

  public String getTitle() {
    return this.title;
  }

  public void setTitle(String title) {
    this.title = title;
  }


  //bi-directional many-to-one association to Section
  @ManyToOne(cascade={CascadeType.PERSIST, CascadeType.MERGE,
CascadeType.REFRESH})
  @JoinTable(name = "ArticleSection",
        joinColumns = {
            @JoinColumn(name="articleId", referencedColumnName="ID")},
            inverseJoinColumns = { @JoinColumn(name="sectionId",
referencedColumnName="ID")})
  public Section getSection() {
    return this.section;
  }
  public void setSection(Section section) {
    this.section = section;
  }

}
```

In the **Project Explorer**, the entity beans will show some errors if the sequences or join tables have not yet been created.

# Creating the JPA persistence configuration file

The `persistence.xml` configuration file specifies a persistence provider to be used for persisting the entities to the database. The persistence unit is specified using the `persistence-unit` element. The `transaction-type` is set to `JTA` by default. The persistence provider is specified as `org.eclipse.persistence.jpa.PersistenceProvider`. The `jta-data-source` element specifies the JTA data source. The entity classes are specified using the class element. The `eclipselink.target-server` property specifies the target server as `WebLogic 10g`. The `eclipselink.target-database` property specifies the target database as `Oracle`. The DDL generation strategy is set to `create-tables` using the `eclipselink.ddl-generation` property. Other EclipseLink properties (`http://wiki.eclipse.org/Using_EclipseLink_JPA_Extensions_%28ELUG%29#Using_EclipseLink_JPA_Extensions_for_Sch`) may also be specified as required. The `persistence.xml` configuration file is listed as follows:

```xml
<?xml version="1.0" encoding="UTF-8"?>
<persistence version="1.0" xmlns="http://java.sun.com/xml/ns/
persistence" xmlns:xsi="http://www.w3.org/2001/XMLSchema-instance"
xsi:schemaLocation="http://java.sun.com/xml/ns/persistence http://
java.sun.com/xml/ns/persistence/persistence_1_0.xsd">
  <persistence-unit name="em" transaction-type="JTA">
    <provider>org.eclipse.persistence.jpa.PersistenceProvider</
provider>
    <jta-data-source>jdbc/OracleDS</jta-data-source>
    <class>ejb3.Article</class>
    <class>ejb3.Catalog</class>
    <class>ejb3.Edition</class>
    <class>ejb3.Section</class>
    <properties>
      <property name="eclipselink.target-server" value="WebLogic_10"/>
      <property name="eclipselink.target-database" value="Oracle"/>
      <property name="eclipselink.ddl-generation" value="create-
tables"/>
      <property name="eclipselink.logging.level" value="FINEST"/>
    </properties>
  </persistence-unit>
</persistence>
```

The `eclipselink.ddl-generation` property may be set to `create-tables` or `drop-and-create-tables`, which drops tables if already created and creates new tables. In development the `drop-and-create-tables` may be used as the schema may need to be updated and data cleared. We have set `eclipselink.ddl-generation` to `create-tables`, which creates tables only if the tables are not already created. The JPA specification does not mandate the creating of tables and only some JPA persistence providers create tables. If it is not known whether a persistence provider supports table generation it is better to create the tables, sequences, and join tables as we have also set the `eclipselink.ddl-generation` value to `create-tables`.

# Creating a session bean facade

For better performance, wrap the entity bean in a session bean facade. The performance benefits of a session facade are fewer remote method calls and an outer transaction context with which each getter method invocation does not start a new transaction. Session facade is one of the core Java EE design patterns (`http://www.oracle.com/technetwork/java/sessionfacade-141285.html`). To create a session bean, go to **File | New | Other** and select **EJB | Session Bean (EJB 3.X)** and click on **Next** as shown in the following screenshot:

Select the EJB project in which you want to create a session bean. The **Source folder** and package are the same as the folder for the entity classes. Specify **Class name** as `CatalogSessionBeanFacade`. Select the session bean **State type** as **Stateless**, which does not incur the overhead of keeping the state of the session bean. Select **Remote** for the **Create business** interface option and specify the remote class name as **CatalogSessionBeanFacadeRemote**. Now, click on **Next** as shown in the following screenshot:

Specify **Mapped name** as **EJB3-SessionEJB**, **Transaction Type** as **Container**. The mapped name is used to look up the session bean from a client. Now, click on **Finish** as shown in the following screenshot:

A session bean class and the remote business interface get created. The session bean class is annotated with the `@Stateless` annotation with name and `mappedName` elements.

```
@Stateless(name="CatalogSessionBean", mappedName="EJB3-SessionEJB")
public class CatalogSessionBeanFacade implements
CatalogSessionBeanFacadeRemote { }
```

Next, we will modify the default session bean generated by the session bean wizard.

# Creating an EntityManager

An **EntityManager** is used to create, remove, find, and query persistence entity instances. Inject an `EntityManager`, using the `@PersistenceContext` annotation. Specify the `unitName` as the `unitName` configured in `persistence.xml`.

```
@PersistenceContext(unitName = "em")
    EntityManager em;
```

# Specifying getter methods

In this section, we shall specify getter methods for `Collections` of entities. For example, the `getAllEditions` method gets all `Edition` entities using the named query `findEditionAll`. The `createNamedQuery` method of `EntityManager` is used to create a `Query` object from a named query. Specify the `TransactionAttribute` annotation's `TransactionAttributeType` enum to `REQUIRES_NEW`, with which the EJB container invokes a session bean method with a new transaction context. `REQUIRES_NEW` has the advantage that if a transaction is rolled back due to an error in a different transaction context from which the session bean is invoked it does not effect the session bean that has the `TransactionAttributeType` set to `REQUIRES_NEW`.

```
@TransactionAttribute(TransactionAttributeType.REQUIRES_NEW)
    public List<Edition> getAllEditions() {
        ArrayList<Edition> editions = new ArrayList<Edition>();
        Query q = em.createNamedQuery("findEditionAll");
        for (Object ed : q.getResultList()) {
            editions.add((Edition)ed);
        }
        return editions;
    }
```

# Creating test data

As we have EJB relationships between different entities, making modifications such as updating or deleting data would affect the associated entities. To demonstrate the use of the entities, we shall create some test data and subsequently delete the data. Create test data with the `createTestData` convenience method in the session bean. Alternatively, a unit test or an extension class may also be used. Create a `Catalog` entity and set the journal using the `setJournal` method. Persist the entity using the `persist` method of the `EntityManager` object and synchronize the entity with the database using the `flush` method.

```
Catalog catalog1 = new Catalog();
        catalog1.setId(1);
        catalog1.setJournal("Oracle Magazine");
        em.persist(catalog1);
        em.flush();
```

Similarly, we can use the create, persist, and flush methods in an `Edition` entity object. Before adding the `Edition` object to the database merge the `Catalog` entity with the persistence context using the `merge` method.

```
Edition edition = new Edition();
        edition.setEdition("January/February 2009");
        em.persist(edition);

        em.flush();
        em.merge(catalog1);
        catalog1.addEdition(edition);
```

Similarly, add the `Section` and `Article` entity instances. Delete some data with the `deleteSomeData` method in which we shall create a `Query` object using the named query `findArticleByTitle`. Specify the article title using the `setParameter` method of the `Query` object. Get the result `List` using the `getResultList` method of the `Query` object. Iterate over the result `List` and remove the article using the `remove` method of the `EntityManager` object.

```
public void deleteSomeData() {
        // remove an article
    Query q = em.createNamedQuery("findArticleByTitle");
        q.setParameter("title", "Launching Performance");
        List list = q.getResultList();
        for (Object article : list) {
            em.remove(article);
        }
    }
```

Also, add `remove<>` methods to remove entities.

# The session bean class

The session bean class is listed as follows:

```
package ejb3;

import javax.ejb.*;
import javax.persistence.*;
import java.util.*;
```

Annotate the session bean with the `@Stateless` annotation, which includes the `mappedName` used to look up the session bean from a client:

```
@Stateless(name = "CatalogSessionBean", mappedName = "EJB3-
SessionEJB")
public class CatalogSessionBeanFacade implements
CatalogSessionBeanFacadeRemote {
  @PersistenceContext(unitName = "em")
  EntityManager em;
```

Specify the getter collections methods for the different entities:

```java
@TransactionAttribute(TransactionAttributeType.REQUIRES_NEW)
public List<Edition> getAllEditions() {
  ArrayList<Edition> editions = new ArrayList<Edition>();
  Query q = em.createNamedQuery("findEditionAll");
  for (Object ed : q.getResultList()) {
    editions.add((Edition) ed);
  }
  return editions;
}

@TransactionAttribute(TransactionAttributeType.REQUIRES_NEW)
public List<Section> getAllSections() {
  ArrayList<Section> sections = new ArrayList<Section>();
  Query q = em.createNamedQuery("findSectionAll");
  for (Object ed : q.getResultList()) {
    sections.add((Section) ed);
  }
  return sections;
}

@TransactionAttribute(TransactionAttributeType.REQUIRES_NEW)
public List<Article> getAllArticles() {
  ArrayList<Article> articles = new ArrayList<Article>();
  Query q = em.createNamedQuery("findArticleAll");
  for (Object ed : q.getResultList()) {
    articles.add((Article) ed);
  }
  return articles;
}

@TransactionAttribute(TransactionAttributeType.REQUIRES_NEW)
public List<Catalog> getAllCatalogs() {

  Query q = em.createNamedQuery("findCatalogAll");
  List<Catalog> catalogs = q.getResultList();
  ArrayList<Catalog> catalogList = new ArrayList<Catalog>(catalogs.
size());
  for (Catalog catalog : catalogs) {
    catalogList.add(catalog);
  }
  return catalogList;
}
```

```
  @TransactionAttribute(TransactionAttributeType.REQUIRES_NEW)
  public List<Edition> getCatalogEditions(Catalog catalog) {
    em.merge(catalog);
    List<Edition> editions = catalog.getEditions();
    ArrayList<Edition> editionList = new ArrayList<Edition>(editions.
size());
    for (Edition edition : editions) {
      editionList.add(edition);
    }
    return editionList;
  }

  @TransactionAttribute(TransactionAttributeType.REQUIRES_NEW)
  public List<Section> getEditionSections(Edition edition) {
    em.merge(edition);
    List<Section> sections = edition.getSections();
    ArrayList<Section> sectionList = new ArrayList<Section>(sections.
size());
    for (Section section : sections) {
      sectionList.add(section);
    }
    return sectionList;
  }

  @TransactionAttribute(TransactionAttributeType.REQUIRES_NEW)
  public List<Article> getSectionArticles(Section section) {
    em.merge(section);
    List<Article> articles = section.getArticles();
    ArrayList<Article> articleList = new ArrayList<Article>(articles.
size());
    for (Article article : articles) {
      articleList.add(article);
    }
    return articleList;
  }
```

Add a convenience method to create test data.

```
  public void createTestData() {
    // create catalog for Oracle Magazine
    Catalog catalog1 = new Catalog();
    // catalog1.setId(1);
    catalog1.setJournal("Oracle Magazine");
    em.persist(catalog1);
    em.flush();
```

```
        // Add an Edition
        Edition edition = new Edition();
        // edition.setId(2);
        edition.setEdition("January/February 2009");
        em.persist(edition);
        // em.refresh(edition);
        em.flush();
        em.merge(catalog1);
        catalog1.addEdition(edition);

        // Add a Features Section
        Section features = new Section();
        // features.setId(31);
        features.setSectionname("FEATURES");
        em.persist(features);
        em.merge(edition);
        edition.addSection(features);

        // add an article to Features section
        Article article = new Article();
        // article.setId(41);
        article.setTitle("Launching Performance");
        article.setSection(features);
        em.persist(article);
        em.merge(features);
        features.addArticle(article);
        em.flush();

        // add a Technology section
        Section technology = new Section();
        // technology.setId(32);
        technology.setSectionname("Technology");
        em.persist(technology);
        em.merge(edition);
        edition.addSection(technology);
        // add an article to Technology section
        article = new Article();
        // article.setId(42);
        article.setSection(technology);
        article.setTitle("On Dynamic Sampling");
        em.persist(article);
        em.merge(technology);
        technology.addArticle(article);
        em.flush();
    }
```

Add another convenience method to delete some data.

```
public void deleteSomeData() {
  // remove an article
  Query q = em.createNamedQuery("findArticleByTitle");
  q.setParameter("title", "Launching Performance");
  List list = q.getResultList();
  for (Object article : list) {
    em.remove(article);
  }
}
```

Add some remove<Entity> methods to remove entities:

```
public void removeEdition(Edition edition) {
  Catalog catalog = edition.getCatalog();
  catalog.removeEdition(edition);

  em.remove(edition);
}

public void removeSection(Section section) {
  Edition edition = section.getEdition();
  edition.removeSection(section);
  em.remove(section);
}

public void removeArticle(Article article) {
  Section section = article.getSection();
  section.removeArticle(article);
  em.remove(article);
}
```

# The remote business interface

The remote business interface is listed as follows:

```
package ejb3;

import javax.ejb.*;
import java.util.*;

@Remote
public interface CatalogSessionBeanFacadeRemote {
```

```
    public List<Edition> getAllEditions();

    public List<Section> getAllSections();

    public List<Article> getAllArticles();

    public List<Catalog> getAllCatalogs();

    public List<Edition> getCatalogEditions(Catalog catalog);

    public List<Section> getEditionSections(Edition edition);

    public List<Article> getSectionArticles(Section section);

    public void createTestData();

    public void deleteSomeData();

    public void removeEdition(Edition edition);

    public void removeSection(Section section);

    public void removeArticle(Article article);
}
```

# Creating the application.xml descriptor

We also need to create an `application.xml` deployment descriptor to generate an EAR application to be deployed to the WebLogic Server. First, create a META-INF folder by going to **File | New | Folder**. Subsequently, create an XML file going to **File | New | Other** and then click on **XML | XML File** in the **New** wizard. Click on **Next**.

Specify the **META-INF** folder and specify the filename as `application.xml`. Click on **Next** as shown in the following screenshot:

Click on **Create an XML file from an XML template** and then click on **Next**. In **Select XML Template**, select the checkbox **Use XML Template**. Select the **xml declaration** in the **XML Template** and click on **Finish**. An `application.xml` file gets added to the `META-INF` folder. Specify an EJB module and a web module in the deployment descriptor. The `application.xml` descriptor is listed as follows:

```xml
<?xml version="1.0" encoding="UTF-8"?>
<application>
  <display-name></display-name>
  <module>
    <ejb>ejb3example.jar</ejb>
  </module>
  <module>
    <web>
      <web-uri>weblogicexample.war</web-uri>
      <context-root>weblogic</context-root>
    </web>
  </module>
</application>
```

The following screenshot shows `application.xml` in the EJB project:

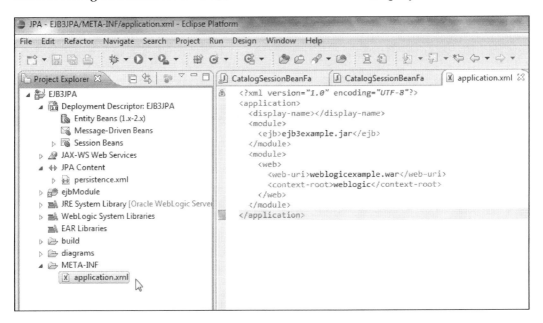

# Creating a test client

Next, we shall create a JSP client to test the entity bean. We shall look up the session bean using the global JNDI name, which includes the mapped name for the session bean. Subsequently, we shall invoke the `testData` method of the session bean to test database persistence using the entity bean. First, create a JSP file. Create a `webModule` folder for the JSP file by going to **File | New | Folder**. Specify **Folder name** as `webModule` in the **EJB3JPA** folder and click on **Finish**. Go to **File | New | Other** and select **JSP File** in **Web** and click on **Next**. Specify **JSP File name** as `catalog.jsp` and click on **Next** as shown in the following screenshot:

Select the **New JSP File (html)** template and click on **Finish**. A JSP client `catalog.jsp` gets created. Create an `InitialContext` object.

```
InitialContext context = new InitialContext();
```

Look up the remote business interface of the session bean using the global JNDI name:

```
CatalogSessionBeanFacadeRemote beanRemote =
(CatalogSessionBeanFacadeRemote) context.lookup("EJB3-SessionEJB#ejb3.
CatalogSessionBeanFacadeRemote");
```

Invoke the `createTestData` method and retrieve the `List` of `Catalog` entities:

```
beanRemote.createTestData();
List<Catalog> catalogs=beanRemote.getAllCatalogs();
```

Iterate over the `Catalog` entities and output the catalog ID, journal name. Similarly, obtain the `Entity`, `Section`, and `Article` entities and output the entity property values.

# The catalog.jsp file

The `catalog.jsp` file is listed as follows:

```
<%@ page language="java" contentType="text/html; charset=ISO-8859-1"
  pageEncoding="ISO-8859-1"%>
<!DOCTYPE HTML PUBLIC "-//W3C//DTD HTML 4.01 Transitional//EN"
"http://www.w3.org/TR/html4/loose.dtd">
<%@ page import="ejb3.*,java.util.*,javax.naming.*"%>
<html>
<head>
<meta http-equiv="Content-Type"
  content="text/html; charset=windows-1252" />
<title>EJB3 Client</title>
</head>
<body>
```

Create an `InitialContext` method to look up the session bean facade:

```
<%
    InitialContext context = new InitialContext();
    CatalogSessionBeanFacadeRemote beanRemote =
(CatalogSessionBeanFacadeRemote) context
        lookup("EJB3-SessionEJB#ejb3.CatalogSessionBeanFacadeRemote");
```

Invoke the session bean method to create test data. Subsequently, retrieve the entity beans and output the values of entities' properties:

```
    beanRemote.createTestData();
    List<Catalog> catalogs = beanRemote.getAllCatalogs();

    out.println("<br/>" + "List of Catalogs" + "<br/>");
    for (Catalog catalog : catalogs) {
      out.println("Catalog Id:");
      out.println("<br/>" + catalog.getId() + "<br/>");
      out.println("Catalog Journal:");
      out.println(catalog.getJournal() + "<br/>");
    }

    out.println("<br/>" + "List of Editions" + "<br/>");
    List<Edition> editions = beanRemote.getAllEditions();
    for (Edition edition : editions) {
      out.println("Edition Id:");
      out.println(edition.getId() + "<br/>");
      out.println("Edition Date:");
      out.println(edition.getEdition() + "<br/>");
```

```
    }
    out.println("<br/>" + "List of Sections" + "<br/>");
    List<Section> sections = beanRemote.getAllSections();
    for (Section section : sections) {
      out.println("Section Id:");
      out.println(section.getId() + "<br/>");
      out.println("Section Name:");
      out.println(section.getSectionname() + "<br/>");

    }


    out.println("<br/>" + "List of Articles" + "<br/>");
    List<Article> articles = beanRemote.getAllArticles();
    for (Article article : articles) {
      out.println("Article Id:");
      out.println(article.getId() + "<br/>");
      out.println("Article Title:");
      out.println(article.getTitle() + "<br/>");

    }
    out.println("Delete some Data" + "<br/>");
```

Invoke the session bean method to delete some data. Subsequently, retrieve the entities and output the properties of different entities:

```
    beanRemote.deleteSomeData();

    catalogs = beanRemote.getAllCatalogs();
    out.println("<br/>" + "List of Catalogs" + "<br/>");
    for (Catalog catalog : catalogs) {
      out.println("Catalog Id:");
      out.println(catalog.getId() + "<br/>");
      out.println("Catalog Journal:");
      out.println(catalog.getJournal() + "<br/>");
    }

    out.println("<br/>" + "List of Editions" + "<br/>");
    editions = beanRemote.getAllEditions();
    for (Edition edition : editions) {
      out.println("Edition Id:");
      out.println(edition.getId() + "<br/>");
      out.println("Edition Date:");
      out.println(edition.getEdition() + "<br/>");

    }
```

```
      out.println("<br/>" + "List of Sections" + "<br/>");
      sections = beanRemote.getAllSections();
      for (Section section : sections) {
        out.println("Section Id:");
        out.println(section.getId() + "<br/>");
        out.println("Section Name:");
        out.println(section.getSectionname() + "<br/>");


      }
      out.println("<br/>" + "List of Articles" + "<br/>");
      articles = beanRemote.getAllArticles();
      for (Article article : articles) {
        out.println("Article Id:");
        out.println(article.getId() + "<br/>");
        out.println("Article Title:");
        out.println(article.getTitle() + "<br/>");
      }
    %>
  </body>
</html>
```

# Packaging and deploying the entity bean application

In this section, we shall compile, package, and deploy the EJB application to the WebLogic server using an Ant build file. First, add the web.xml deployment descriptor. Create a WEB-INF folder in the webModule folder and add web.xml to the WEB-INF folder. The web.xml is an optional deployment descriptor for a web application deployed to the WebLogic descriptor and is listed as follows:

```
<?xml version="1.0" encoding="UTF-8"?>
<web-app xmlns="http://java.sun.com/xml/ns/javaee" xmlns:xsi="http://
www.w3.org/2001/XMLSchema-instance"
  xsi:schemaLocation="http://java.sun.com/xml/ns/javaee/web- app_2_5.
xsd" version="2.5">
</web-app>
```

If we were using servlets or other web application artifacts, we would have configured those in web.xml. We need a build.xml file for the tasks involved in assembling and deploying the entity bean application. Create a build.xml file in the project EJB3JPA by going to **File | New | Other** and in the **New** wizard, in **XML**, select **XML file**. Specify the following properties in the build.xml file:

| Property | Value | Description |
|---|---|---|
| `src.dir` | `${basedir}/ejbModule` | Source directory |
| `web.module` | `${basedir}/webModule` | Web module directory |
| `weblogic.home` | `C:/Oracle/Middleware` | WebLogic home directory |
| `weblogic.server` | `${weblogic.home}/wlserver_12.1/server` | WebLogic Server directory |
| `build.dir` | `${basedir}/build` | Build directory |
| `deploy.dir` | `${weblogic.home}/user_projects/domains/base_domain/autodeploy` | Deploy directory |

Specify a `path` element to include the WebLogic JAR files. Add the following tasks in the build file:

| Task | Description |
|---|---|
| `prepare` | Makes the required directories |
| `compile` | Compiles the Java classes |
| `jar` | Creates a EJB JAR |
| `war` | Creates a web application WAR file |
| `assemble-app` | Assembles the JAR and the WAR files into an EAR file |
| `deploy` | Deploy the EAR file to WebLogic server |
| `clean` | Deletes directories when recompiling |

# The build script

The `build.xml` file is listed as follows:

```
<?xml version="1.0" encoding="UTF-8"?>
  <!--
    WebLogic build file
  -->
```

First, declare the different properties used in the build script:

```
<project name="EJB3" default="deploy" basedir=".">
  <property environment="env" />
  <property name="src.dir" value="${basedir}/ejbModule" />
  <property name="web.module" value="${basedir}/webModule" />
    <property name="weblogic.home" value="C:/Oracle/Middleware/" />
```

```
    <property name="weblogic.server" value="${weblogic.
home}/wlserver_12.1/server" />  <property name="build.dir"
value="${basedir}/build" />

    <property name="deploy.dir"
      value="${weblogic.home}/user_projects/domains/base_domain/
autodeploy" />
```

Specify the class path for the classes to be compiled:

```
    <path id="classpath">
      <fileset dir="${weblogic.home}/modules">
        <include name="*.jar" />
      </fileset>
      <fileset dir="${weblogic.server}/lib">
        <include name="*.jar" />
      </fileset>

      <pathelement location="${build.dir}" />
    </path>
    <property name="build.classpath" refid="classpath" />
    <target name="prepare">
      <mkdir dir="${build.dir}" />
    </target>
```

Compile the Java classes, which include the entity beans and the session bean facade:

```
    <target name="compile" depends="prepare">
      <javac srcdir="${src.dir}" destdir="${build.dir}" debug="on"
        includes="**/*.java">
        <classpath refid="classpath" />
      </javac>
    </target>
```

Generate the EJB JAR file, which includes the compiled EJB classes and the deployment descriptors:

```
    <target name="jar" depends="compile">
      <jar destfile="${build.dir}/ejb3.jar">
        <fileset dir="${build.dir}">
          <include name="**/*.class" />
        </fileset>
        <fileset dir="${src.dir}">
```

```
            <include name="META-INF/*.xml" />
        </fileset>
    </jar>
</target>
```

Generate the web application WAR file, which includes the JSP client:

```
<target name="war" depends="jar">
  <war warfile="${build.dir}/weblogic.war">
    <fileset dir="webModule">
      <include name="*.jsp" />
    </fileset>
    <fileset dir="webModule">
      <include name="WEB-INF/web.xml" />
    </fileset>
  </war>
</target>
```

Assemble the application into an EAR file, which includes the EJB JAR and the WAR files and the `application.xml` deployment descriptor:

```
<target name="assemble-app" depends="war">
  <jar jarfile="${build.dir}/ejb3.ear">
    <metainf dir="META-INF">
      <include name="application.xml" />
    </metainf>
    <fileset dir="${build.dir}" includes="*.jar,*.war" />
  </jar>
</target>
```

Deploy the application to the WebLogic Server deploy directory, the `autodeployed` directory:

```
<target name="deploy" depends="assemble-app">
  <copy file="${build.dir}/ejb3.ear" todir="${deploy.dir}" />
</target>
<target name="clean">
  <delete file="${build.dir}/ejb3.ear" />
  <delete file="${build.dir}/ejb3.jar" />
  <delete file="${build.dir}/weblogic.war" />
</target>
</project>
```

# Running the build script

Having created a build script, now we shall run it. Right-click on **build.xml** and select **Run As | Ant Build** as shown in the following screenshot:

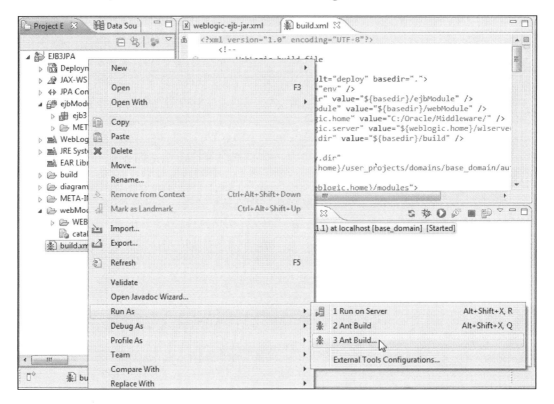

Select the **deploy** task and click on **Run** as shown in the following screenshot. As dependence is declared between tasks all the preceding tasks will also get run.

The EJB application gets compiled, built, assembled, and deployed to WebLogic Server's autodeployed directory as an EAR file. The **BUILD SUCCESSFUL** message indicates that the build and deployment was without error. If the build needs to be re-run first run the `clean` task, which deletes any previously generated EAR, WAR, and JAR files.

Start the WebLogic Server if not already started. In the WebLogic Server's Admin Server Console, the EAR file is shown deployed in **Deployments**. On expanding the EAR file the EJB JAR and web module WAR get listed as shown in the following screenshot:

# Testing the JSP client

Next, we shall run the JSP client to invoke the session bean facade, which subsequently invokes the entity beans. Test the JSP client with the URL `http://localhost:7001/weblogic/catalog.jsp`. The test data gets generated and the entity properties get listed for the `Catalog`, `Edition`, `Section`, and `Article` entities as shown in the following screenshot:

# Summary

In this chapter, we discussed creating an EJB project using the EJB 3.0 Module project facet provided by the Oracle Enterprise Pack for Eclipse. To create an entity bean, we added the JPA project facet. Subsequently, we generated entity beans from tables. We created a session bean facade for the entity beans; wrapping an entity bean in a session bean facade is a best practice. We created a JSP client for the EJB application. We packaged and deployed the EJB application to WebLogic Server and ran the test client on the WebLogic Server.

In the next chapter, we will discuss the **Object/XML (O/X)** mapping provided by the JAXB 2.0 framework using the Oracle WebLogic web services project facet.

# 2
# O/X Mapping with JAXB 2.x

**Java Architecture for XML Binding (JAXB)** is an API/framework used for **Object/XML (O/X)** mapping. JAXB provides an XML Schema compiler to create Java objects from an XML Schema. Subsequently, the Java classes may be used to marshal/unmarshal XML documents. A common application of JAXB is in web services; JAXB 2.x is a component of the API stack for web services. The schema types within a WSDL document are compiled to Java types using JAXB 2.x. This chapter has the following sections:

- JAXB 2.x advantages
- Creating a JAXB project
- Creating an XML Schema
- Compiling the XML Schema
- Marshalling an XML document
- Unmarshalling an XML document
- Java to XML mapping

# JAXB 2.x advantages

JAXB 2.x has the following advantages over JAXB 1.0:

- Smaller runtime libraries that require lesser runtime memory
- Fewer Java classes generated from an XML Schema, which implies fewer classes to process
- Support for all of the W3C XML Schema constructs
- Support for JAXP 1.3 validation
- Support for bidirectional Java to XML mapping
- Support for using parameterized types for which casts are not required and type checking is performed at compile time

# Creating a JAXB project

In this section we shall create a JAXB project. Select **File | New | Other**. In the **New** wizard select **JAXB Project** under **JAXB** and click on **Next**, as shown in the following screenshot:

In the **New JAXB Project** window specify a project name in the **Project name** field, and select **<None>** for **Target Runtime**, because the JAXB application is run as a Java application and does not require a target server. Specify **2.1** as **JAXB version** and click on **Next**, as shown in the following screenshot:

In Java configuration, source folders on the build path have the names as `src`, and the default output folder is `build/classes`. Click on **Next**. In the **JAXB Facet** dialog box select **Generic JAXB 2.1** as **Platform**, and select **User Library** for the **Type** field under **JAXB implementation**. Click on the **Download Library** button, as follows:

In the **Download Library** window select **EclipseLink 2.4.0 – Juno** and click on **Next**, as shown in the following screenshot:

In **Library License** select **I accept the terms of this license** and click on **Finish**. **EclipseLink 2.4.0 – Juno** gets added to the **JAXB Facet** dialog box. Click on **Finish**, as follows:

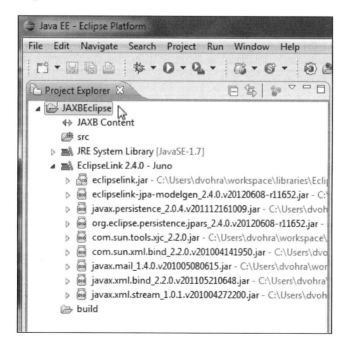

A JAXB 2.1 project gets created.

Right-click on the project node and select **Project Properties**. In **Project Properties** select the **Project Facets** node. The **JAXB** project facet should be shown as selected, because we created a JAXB project:

| Project Facets | | |
|---|---|---|
| **Configuration:** `<custom>` | | |
| **Project Facet** | **Version** | |
| ▷ ☐ Apache XMLBeans | | |
| ☐ Application Client module | 6.0 | ▾ |
| ▷ ☐ Axis2 Web Services | | |
| ☐ CXF 2.x Web Services | 1.0 | |
| ☐ Dynamic Web Module | 3.0 | ▾ |
| ☐ EJB Module | 3.1 | ▾ |
| ☐ EJBDoclet (XDoclet) | 1.2.3 | ▾ |
| ☐ GlassFish Deployment Descriptors Files | 9 | |
| ☑ Java | 1.7 | ▾ |
| ☐ Java Annotation Processing Support | 5.0 | |
| ☐ JavaScript | 1.0 | |
| ☐ JavaServer Faces | 2.0 | ▾ |
| ☐ JAX-RS (REST Web Services) | 1.1 | ▾ |
| ☑ JAXB | 2.1 | ▾ |
| ☐ JCA Module | 1.6 | ▾ |
| ☐ JPA | 2.0 | ▾ |
| ☐ JSTL | 1.2 | ▾ |
| ☐ Oracle ADF Web | 11.1.1 | |
| ☐ Oracle Coherence | 3.7.1 | ▾ |
| ☐ Oracle WebLogic EJB Extensions | 12.1.1 | ▾ |
| ☐ Oracle WebLogic EJBGen Support | 12.1.1 | ▾ |
| ☐ Oracle WebLogic SCA | 12.1.1 | ▾ |
| ☐ Oracle WebLogic Scripting Tools (WLST) Support | 12.1.1 | ▾ |
| ☐ Oracle WebLogic Utility Module Extensions | 12.1.1 | ▾ |
| ☐ Oracle WebLogic Web App Extensions | 12.1.1 | ▾ |
| ☐ Oracle WebLogic Web Service Clients | 2.1 | |

# Creating an XML Schema

We shall be generating Java classes from an XML Schema. In this section we create the XML Schema. To create an XML Schema select **File | New | Other**. In the **New** wizard select **XML Schema File** under **XML**. Click on **Next**, as shown in the following screenshot:

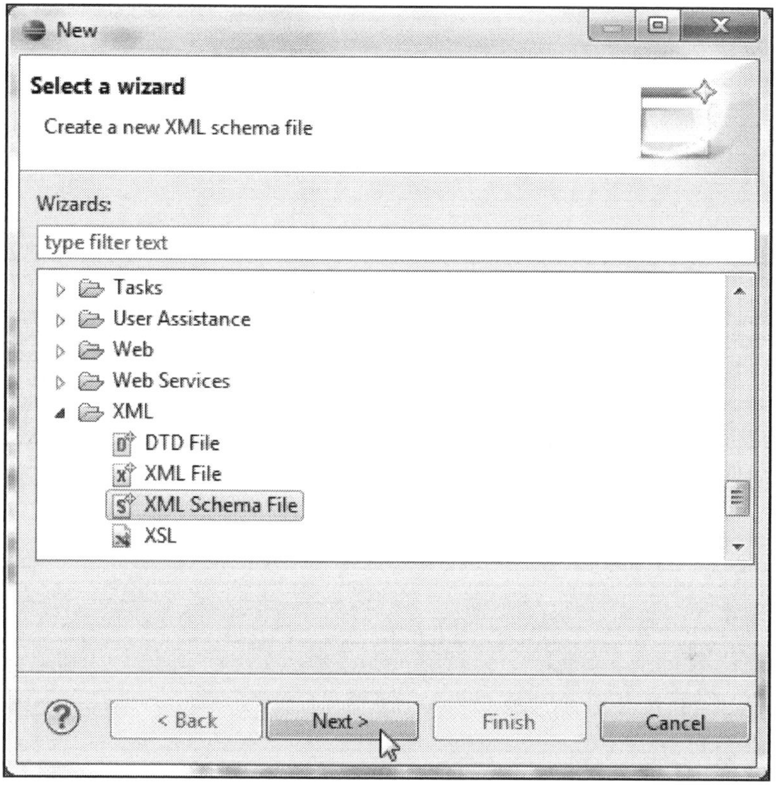

In the new XML Schema wizard select the JAXBEclipse/src folder. Specify the XML Schema name as **catalog.xsd** in the **File name** field. Click on **Finish**. An XML Schema template gets added to the **JAXBEclipse** project. The example XML Schema represents a catalog and specifies some complexType elements, an optional element of the xsd:int type, and an attribute. The **TargetNamespace** field is set to http://www.example.org/catalog. Copy the following XML Schema to **catalog.xsd**:

```
<?xml version="1.0" encoding="UTF-8"?>
<xsd:schema xmlns:xsd="http://www.w3.org/2001/XMLSchema"
  targetNamespace="http://www.example.org/catalog"
xmlns:catalog="http://www.example.org/catalog"
  elementFormDefault="qualified">
  <xsd:element name="catalog" type="catalog:catalogType" />
  <xsd:element name="catalogid" type="xsd:int" />
  <xsd:complexType name="catalogType">
    <xsd:sequence>
      <xsd:element ref="catalog:catalogid" minOccurs="0"
        maxOccurs="1" />
      <xsd:element name="journal" type="catalog:journalType"
        minOccurs="0" maxOccurs="unbounded" />
    </xsd:sequence>
    <xsd:attribute name="title" type="xsd:string" />
    <xsd:attribute name="publisher" type="xsd:string" />
  </xsd:complexType>

  <xsd:complexType name="journalType">
    <xsd:sequence>
      <xsd:element name="article" type="catalog:articleType"
        minOccurs="0" maxOccurs="unbounded" />
    </xsd:sequence>
    <xsd:attribute name="date" type="xsd:string" />
  </xsd:complexType>
  <xsd:complexType name="articleType">
    <xsd:sequence>
      <xsd:element name="title" type="xsd:string" />
      <xsd:element name="author" type="xsd:string" />
    </xsd:sequence>
    <xsd:attribute name="section" type="xsd:string" />
  </xsd:complexType>

</xsd:schema>
```

The **catalog.xsd** XML Schema is shown under the **JAXBEclipse** project in the following screenshot:

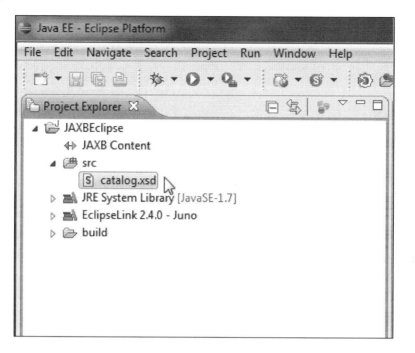

In the next section we shall compile the XML Schema into Java classes using the built-in JAXB compiler.

# Compiling the XML Schema

An XML Schema gets compiled to Java classes representing the DOM structure of the schema using the JAXB compiler. To compile the **catalog.xsd** XML Schema, select **File | New | Other**, and select **JAXB Classes from Schema** under **JAXB**, as shown in the following screenshot:

In the **New JAXB Classes from schema** window, select the JAXB project— **JAXBEclipse** and click on **Next**, as shown in the following screenshot:

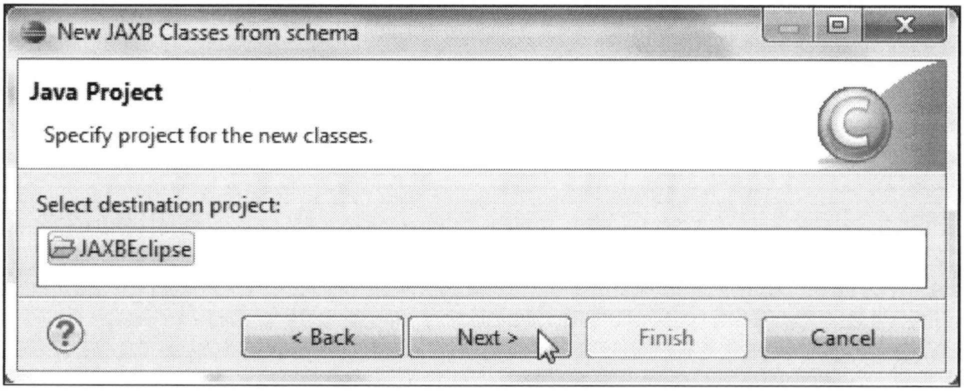

In the **Configure JAXB class generation** dialog box, specify JAXBEclipse/src in the **Source folder** field, specify the package name as jaxbeclipse in the **Package** field, and click on **Next**, as shown in the following screenshot:

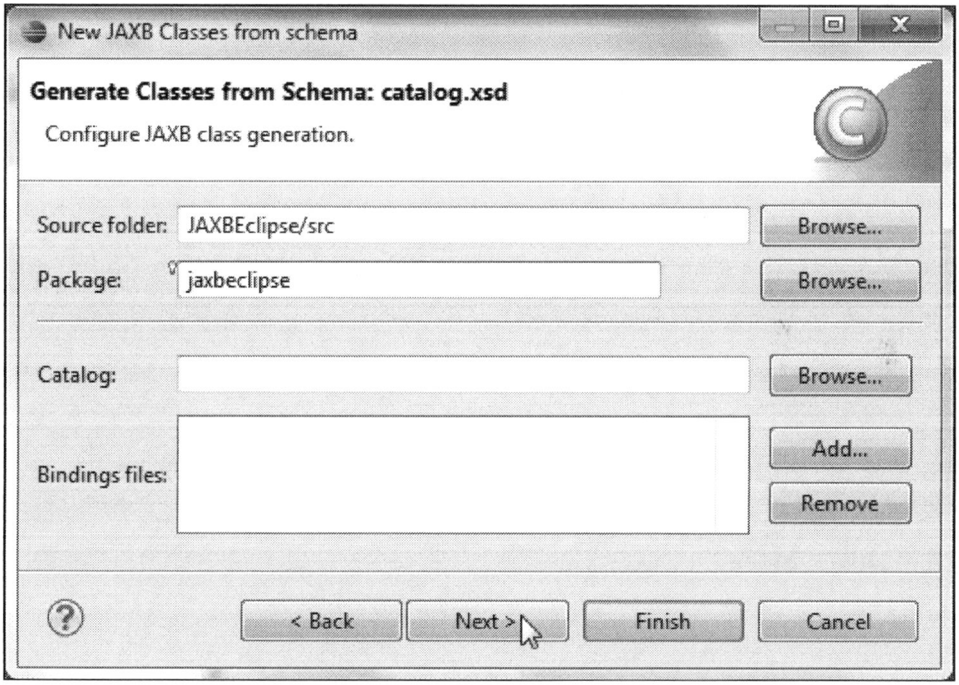

In the **Classes Generation Options** dialog box, check the **Use strict validation** and **Treat input as XML schema** checkboxes and click on **Next**, as shown in the following screenshot:

In the **Classes Generator Extension Configuration** dialog box, specify **-target 2.1** in the **Additional arguments** field. Click on **Finish**:

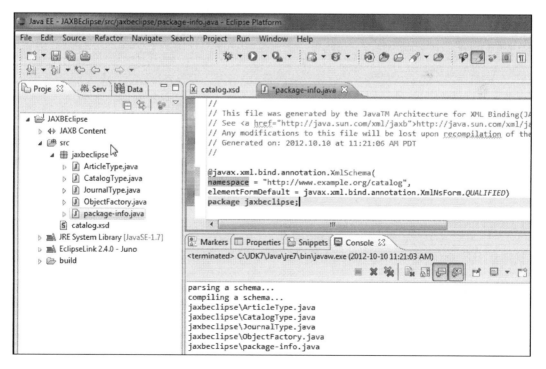

The `catalog.xsd` schema gets parsed and compiled. For each top-level element
an `ObjectFactory` class is generated. For each top-level `complexType` element
a value class gets generated; value classes — `CatalogType.java`, `ArticleType.`
`java`, and `JournalType.java` get generated. `package-info.java` consists of
package-level declarations, annotations, and comments. In `package-info.`
`java` the target namespace of the schema and package declaration are specified.
`elementFormDefault` is set to `javax.xml.bind.annotation.XmlNsForm.`
`QUALIFIED`, as shown in the following screenshot:

Alternatively, the Java classes may be generated from the **Project Explorer** tab; right-click on the schema file—`catalog.xsd`—and click on **Generate | JAXB Classes...**, as shown in the following screenshot:

The `ObjectFactory` class consists of `create<complexType>` method for each of the `complexType` elements. A `createCatalog(CatalogType)` method is included to create `JAXBElement<CatalogType>` from a `CatalogType` object. The `ObjectFactory` class is listed, as follows:

```
package jaxbeclipse;

import javax.xml.bind.JAXBElement;
import javax.xml.bind.annotation.XmlElementDecl;
import javax.xml.bind.annotation.XmlRegistry;
import javax.xml.namespace.QName;


@XmlRegistry
public class ObjectFactory {

    private final static QName _Catalogid_QNAME = new QName("http://
www.example.org/catalog", "catalogid");
    private final static QName _Catalog_QNAME = new QName("http://www.
example.org/catalog", "catalog");


    public ObjectFactory() {
    }


    public CatalogType createCatalogType() {
        return new CatalogType();
    }


    public ArticleType createArticleType() {
        return new ArticleType();
    }

    public JournalType createJournalType() {
        return new JournalType();
    }


    @XmlElementDecl(namespace = "http://www.example.org/catalog", name
= "catalogid")
    public JAXBElement<Integer> createCatalogid(Integer value) {
        return new JAXBElement<Integer>(_Catalogid_QNAME, Integer.
class, null, value);
    }


    @XmlElementDecl(namespace = "http://www.example.org/catalog", name
= "catalog")
```

```
        public JAXBElement<CatalogType> createCatalog(CatalogType value) {
            return new JAXBElement<CatalogType>(_Catalog_QNAME,
    CatalogType.class, null, value);
        }


    }
```

The CatalogType.java class consists of getter/setter methods for the catalogid, journal, title, and publisher properties. For example, the accessor method for journal is getJournalType, which returns List<JournalType>. The accessor (getter/setter) methods for title are getTitle and setTitle, as follows:

```
    package jaxbeclipse;

    import java.util.ArrayList;
    import java.util.List;
    import javax.xml.bind.annotation.XmlAccessType;
    import javax.xml.bind.annotation.XmlAccessorType;
    import javax.xml.bind.annotation.XmlAttribute;
    import javax.xml.bind.annotation.XmlType;


    @XmlAccessorType(XmlAccessType.FIELD)
    @XmlType(name = "catalogType", propOrder = {
        "catalogid",
        "journal"
    })
    public class CatalogType {

        protected Integer catalogid;
        protected List<JournalType> journal;
        @XmlAttribute(name = "title")
        protected String title;
        @XmlAttribute(name = "publisher")
        protected String publisher;


        public Integer getCatalogid() {
            return catalogid;
        }

        public void setCatalogid(Integer value) {
            this.catalogid = value;
        }
```

```
    public List<JournalType> getJournal() {
        if (journal == null) {
            journal = new ArrayList<JournalType>();
        }
        return this.journal;
    }

    public String getTitle() {
        return title;
    }


    public void setTitle(String value) {
        this.title = value;
    }


    public String getPublisher() {
        return publisher;
    }
    public void setPublisher(String value) {
        this.publisher = value;
    }

}
```

The `JournalType.java` class consists of the `article` and `date` properties, and accessor methods for the `article` and `date` properties. For example, the accessor method for `article` is `getArticle()`, which returns `List<ArticleType>`. The accessor (getter/setter) methods for `date` are `getDate` and `setDate`, as follows:

```
package jaxbeclipse;

import java.util.ArrayList;
import java.util.List;
import javax.xml.bind.annotation.XmlAccessType;
import javax.xml.bind.annotation.XmlAccessorType;
import javax.xml.bind.annotation.XmlAttribute;
import javax.xml.bind.annotation.XmlType;


@XmlAccessorType(XmlAccessType.FIELD)
```

```
@XmlType(name = "journalType", propOrder = {
    "article"
})
public class JournalType {

    protected List<ArticleType> article;
    @XmlAttribute(name = "date")
    protected String date;


    public List<ArticleType> getArticle() {
        if (article == null) {
            article = new ArrayList<ArticleType>();
        }
        return this.article;
    }

    public String getDate() {
        return date;
    }

    public void setDate(String value) {
        this.date = value;
    }


}
```

The `ArticleType.java` class consists of the `title`, `author`, and `section` properties, and getter and setter methods for these properties, as follows:

```
package jaxbeclipse;

import javax.xml.bind.annotation.XmlAccessType;
import javax.xml.bind.annotation.XmlAccessorType;
import javax.xml.bind.annotation.XmlAttribute;
import javax.xml.bind.annotation.XmlElement;
import javax.xml.bind.annotation.XmlType;


@XmlAccessorType(XmlAccessType.FIELD)
@XmlType(name = "articleType", propOrder = {
    "title",
    "author"
})
public class ArticleType {
```

```
    @XmlElement(required = true)
    protected String title;
    @XmlElement(required = true)
    protected String author;
    @XmlAttribute(name = "section")
    protected String section;


    public String getTitle() {
        return title;
    }

    public void setTitle(String value) {
        this.title = value;
    }


    public String getAuthor() {
        return author;
    }

    public void setAuthor(String value) {
        this.author = value;
    }


    public String getSection() {
        return section;
    }

    public void setSection(String value) {
        this.section = value;
    }

}
```

jaxb.properties also gets generated with the following property specified for the JAXB context factory for MOXy:

```
javax.xml.bind.context.factory=org.eclipse.persistence.jaxb.
JAXBContextFactory
```

The implementation class for JAXBContextFactory is com.sun.xml.bind.
v2.runtime.JAXBContextImpl.

# Marshalling an XML document

In this section we marshal a Java representation of an XML document constructed using the compiled Java classes to an XML document. Create the Java class by going to **File | New | Other** and selecting **Java | Class**. Provide a JAXB context for implementing the JAXB framework with a JAXBContext object. Create a Marshaller object from the JAXBContext object and set the jaxb.formatted.output to true. The newInstance() static method of the JAXBContext class takes a list of packages, separated by a colon (:), that are to be added to the JAXB context. A package to be added to the JAXB context must contain either an ObjectFactory class or a jaxb.index file. As we compile the catalog.xsd XML Schema into the jaxbeclipse package, add the package to JAXB context. Create a Marshaller object using the createMarshaller() method of JAXBContext, as follows:

```
JAXBContext jaxbContext = JAXBContext.newInstance("jaxbeclipse");
Marshaller marshaller = jaxbContext.createMarshaller();
marshaller.setProperty("jaxb.formatted.output", new Boolean(true));
```

Create an ObjectFactory object using its constructor. Create the CatalogType, JournalType, and ArticleType objects from the ObjectFactory object using the createCatalogType, createJournalType, and createArticleType methods, respectively.

```
jaxb.ObjectFactory factory = new jaxb.ObjectFactory();
CatalogType catalog = factory.createCatalogType();
```

Construct a DOM representation of an XML document using the accessor methods. For example, set the catalogid, title, and publisher methods, as follows:

```
catalog.setCatalogid(1);
catalog.setTitle("Oracle Magazine");
catalog.setPublisher("Oracle Publishing");
```

For elements that have a cardinality greater than 1, such as the journal and article elements, obtain the parameterized List for the element's type using the getter method and add a new element using the add() method. For example, a journal element is added by first creating a JournalType object using the createJournalType() method of the ObjectFactory, setting its properties using setter methods, and subsequently adding the JournalType object to the List<JournalType> parameterized List.

```
JournalType journal = factory.createJournalType();
journal.setDate("September-October 2008");
List<JournalType> journalList = catalog.getJournal();
journalList.add(journal);
```

To output the DOM representation of constructed XML document, create a
JAXBElement<CatalogType> instance from the CatalogType instance. Marshal
the JAXBElement object using the marshal method of the Marshaller class.

```
JAXBElement<CatalogType> catalogElement = factory.
createCatalog(catalog);
String xmlDocument = "src/jaxbeclipse/catalog.xml";
marshaller.marshal(catalogElement, new FileOutputStream(xmlDocument));
```

The JAXB2Marshaller class is listed, as follows:

```
package jaxbeclipse;

import javax.xml.bind.*;
import java.io.File;
import java.io.FileOutputStream;
import java.io.IOException;
import java.util.List;

public class JAXB2Marshaller {

   public void generateXMLDocument(File xmlDocument) {
     try {

       JAXBContext jaxbContext = JAXBContext.
newInstance("jaxbeclipse");

       Marshaller marshaller = jaxbContext.createMarshaller();

       marshaller.setProperty("jaxb.formatted.output", new
Boolean(true));

       jaxbeclipse.ObjectFactory factory = new jaxbeclipse.
ObjectFactory();

       CatalogType catalog = factory.createCatalogType();
       catalog.setCatalogid(1);
       catalog.setTitle("Oracle Magazine");
       catalog.setPublisher("Oracle Publishing");
       JournalType journal = factory.createJournalType();
       journal.setDate("September-October 2008");
       List<JournalType> journalList = catalog.getJournal();
       journalList.add(journal);
```

```
        ArticleType article = factory.createArticleType();
        article.setSection("FEATURES");
        article.setTitle("Share 2.0");
        article.setAuthor("Alan Joch");
        List<ArticleType> articleList = journal.getArticle();
        articleList.add(article);
        journal = factory.createJournalType();
        journal.setDate("March-April 2008");

        journalList.add(journal);
        article = factory.createArticleType();
        article.setSection("ORACLE DEVELOPER");
        article.setTitle("Declarative Data Filtering");
        article.setAuthor("Steve Muench");
        articleList = journal.getArticle();
        articleList.add(article);

        JAXBElement<CatalogType> catalogElement = factory
            .createCatalog(catalog);

        marshaller.marshal(catalogElement,
            new FileOutputStream(xmlDocument));

    } catch (IOException e) {
      System.err.println(e.toString());

    } catch (JAXBException e) {

      System.err.println(e.toString());

    }

  }

  public static void main(String[] argv) {
    String xmlDocument = "src/jaxbeclipse/catalog.xml";
    JAXB2Marshaller jaxbMarshaller = new JAXB2Marshaller();
    jaxbMarshaller.generateXMLDocument(new File(xmlDocument));
  }
}
```

To marshal the XML document, right-click on the **JAXBMarshaller.java** class and select **Run As | Java Application**, as shown in the following screenshot:

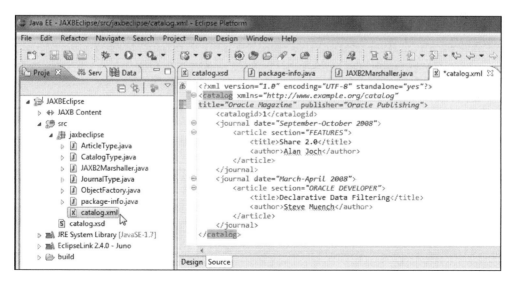

The Java DOM structure representation gets marshalled to an XML document—`catalog.xml`. Because we used `targetNamespace` in the `catalog.xsd` schema, the `catalog.xml` document is created in the target namespace—`http://www.example.org/catalog`, as follows:

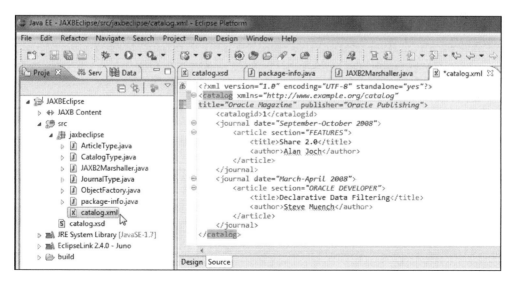

The **catalog.xml** XML document generated is listed, as follows:

```
<?xml version="1.0" encoding="UTF-8" standalone="yes"?>
<catalog xmlns="http://www.example.org/catalog" title="Oracle
Magazine" publisher="Oracle Publishing">
    <catalogid>1</catalogid>
    <journal date="September-October 2008">
        <article section="FEATURES">
            <title>Share 2.0</title>
            <author>Alan Joch</author>
        </article>
    </journal>
    <journal date="March-April 2008">
        <article section="ORACLE DEVELOPER">
            <title>Declarative Data Filtering</title>
            <author>Steve Muench</author>
        </article>
    </journal>
</catalog>
```

# Unmarshalling an XML document

For unmarshalling the same XML document that we created in the previous section, create a Java class—JAXB2UnMarshaller.java. In the unmarshaller class create a JAXBContext object as in the previous section and create an Unmarshaller object using the createUnmarshaller() method:

```
JAXBContext jaxbContext = JAXBContext.newInstance("jaxbeclipse");
Unmarshaller unMarshaller = jaxbContext.createUnmarshaller();
```

For XML Schema validation we need to set an XML Schema on the Unmarshaller object. Create a SchemaFactory object using the static method newInstance(), a Schema object from the SchemaFactory object using the newSchema() method, and set the schema on the Unmarshaller object using the setSchema() method:

```
SchemaFactory schemaFactory = SchemaFactory
        .newInstance("http://www.w3.org/2001/XMLSchema");
Schema schema = schemaFactory.newSchema(new File("src/catalog.xsd"));
unMarshaller.setSchema(schema);
```

Create a custom validation handler class, CustomValidationEventHandler, which implements the ValidationEventHandler class, as an inner class. Create a CustomValidationEventHandler object and set the event handler on the Unmarshaller object using the setEventHandler() method. CustomValidationEventHandler validates the XML document to be unmarshalled with the XML Schema and outputs validation errors, if any:

```
CustomValidationEventHandler validationEventHandler = new
CustomValidationEventHandler();
unMarshaller.setEventHandler(validationEventHandler);
```

Create a `JAXBElement<CatalogType>` object from the XML document to be unmarshalled using the `unmarshal()` method of the `Unmarshaller` class and create a `CatalogType` object using the `getValue()` method:

```
File xmlDocument = new File("src/jaxbeclipse/catalog.xml");
JAXBElement<CatalogType> catalogElement = (JAXBElement<CatalogType>)
unMarshaller.unmarshal(xmlDocument);
CatalogType catalog = catalogElement.getValue();
```

Output the `CatalogType` object properties using getter methods. Get a `JournalType` object and output its properties, and create an `ArticleType` object and output its properties. The `JAXB2UnMarshaller` class is listed, as follows:

```
package jaxbeclipse;

import javax.xml.bind.*;
import javax.xml.validation.SchemaFactory;
import javax.xml.validation.Schema;
import org.xml.sax.SAXException;
import java.io.*;
import java.util.List;

public class JAXB2UnMarshaller {

  public void unMarshall(File xmlDocument) {
    try {

      JAXBContext jaxbContext = JAXBContext.
newInstance("jaxbeclipse");
      Unmarshaller unMarshaller = jaxbContext.createUnmarshaller();
      SchemaFactory schemaFactory = SchemaFactory
          .newInstance("http://www.w3.org/2001/XMLSchema");
      Schema schema = schemaFactory.newSchema(new File("src/catalog.
xsd"));
      unMarshaller.setSchema(schema);
      CustomValidationEventHandler validationEventHandler = new
CustomValidationEventHandler();
      unMarshaller.setEventHandler(validationEventHandler);

      JAXBElement<CatalogType> catalogElement =
(JAXBElement<CatalogType>) unMarshaller
          .unmarshal(xmlDocument);
```

```
            CatalogType catalog = catalogElement.getValue();
System.out.println("Catalog id: " + catalog.getCatalogid());
      System.out.println("Journal Title: " + catalog.getTitle());
      System.out.println("Publisher: " + catalog.getPublisher());
      List<JournalType> journalList = catalog.getJournal();
      for (int i = 0; i < journalList.size(); i++) {

        JournalType journal = journalList.get(i);
        System.out.println("Journal Date: " + journal.getDate());
        List<ArticleType> articleList = journal.getArticle();
        for (int j = 0; j < articleList.size(); j++) {
          ArticleType article = articleList.get(j);

          System.out.println("Section: " + article.getSection());
          System.out.println("Title: " + article.getTitle());
          System.out.println("Author: " + article.getAuthor());
        }
      }
    } catch (JAXBException e) {
      System.err.println(e.getMessage());
    } catch (SAXException e) {
      System.err.println(e.getMessage());
    }
  }

  public static void main(String[] argv) {
    File xmlDocument = new File("src/jaxbeclipse/catalog.xml");
    JAXB2UnMarshaller jaxbUnmarshaller = new JAXB2UnMarshaller();

    jaxbUnmarshaller.unMarshall(xmlDocument);

  }

  class CustomValidationEventHandler implements ValidationEventHandler
{
    public boolean handleEvent(ValidationEvent event) {
      if (event.getSeverity() == ValidationEvent.WARNING) {
        return true;
      }
      if ((event.getSeverity() == ValidationEvent.ERROR)
          || (event.getSeverity() == ValidationEvent.FATAL_ERROR)) {
```

```
        System.err.println("Validation Error:" + event.getMessage());

        ValidationEventLocator locator = event.getLocator();
        System.err.println("at line number:" + locator.
getLineNumber());
        System.err.println("Unmarshalling Terminated");
        return false;
    }
    return true;
}


  }
}
```

Right-click on the **JAXB2UnMarshaller** class and select **Run As | Java Application**. The XML document gets unmarshalled and the element values get output, as follows:

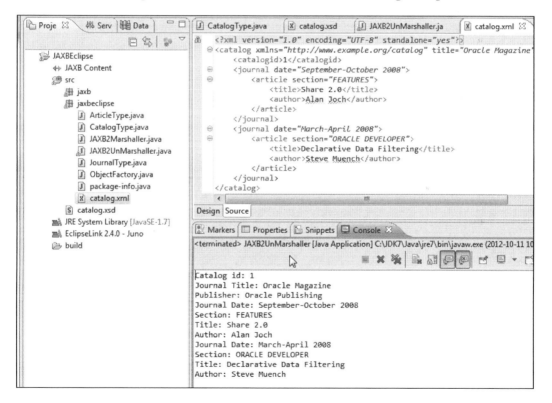

In the next section we shall discuss the support for Java to XML mapping.

# Java to XML mapping

In this section we shall map a Java class, containing elements and attributes declared using the annotations API in the `javax.xml.bind.annotation` package.

Create a Java class—`Catalog.java`. Specify the root element using the `@XmlRootElement` annotation. Specify the root element's name and the namespace. Specify the property order within the root element using the `@XmlType` annotation's `propOrder` element:

```
@XmlRootElement(name="catalog", namespace="http://www.example.org/
catalog")@XmlType(name = "", propOrder = { "publisher", "edition",
"title", "author" })
public class Catalog {


}
```

Specify declarations and getter/setter methods for the properties. Specify a `journal` attribute using the `@XmlAttribute` annotation:

```
@XmlAttribute
public String journal;
```

The annotated class—`Catalog.java` is listed, as follows:

```
package jaxb;

import javax.xml.bind.annotation.XmlRootElement;
import javax.xml.bind.annotation.XmlAttribute;
import javax.xml.bind.annotation.XmlType;

@XmlRootElement(name="catalog", namespace="http://www.example.org/
catalog")
@XmlType(name = "", propOrder = { "publisher", "edition", "title",
"author" })
public class Catalog {

  private String publisher;

  private String edition;

  private String title;

  private String author;

  public Catalog() {
```

```java
}

public Catalog(String journal, String publisher, String edition,
    String title, String author) {

  this.journal = journal;
  this.publisher = publisher;
  this.edition = edition;
  this.title = title;
  this.author = author;
}

@XmlAttribute
public String journal;

private String getJournal() {
  return this.journal;
}

public void setJournal(String journal) {
  this.journal = journal;
}

public String getPublisher() {
  return this.publisher;
}

public void setPublisher(String publisher) {
  this.publisher = publisher;
}

public String getEdition() {
  return this.edition;
}

public void setEdition(String edition) {
  this.edition = edition;
}

public String getTitle() {
  return this.title;
}

public void setTitle(String title) {
```

```
      this.title = title;
   }

   public String getAuthor() {
      return this.author;
   }

   public void setAuthor(String author) {
      this.author = author;
   }
}
```

Create a Java class—JavaToXML.java for marshalling the Catalog.java annotated class to an XML document. The procedure to marshall the Java class is the same as discussed previously in the JAXB2Marshaller class. A JAXBContext object is created using the newInstance() method with the argument as Catalog.class, as follows:

```
JAXBContext jaxbContext = JAXBContext.newInstance(Catalog.class);
```

After creating a JAXBContext object create a Marshaller object with the jaxb. formatted.output property set to true. Create a Catalog object and set its properties using setter methods. Marshal the Catalog object using the marshal method:

```
Catalog catalog = new Catalog();
catalog.setJournal("Oracle Magazine");
catalog.setPublisher("Oracle Publishing");
String xmlDocument = "src/catalog.xml";
marshaller.marshal(catalog, new FileOutputStream(xmlDocument));
```

The JavaToXML.java class is listed, as follows:

```
package jaxb;

import javax.xml.bind.*;
import java.io.File;
import java.io.FileOutputStream;
import java.io.IOException;

public class JavaToXML {
   public void marshalXMLDocument(File xmlDocument) {
      try {
         JAXBContext jaxbContext = JAXBContext.newInstance(Catalog.
class);
         Marshaller marshaller = jaxbContext.createMarshaller();
         marshaller.setProperty("jaxb.formatted.output",
            Boolean.valueOf(true));
         Catalog catalog = new Catalog();
         catalog.setJournal("Oracle Magazine");
```

```
            catalog.setPublisher("Oracle Publishing");
            catalog.setEdition("March-April 2008");
            catalog.setTitle("Declarative Data Filtering");
            catalog.setAuthor("Steve Muench");
            marshaller.marshal(catalog, new FileOutputStream(xmlDocument));
        } catch (IOException e) {
            System.err.println(e.toString());
        } catch (PropertyException e) {
            System.err.println(e.toString());
        } catch (JAXBException e) {
            System.err.println(e.toString());
        }
    }

    public static void main(String[] argv) {
        String xmlDocument = "src/catalog.xml";
        JavaToXML javaToXML = new JavaToXML();
        javaToXML.marshalXMLDocument(new File(xmlDocument));
    }
}
```

Right-click on **JavaToXML.java** and select **Run As | Java Application**, as follows:

The `catalog.xml` file gets generated. As we had specified a namespace for the root element, the `Catalog` element has a namespace declaration, as shown in the following screenshot:

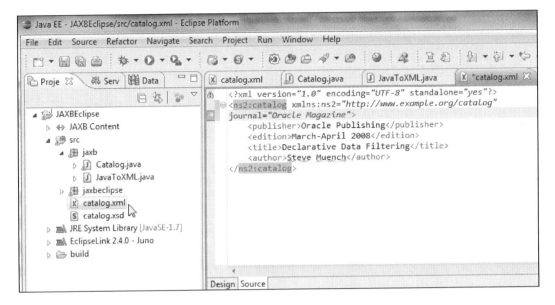

The **catalog.xml** file generated is listed, as follows:

```
<?xml version="1.0" encoding="UTF-8" standalone="yes"?>
<ns2:catalog xmlns:ns2="http://www.example.org/catalog"
journal="Oracle Magazine">
    <publisher>Oracle Publishing</publisher>
    <edition>March-April 2008</edition>
    <title>Declarative Data Filtering</title>
    <author>Steve Muench</author>
</ns2:catalog>
```

The JAXB project facet also provides built-in support for mapping JAXB classes to an XML Schema. Next, we shall map the `Catalog.java` class to an XML Schema. Select **File | New**. In **New** select **Schema from JAXB Classes** under **JAXB**. Click on **Next**, as shown in the following screenshot:

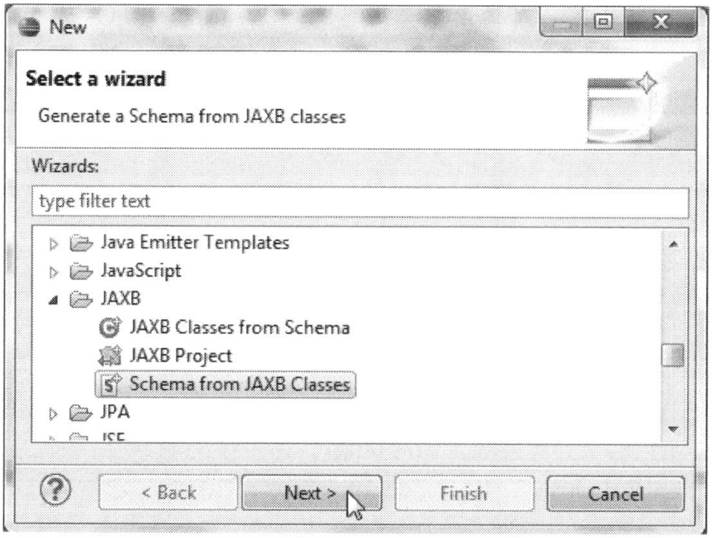

In the **New JAXB Schema File** dialog box, specify the folder to generate the schema and specify the schema filename in the **File name** field. Click on **Next**, as shown in the following screenshot:

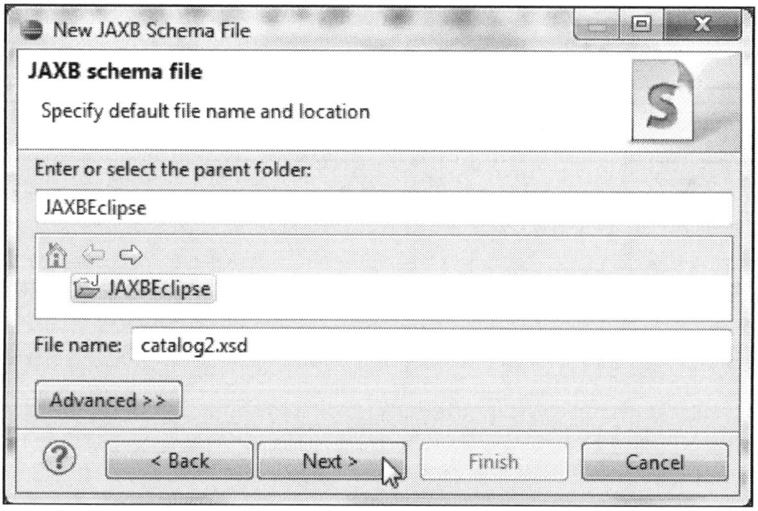

In the **Generate Schema from Classes** dialog box select the classes to include in the schema; select the folder containing the classes, which is the **jaxb** package folder. Click on **Finish**, as shown in the following screenshot:

Two XML Schemas get generated by MOXy—**catalog21.xsd** and **www.example.org_catalog.xsd**. The **catalog21.xsd** schema specifies `complexType` for the `JavaToXML.java` class, as follows:

The second schema—**www.example.org_catalog.xsd**—is the XML Schema representing the `Catalog.java` class. The second schema imports the first schema.

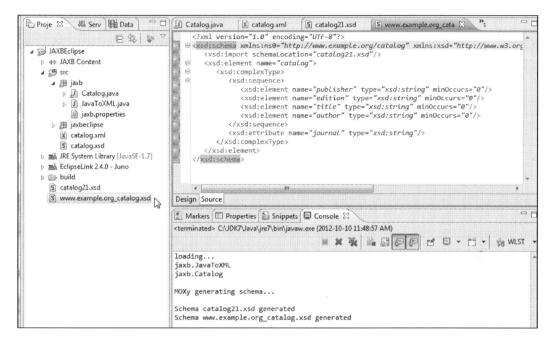

The **www.example.org_catalog.xsd** schema is listed, as follows:

```xml
<?xml version="1.0" encoding="UTF-8"?>
<xsd:schema xmlns:ns0="http://www.example.org/catalog"
xmlns:xsd="http://www.w3.org/2001/XMLSchema" targetNamespace="http://
www.example.org/catalog">
    <xsd:import schemaLocation="catalog21.xsd"/>
    <xsd:element name="catalog">
        <xsd:complexType>
            <xsd:sequence>
                <xsd:element name="publisher" type="xsd:string"
minOccurs="0"/>
                <xsd:element name="edition" type="xsd:string"
minOccurs="0"/>
                <xsd:element name="title" type="xsd:string"
minOccurs="0"/>
                <xsd:element name="author" type="xsd:string"
minOccurs="0"/>
            </xsd:sequence>
            <xsd:attribute name="journal" type="xsd:string"/>
        </xsd:complexType>
    </xsd:element>
</xsd:schema>
```

JAXB has the advantage that the data objects are properly linked to the XML Schema grammar and the schema types may be used to generate Java classes with the required data types. JAXB has its drawbacks; the tight coupling between an XML Schema and the serialized classes is not the best design, as modifying either requires the other to be modified as well. JAXB is not the only option available for Object/XML mapping. Apache XMLBeans is also supported in Oracle Enterprise Pack for Eclipse as a project facet.

# Summary

In this chapter we discussed the O/X mapping provided by the JAXB 2.x framework. We discussed the advantages of JAXB 2.x over JAXB 1.0. We created a JAXB project. We created an XML Schema and generated JAXB classes from the XML Schema using JAXB Schema compilation. Subsequently, we marshalled an XML document from a DOM document object, and also unmarshalled an XML document using the compiled Java classes. We also mapped an annotated Java class to an XML document using the annotations API and to an XML Schema using the built-in support for schema from JAXB classes.

In the next chapter we will create PDF and Excel reports using the JasperReports reporting engine in a Dynamic Web Module project. We will use WebLogic Server to deploy and run the web project to create JasperReports reports.

# 3
# Developing a Web Project for JasperReports

Eclipse IDE for Java EE provides project facets for various types of projects. In *Chapter 1, EJB 3.0 Database Persistence*, we used the EJB Module project facet and the JPA project facet to create an EJB project. In *Chapter 2, O/X Mapping with JAXB 2.x*, we used the JAXB project facet to create a JAXB project. In this chapter, we shall discuss a more generic project facet for web applications called the **Dynamic Web Module** project facet that adds support for Java Servlet API to build web applications. To demonstrate the use of the Dynamic Web project, we shall be using JasperReports as an example. Preparing presentation-quality reports is a routine occurrence, and several tools and APIs for creating reports are available. For Java developers, one of the most commonly used API is JasperSoft's open source JasperReports, which is capable of producing a range of outputs, including HTML, PDF, and presentations from either static data or data retrieved from a database table using a SQL query, and is designed to be integrated directly into Java/J2EE applications.

This chapter sets out to demonstrate the essentials of how JasperReports can be used in a web application created with Eclipse. The examples created in this chapter are a PDF report and an Excel report. This chapter has the following sections:

- Setting the environment
- Creating a Dynamic Web project in Eclipse
- Creating the configuration file
- Creating a web application
- Packaging and deploying the web application
- Running the web application

# Setting the environment

First, we need to install the required software, Oracle Enterprise Pack for Eclipse 12*c*, from `http://www.oracle.com/technetwork/middleware/ias/downloads/wls-main-097127.html` using Installers with Oracle WebLogic Server, Oracle Coherence and Oracle Enterprise Pack for Eclipse, and download the Oracle Database 11g Express Edition from `http://www.oracle.com/technetwork/products/express-edition/overview/index.html`. Setting the environment requires the following tasks:

- Creating database tables
- Configuring a data source in WebLogic Server 12*c*
- Copying JasperReports required JAR files to the server classpath

First, create a database table, which shall be the data source for creating the reports, with the following SQL script. If a database table for another chapter has already been created, that table may be used for this chapter too.

```
CREATE TABLE OE.Catalog(CatalogId INTEGER PRIMARY KEY, Journal
VARCHAR(25), Publisher VARCHAR(25),Edition VARCHAR(25), Title
Varchar(45), Author Varchar(25));
INSERT INTO OE.Catalog VALUES('1', 'Oracle Magazine',  'Oracle
Publishing', 'Nov-Dec 2004', 'Database Resource  Manager', 'Kimberly
Floss');
INSERT INTO OE.Catalog VALUES('2', 'Oracle Magazine',   'Oracle
Publishing', 'Nov-Dec 2004', 'From ADF UIX to JSF',  'Jonas Jacobi');
INSERT INTO OE.Catalog VALUES('3', 'Oracle Magazine',   'Oracle
Publishing', 'March-April 2005', 'Starting with  Oracle ADF ', 'Steve
Muench');
```

Next, configure a data source in WebLogic Server with the JNDI name `jdbc/OracleDS` as discussed in *Chapter 1, EJB 3.0 Database Persistence*. Next, we need to download some JasperReports JAR files including dependencies. Download the JAR/ZIP files listed in the following table and extract the ZIP/TAR.CZ to a directory, `c:\jasperreports`, for example.

| JAR/ZIP file | Download URL |
|---|---|
| `jasperreports-4.7.0.jar` | `http://sourceforge.net/projects/jasperreports/files/jasperreports/JasperReports%204.7.0/` |
| `itext-2.1.0` | `http://mirrors.ibiblio.org/pub/mirrors/maven2/com/lowagie/itext/2.1.0/itext-2.1.0.jar` |

| JAR/ZIP file | Download URL |
|---|---|
| `commons-beanutils-1.8.3-bin.zip` | `http://commons.apache.org/beanutils/download_beanutils.cgi` |
| `commons-digester-2.1.jar` | `http://commons.apache.org/digester/download_digester.cgi` |
| `commons-logging-1.1.1-bin` | `http://commons.apache.org/logging/download_logging.cgi` |
| `poi-bin-3.8-20120326 zip or tar.gz` | `http://poi.apache.org/download.html#POI-3.8` |

All the JasperReports libraries are open source. We shall be using the following JAR files to create a JasperReports report:

| JAR File | Description |
|---|---|
| `commons-beanutils-1.8.3.jar` | JavaBeans utility classes |
| `commons-beanutils-bean-collections-1.8.3.jar` | Collections framework extension classes |
| `commons-beanutils-core-1.8.3.jar` | JavaBeans utility core classes |
| `commons-digester-2.1.jar` | Classes for processing XML documents |
| `commons-logging-1.1.1.jar` | Logging classes |
| `iText-2.1.0.jar` | PDF library |
| `jasperreports-4.7.0.jar` | JasperReports API |
| • `poi-3.8-20120326.jar`<br>• `poi-excelant-3.8-20120326.jar`<br>• `poi-ooxml-3.8-20120326.jar`<br>• `poi-ooxml-schemas-3.8-20120326.jar`<br>• `poi-scratchpad-3.8-20120326.jar` | Apache Jakarta POI classes and dependencies |

Add the Jasper Reports required by the JAR files to the `\\user_projects\domains\base_domain\bin\startWebLogic.bat` script's `CLASSPATH` variable:

```
set SAVE_CLASSPATH=%CLASSPATH%;C:\jasperreports\commons-
beanutils-1.8.3\commons-beanutils-1.8.3.jar;C:\jasperreports\commons-
beanutils-1.8.3\commons-beanutils-bean-collections-1.8.3.jar;C:\
jasperreports\commons-beanutils-1.8.3\commons-beanutils-core-
1.8.3.jar;C:\jasperreports\commons-digester-2.1.jar;C:\jasperreports\
commons-logging-1.1.1\commons-logging-1.1.1.jar;C:\jasperreports\
itext-2.1.0.jar;C:\jasperreports\jasperreports-4.7.0.jar;C:\
jasperreports\poi-3.8\poi-3.8-20120326.jar;C:\jasperreports\poi-
3.8\poi-scratchpad-3.8-20120326.jar;C:\jasperreports\poi-3.8\poi-
ooxml-3.8-20120326.jar;C:\jasperreports\poi-3.8.jar;C:\jasperreports\
poi-3.8\poi-excelant-3.8-20120326.jar;C:\jasperreports\poi-3.8\poi-
ooxml-schemas-3.8-20120326.jar
```

# Creating a Dynamic Web project in Eclipse

First, we need to create a web project for generating JasperReports reports.

Now, go to **File** | **New** | **Other**. In the **New** wizard, expand **Web** and select **Dynamic Web Project**. In **Dynamic Web Project** configuration, specify **Project name** (for example, `PDFExcelReports`), and select the **Target Runtime** server as **Oracle WebLogic Server 12c (12.1.1)** as discussed in *Chapter 1, EJB 3.0 Database Persistence*. Click on **Next** as shown in the following screenshot:

Select the default Java settings; that is, **Default output folder** as **build/classes**, and then click on **Next**. In **WebModule**, specify **ContextRoot** as `PDFExcelReports` and **Content Directory** as `WebContent`. Click on **Finish**. A web project for **PDFExcelReports** gets generated. Right-click on the project node in **ProjectExplorer** and select **Project Properties**. In **Properties**, select **Project Facets**. The **Dynamic Web Module** project facet should be selected by default as shown in the following screenshot:

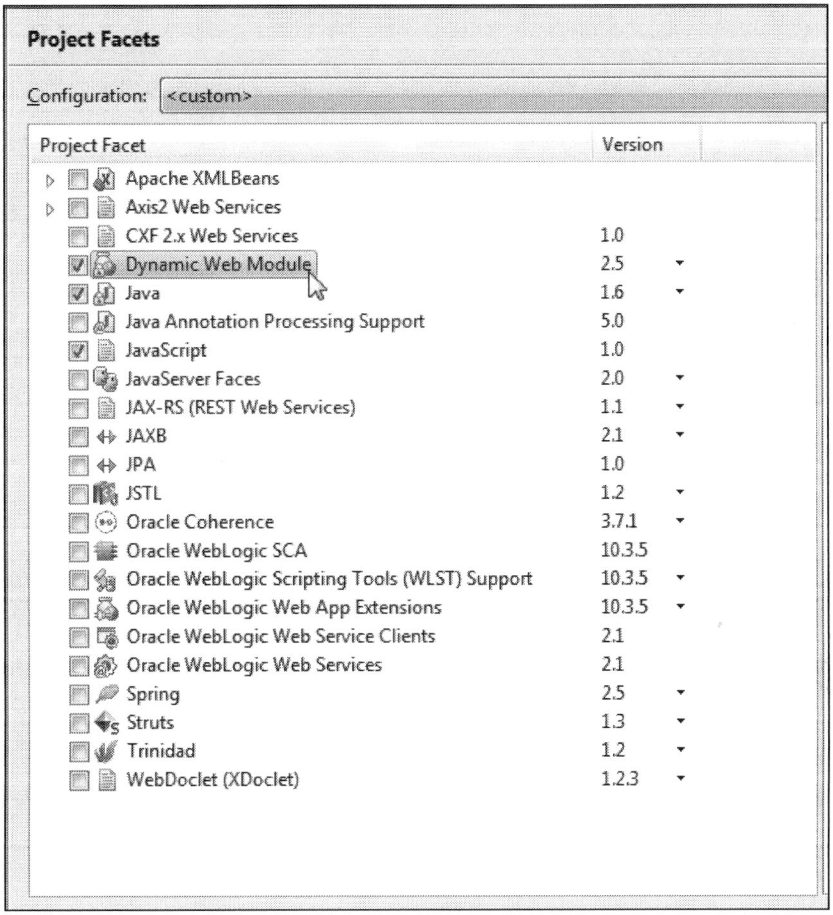

Next, create a **User Library** for JasperReports JAR files and dependencies. Select **Java Build Path** in **Properties**. Click on **Add Library**. In **Add Library**, select **User Library** and click on **Next**. In **User Library**, click on **User Libraries**. In **User Libraries**, click on **New**. In **New User Library**, specify a **User library name** (JasperReports) and click on **OK**. A new user library gets added to **User Libraries**. Click on **Add JARs** to add JAR files to the library. The following screenshot shows the **JasperReports** that are added:

# Creating the configuration file

We require a JasperReports configuration file for generating reports. JasperReports XML configuration files are based on the jasperreport.dtd DTD, with a root element of jasperReport. We shall specify the JasperReports report design in an XML configuration bin file, which we have called config.xml. Create an XML file config.xml in the webContent folder by selecting **XML | XML File** in the **New** wizard.

Some of the other elements (with commonly used subelements and attributes) in a JasperReports configuration XML file are listed in the following table:

| XML element | Description | Subelements | Attributes |
|---|---|---|---|
| `jasperReport` | Root element | `reportFont`, `parameter`, `queryString`, `field`, `variable`, `group`, `title`, `pageHeader`, `columnHeader`, `detail`, `columnFooter`, `pageFooter` | `name`, `columnCount`, `pageWidth`, `pageHeight`, `orientation`, `columnWidth`, `columnSpacing`, `leftMargin`, `rightMargin`, `topMargin`, `bottomMargin` |
| `reportFont` | Report level font definitions | | `name`, `isDefault`, `fontName`, `size`, `isBold`, `isItalic`, `isUnderline`, `isStrikeThrough`, `pdfFontName`, `pdfEncoding`, `isPdfEmbedded` |
| `parameter` | Object references used in generating a report. Referenced with `P${name}` | `parameterDescription`, `defaultValueExpression` | `name`, `class` |
| `queryString` | Specifies the SQL query for retrieving data from a database | | |
| `field` | Database table columns included in report. Referenced with `F${name}` | `fieldDescription` | `name`, `class` |

| XML element | Description | Subelements | Attributes |
|---|---|---|---|
| variable | Variable used in the report XML file. Referenced with V$*{name}* | variableExpression, initialValueExpression | name, class. |
| title | Report title | band | |
| pageHeader | Page header | band | |
| columnHeader | Specifies the different columns in the report generated | band | |
| detail | Specifies the column values | band | |
| columnFooter | Column footer | band | |

A report section is represented with the band element. A band element includes staticText and textElement elements. A staticText element is used to add static text to a report (for example, column headers) and a textElement element is used to add dynamically generated text to a report (for example, column values retrieved from a database table). We won't be using all or even most of these element and attributes. Specify the page width with the pageWidth attribute in the root element jasperReport. Specify the report fonts using the reportFont element. The reportElement elements specify the ARIAL_NORMAL, ARIAL_BOLD, and ARIAL_ITALIC fonts used in the report. Specify a ReportTitle parameter using the parameter element. The queryString of the example JasperReports configuration XML file catalog.xml specifies the SQL query to retrieve the data for the report.

```
<queryString><![CDATA[SELECT CatalogId, Journal,
  Publisher, Edition, Title,
  Author FROM OE.Catalog]]> </queryString>
```

The PDF report has the columns CatalogId, Journal, Publisher, Edition, Title, and Author. Specify a report band for the report title. The ReportTitle parameter is invoked using the $P{ReportTitle} expression. Specify a column header using the columnHeader element. Specify static text with the staticText element. Specify the report detail with the detail element. A column text field is defined using the textField element. The dynamic value of a text field is defined using the textFieldExpression element:

```
<textField>
        <reportElement x="0" y="0" width="100" height="20"/>
        <textFieldExpression class="java.lang.String"><![CDATA[$F{Cata
logId}]]></textFieldExpression>
        </textField>
```

Specify a page footer with the `pageFooter` element. Report parameters are defined using $P{}, report fields using $F{}, and report variables using $V{}. The `config.xml` file is listed as follows:

```
<?xml version='1.0' encoding='utf-8'?>
<!DOCTYPE jasperReport PUBLIC "-//JasperReports//DTD Report Design//
EN"
"http://jasperreports.sourceforge.net/dtds/jasperreport.dtd">
<jasperReport name="PDFReport" pageWidth="975">
```

The following code snippet specifies the report fonts:

```
<reportFont name="Arial_Normal" isDefault="true" fontName="Arial"
size="15" isBold="false" isItalic="false" isUnderline="false"
isStrikeThrough="false" pdfFontName="Helvetica" pdfEncoding="Cp1252"
isPdfEmbedded="false"/>
<reportFont name="Arial_Bold" isDefault="false" fontName="Arial"
size="15" isBold="true" isItalic="false" isUnderline="false"
isStrikeThrough="false" pdfFontName="Helvetica-Bold"
pdfEncoding="Cp1252" isPdfEmbedded="false"/>
<reportFont name="Arial_Italic" isDefault="false" fontName="Arial"
size="12" isBold="false" isItalic="true" isUnderline="false"
isStrikeThrough="false" pdfFontName="Helvetica-Oblique"
pdfEncoding="Cp1252" isPdfEmbedded="false"/>
```

The following code snippet specifies the parameter for the report title, the SQL query to generate the report with, and the report fields. The `resultset` from the SQL query gets bound to the fields.

```
<parameter name="ReportTitle" class="java.lang.String"/>
<queryString><![CDATA[SELECT CatalogId, Journal, Publisher, Edition,
Title, Author FROM Catalog]]></queryString>
<field name="CatalogId" class="java.lang.String"/>
<field name="Journal" class="java.lang.String"/>
<field name="Publisher" class="java.lang.String"/>
<field name="Edition" class="java.lang.String"/>
<field name="Title" class="java.lang.String"/>
<field name="Author" class="java.lang.String"/>
```

Add the report title to the report as follows:

```
<title>
    <band height="50">
      <textField>
        <reportElement x="350" y="0" width="200" height="50" />
        <textFieldExpression class="java.lang.
String">$P{ReportTitle}</textFieldExpression>
      </textField>
    </band>
</title>
  <pageHeader>
    <band>
    </band>
  </pageHeader>
```

Add the column's header as follows:

```
<columnHeader>
    <band height="20">
      <staticText>
        <reportElement x="0" y="0" width="100" height="20"/>
        <textElement>
          <font isUnderline="false" reportFont="Arial_Bold"/>
        </textElement>
        <text><![CDATA[CATALOG ID]]></text>
      </staticText>
    <staticText>
        <reportElement x="125" y="0" width="100" height="20"/>
        <textElement>
          <font isUnderline="false" reportFont="Arial_Bold"/>
        </textElement>
        <text><![CDATA[JOURNAL]]></text>
      </staticText>
      <staticText>
        <reportElement x="250" y="0" width="150" height="20"/>
        <textElement>                    <font isUnderline="false"
reportFont="Arial_Bold"/>
        </textElement>
        <text><![CDATA[PUBLISHER]]></text>
      </staticText>
      <staticText>
        <reportElement x="425" y="0" width="100" height="20"/>
        <textElement>
          <font isUnderline="false" reportFont="Arial_Bold"/>
```

```
        </textElement>
        <text><![CDATA[EDITION]]></text>
      </staticText>
<staticText>
        <reportElement x="550" y="0" width="200" height="20"/>
        <textElement>
          <font isUnderline="false" reportFont="Arial_Bold"/>
        </textElement>
        <text><![CDATA[TITLE]]></text>
      </staticText>
      <staticText>
        <reportElement x="775" y="0" width="200" height="20"/>
        <textElement>
          <font isUnderline="false" reportFont="Arial_Bold"/>
        </textElement>
        <text><![CDATA[AUTHOR]]></text>
      </staticText>

    </band>
  </columnHeader>
```

The following code snippet shows how to add the report detail, which consists of values retrieved using the SQL query from the Oracle database:

```
<detail>
    <band height="20">
      <textField>
        <reportElement x="0" y="0" width="100" height="20"/>
        <textFieldExpression class="java.lang.String"><![CDATA[$F{Cata
logId}]]></textFieldExpression>
      </textField>
      <textField pattern="0.00">
        <reportElement x="125" y="0" width="100" height="20"/>
        <textFieldExpression class="java.lang.String"><![CDATA[$F{Jour
nal}]]></textFieldExpression>
      </textField>

      <textField pattern="0.00">
        <reportElement x="250" y="0" width="150" height="20"/>
        <textFieldExpression class="java.lang.String"><![CDATA[$F{Publ
isher}]]></textFieldExpression>
      </textField>

  <textField>
        <reportElement x="425" y="0" width="100" height="20"/>
```

```
          <textFieldExpression class="java.lang.String"><![CDATA[$F{Edit
ion}]]></textFieldExpression>
        </textField>
      <textField pattern="0.00">
        <reportElement x="550" y="0" width="200" height="20"/>
        <textFieldExpression class="java.lang.
String"><![CDATA[$F{Title}]]></textFieldExpression>
        </textField>
  <textField>
        <reportElement x="775" y="0" width="200" height="20"/>


        <textFieldExpression class="java.lang.
String"><![CDATA[$F{Author}]]></textFieldExpression>
        </textField>


    </band>
   </detail>
```

Add the column and page footer including the page number as follows:

```
<columnFooter>
    <band>
    </band>
  </columnFooter>
<pageFooter>
    <band height="15">
      <staticText>
        <reportElement x="0" y="0" width="40" height="15"/>
         <textElement>
          <font isUnderline="false" reportFont="Arial_Italic"/>
        </textElement>
        <text><![CDATA[Page #]]></text>
      </staticText>
      <textField>
        <reportElement x="40" y="0" width="100" height="15"/>
        <textElement>
          <font isUnderline="false" reportFont="Arial_Italic"/>
        </textElement>
        <textFieldExpression class="java.lang.
Integer"><![CDATA[$V{PAGE_NUMBER}]]></textFieldExpression>
</textField>
    </band>
  </pageFooter>
<summary>
```

```
    <band>
    </band>
  </summary>
</jasperReport>
```

We need to create a JAR file for the `config.xml` file and add the JAR file to the WebLogic Server's domain's `lib` directory. Create a JAR file using the following command from the directory containing the `config.xml` as follows:

```
>jar cf config.jar config.xml
```

Add the `config.jar` file to the `\\user_projects\domains\base_domain\lib` directory, which is in the classpath of the server.

# Creating a web application

We shall be creating a web application for generating JasperReports reports and deploying the web application to WebLogic Server. For the web application, we need to create the JSPs `CatalogPDFReport.jsp` (for the PDF report) and `CatalogExcelReport.jsp` (for the Excel report).

To create a JSP file, go to **File | New | Other**. In **New**, expand **Web** and select **JSP File** and click on **Next,** as shown in the following screenshot:

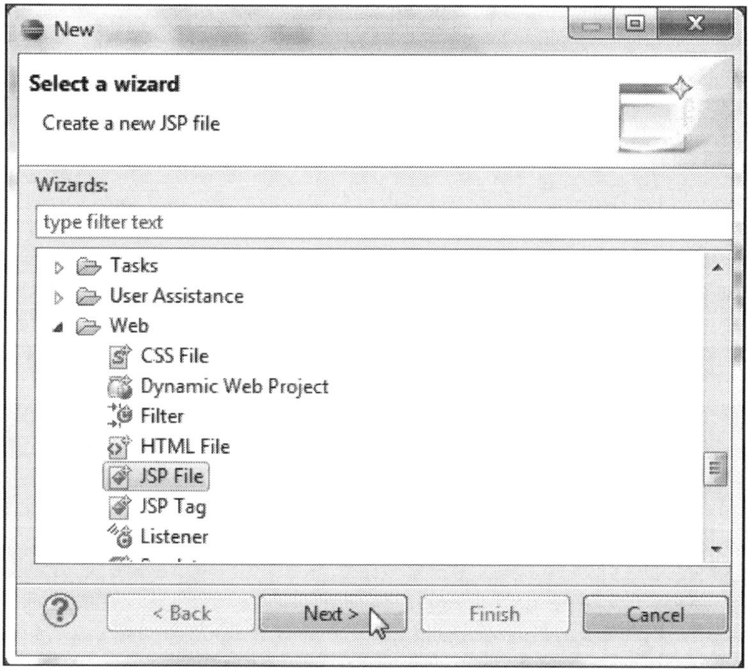

Select the folder to create a JSP file as `WebContent`, specify a **File name** (`CatalogPDFReport.jsp` or `CatalogExcelReport.jsp`), and click on **Next**.

Select the default JSP file template and click on **Finish**. The JSPs get added to the project.

The JasperReports process involves creating a report design, compiling the report design to a runnable format, setting the report parameters, creating a JDBC connection to Oracle database, creating a print of the report, and exporting the print to the required format such as a PDF or an Excel spreadsheet. In the `CatalogPDFReport.jsp`, first import the JasperReports packages and other required packages for creating an `InitialContext` object and obtaining a `Connection` object as follows:

```
<%@ page import="java.io.*,
java.util.*,
java.sql.Connection,
javax.sql.DataSource,
javax.naming.InitialContext,
net.sf.jasperreports.engine.*, net.sf.jasperreports.engine.design.
JasperDesign,
net.sf.jasperreports.engine.xml.JRXmlLoader,
net.sf.jasperreports.engine.export.*"
%>
```

# Creating a report design

In this section, we shall create an `InputStream` for the JasperReports configuration file `config.xml` and load the XML file:

```
InputStream input=this.getClass().getClassLoader().
getResourceAsStream("config.xml");
```

A `JasperDesign` object represents the report design. Compile the report design file to create a `JasperReport` object. The compilation of the report design file validates the JasperReports XML file (`config.xml`) with the `jaspereports.dtd` DTD and converts the report expressions into a ready-to-evaluate form.

```
JasperReport report = JasperCompileManager.compileReport(design);
```

# Setting the report title

We need to set a value for the report title using the `ReportTitle` parameter. Create a `HashMap` for parameters and set the parameter value using the `put` method as follows:

```
Map parameters = new HashMap();
parameters.put("ReportTitle", "PDF JasperReport");
```

# Creating a JDBC connection

Now, obtain a JDBC connection to retrieve data from the database, in order to create your PDF/Excel report. First, create an `InitialContext` object. Subsequently, look up the WebLogic Server data source that we created earlier using the JNDI lookup. Obtain a `Connection` object using the `getConnection` method.

```
InitialContext initialContext = new InitialContext();
DataSource ds = (DataSource)initialContext.lookup("jdbc/OracleDS");
Connection conn = ds.getConnection();
```

The database data binding to the report fields gets applied in the report configuration file `config.xml`, which we created earlier.

# Generating a PDF report

To view the report, generate a `JasperPrint` document, which may be viewed, printed, or exported to other formats, from the compiled report design.

```
JasperPrint print = JasperFillManager.fillReport(report,

        parameters, conn);
```

The `Map` parameters in the `fillReport(JasperReport,Map,Connection)` method consist of the parameter values for the parameters specified in the `parameter` element of the XML configuration file. The `conn` argument is the JDBC connection we generated in the previous section. A JasperReports report may be exported to an XML file, a PDF file, an HTML file, a CSV file, or an Excel XLS file; to export the JasperReports report we've just generated to a PDF file, use the `exportReportToPdfStream` method of the `JasperExportManager` class as follows:

```
OutputStream output=new FileOutputStream(new File("C InputStream
input=this.getClass().getClassLoader().getResourceAsStream("config.
xml");CatalogPDFReport.pdf"));
JasperExportManager.exportReportToPdfStream(print, output);
```

The completed `CatalogPDFReport.jsp` JSP is listed as follows:

```
<%@ page contentType="text/html;charset=windows-1252"%>
<%@ page
   import="java.io.*,java.util.*,java.sql.Connection,javax.sql.
DataSource,javax.naming.InitialContext,net.sf.jasperreports.
engine.*,net.sf.jasperreports.engine.design.JasperDesign,net.
sf.jasperreports.engine.xml.JRXmlLoader"%>
<%
   InputStream input = this.getClass().getClassLoader()
       .getResourceAsStream("config.xml");
```

```
JasperDesign design = JRXmlLoader.load(input);

JasperReport report = JasperCompileManager.compileReport(design);
Map parameters = new HashMap();
parameters.put("ReportTitle", "PDF JasperReport");

InitialContext initialContext = new InitialContext();
DataSource ds = (DataSource) initialContext.lookup("jdbc/OracleDS");
Connection conn = ds.getConnection();
JasperPrint print = JasperFillManager.fillReport(report,
    parameters, conn);
OutputStream output = new FileOutputStream(new File(
    "catalogPDFReport.pdf"));
JasperExportManager.exportReportToPdfStream(print, output);
%>
```

# Creating an Excel report

Similarly, create the `CatalogExcelReport.jsp` file for the Excel report. Create
an `InputStream` for `config.xml`, create a `JasperDesign` object, compile the
design to create a JasperReport, set the `ReportTitle` parameter value, create an
`InitialContext`, look up the WebLogic Server data source, obtain a `Connection`
object, and create a `JasperPrint` with the same procedure as for the PDF report.
Create a `ByteArrayOutputStram` for the `catalogExcelReport.xls` report
as follows:

```
OutputStream ouputStream=new FileOutputStream(new
File("catalogExcelReport.xls"));
    ByteArrayOutputStream byteArrayOutputStream = new
ByteArrayOutputStream();
```

Create a `JRXlsExporter` object and set the parameter values for the `JASPER_PRINT`
and `OUTPUT_STREAM` parameters as follows:

```
JRXlsExporter exporterXLS = new JRXlsExporter();
exporterXLS.setParameter(JRXlsExporterParameter.JASPER_PRINT, print);
exporterXLS.setParameter(JRXlsExporterParameter.OUTPUT_STREAM,
byteArrayOutputStream);
```

Export the Excel report using the `exportReport` method as follows:

```
exporterXLS.exportReport();
```

Just exporting doesn't generate the report. We need to output the Excel report using the OutputStream object. Write the Excel report using the ByteArrayOutputStream object. Subsequently, flush and close the OutputStream object as shown in the following code snippet:

```
ouputStream.write(byteArrayOutputStream.toByteArray());
        ouputStream.flush();
        ouputStream.close();
```

The CatalogExcelReport.jsp is listed as follows:

```
<%@ page contentType="text/html;charset=windows-1252"%>
<%@ page
  import="java.io.*,java.util.*,java.sql.Connection,javax.sql.
DataSource,javax.naming.InitialContext,net.sf.jasperreports.
engine.*,net.sf.jasperreports.engine.design.JasperDesign,net.
sf.jasperreports.engine.xml.JRXmlLoader,net.sf.jasperreports.engine.
export.*"%>
<%
  InputStream input = this.getClass().getClassLoader()
      .getResourceAsStream("config.xml");

  JasperDesign design = JRXmlLoader.load(input);

  JasperReport report = JasperCompileManager.compileReport(design);

  Map parameters = new HashMap();

  parameters.put("ReportTitle", "Excel JasperReport");

  InitialContext initialContext = new InitialContext();

  DataSource ds = (DataSource) initialContext.lookup("jdbc/OracleDS");

  Connection conn = ds.getConnection();

  JasperPrint print = JasperFillManager.fillReport(report,
      parameters, conn);

  OutputStream ouputStream = new FileOutputStream(new File(
      "catalogExcelReport.xls"));
```

```
      ByteArrayOutputStream byteArrayOutputStream = new
  ByteArrayOutputStream();

  JRXlsExporter exporterXLS = new JRXlsExporter();

  exporterXLS
      .setParameter(JRXlsExporterParameter.JASPER_PRINT, print);

  exporterXLS.setParameter(JRXlsExporterParameter.OUTPUT_STREAM,
      byteArrayOutputStream);

  exporterXLS.exportReport();

  ouputStream.write(byteArrayOutputStream.toByteArray());

  ouputStream.flush();

  ouputStream.close();
%>
```

In the following section, we shall package and deploy the web application to
generate a JasperReports PDF report and an Excel report from the example
`Catalog` table.

# Packaging and deploying the web application

In this section, we package the web application and deploy the web application
to WebLogic Server using a `build.xml` file. Create an XML file `build.xml` in the
project folder **JasperReports**. In the `build.xml` file, define the properties listed in
following table:

| Property | Description | Value |
|---|---|---|
| `web.module` | The web module folder | `${basedir}/WebContent` |
| `weblogic.home` | WebLogic home directory | `C:\Oracle\Middleware` |
| `weblogic.server` | WebLogic Server directory | `${weblogic.home}/wlserver_12.1/server` |
| `build.dir` | Build directory | `${basedir}/build` |

| Property | Description | Value |
|---|---|---|
| `weblogic.domain.dir` | WebLogic base domain directory | `${weblogic.home}/user_ projects/ domains/base_domain` |
| `deploy.dir` | WebLogic server deploy directory | `${weblogic.domain.dir}/ autodeploy` |

Define a `path` element to include all the JAR files in the WebLogic `modules` directory, WebLogic server `lib` directory, and WebLogic domain `lib` directory. Add the following tasks to `build.xml`:

| Target | Description |
|---|---|
| prepare | Make the required directories |
| war | Package the JSPs, `catalog.xml`, `WEB-INF/ web.xml` into a WAR file |
| deploy | Deploy the WAR file to WebLogic server |
| clean | Delete the generated artifacts |

The `build.xml` file is listed as follows:

```xml
<?xml version="1.0" encoding="UTF-8"?>
  <!--
    WebLogic build file
  -->
<project name="JasperReports" default="deploy" basedir=".">
  <property name="web.module" value="${basedir}/WebContent" />
  <property name="weblogic.home" value=" C:/Oracle/Middleware/" />
  <property name="weblogic.server" value="${weblogic.home}/
wlserver_12.1/server" />
  <property name="build.dir" value="${basedir}/build" />
  <property name="weblogic.domain.dir"
    value="${weblogic.home}/user_projects/domains/base_domain" />
  <property name="deploy.dir"
    value="${weblogic.domain.dir}/autodeploy" />
  <path id="classpath">
    <fileset dir="${weblogic.home}/modules">
      <include name="*.jar" />
    </fileset>
    <fileset dir="${weblogic.server}/lib">
      <include name="*.jar" />
    </fileset>
```

```xml
        <fileset dir="${weblogic.domain.dir}/lib">
          <include name="*.jar" />
        </fileset>
        <pathelement location="${build.dir}" />
    </path>

    <property name="build.classpath" refid="classpath" />
    <target name="prepare">
      <mkdir dir="${build.dir}" />
    </target>

    <target name="war" depends="prepare">
      <war warfile="${build.dir}/jasperreports.war">
        <fileset dir="WebContent">
          <include name="*.jsp" />
        </fileset>
        <fileset dir="WebContent">
          <include name="catalog.xml" />
        </fileset>
        <fileset dir="WebContent">
          <include name="WEB-INF/web.xml" />
        </fileset>
        <fileset dir="WebContent">
          <include name="WEB-INF/lib/*.jar" />
        </fileset>
      </war>
    </target>


    <target name="deploy" depends="war">
      <copy file="${build.dir}/jasperreports.war" todir="${deploy.dir}"
/>
    </target>
    <target name="clean">

      <delete file="${build.dir}/jasperreports.war" />
    </target>
</project>
```

The directory structure of the project is shown as follows:

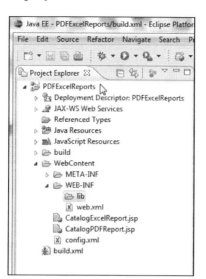

Right-click on `build.xml` and in **Run As** select **3 Ant build...** as shown in the following screenshot:

Select the **deploy** target and click on **Run**.

As the targets have dependency on preceding targets, all the targets except the `clean` target get run.

```
Buildfile: C:\Users\dvohra\workspace\PDFExcelReports\build.xml
prepare:
war:
    [war] Building war: C:\Users\dvohra\workspace\PDFExcelReports\build\jasperreports.war
deploy:
    [copy] Copying 1 file to C:\Oracle\Middleware\user_projects\domains\base_domain\autodeploy
BUILD SUCCESSFUL
Total time: 2 seconds
```

The `clean` target may be run to delete the WAR file and recompile it.

Start the WebLogic server if not already started. The JasperReports WAR file gets deployed to WebLogic Server and gets listed in the **Deployments** table as shown in the following screenshot:

# Running the web application

Run the `CatalogPDFReport.jsp` with the URL `http://loclahost:7001/jasperreports/CatalogPDFReport.jsp`. A PDF report gets generated. The PDF report `catalogPDFReport.pdf` gets generated in the `\\user_projects\domains\base_domain directory` as shown in the following screenshot:

PDF JasperReport

| CATALOG ID | JOURNAL | PUBLISHER | EDITION | TITLE | AUTHOR |
|---|---|---|---|---|---|
| 1 | Oracle Magazine | Oracle Publishing | Nov-Dec 2004 | Database Resource Manager | Kimberly Floss |
| 2 | Oracle Magazine | Oracle Publishing | Nov-Dec 2004 | From ADF UIX to JSF | Jonas Jacobi |
| 3 | Oracle Magazine | Oracle Publishing | March-April 2005 | Starting with Oracle ADF | Steve Muench |

Run `CatalogExcelReport.jsp` with the URL `http://localhost:7001/jasperreports/CatalogExcelReport.jsp`. The `catalogExcelReport.xls` gets generated in the `\\user_projects\domains\base_domain` directory as shown in the following screenshot:

JasperReports is not without its drawbacks. A tight-coupling between the report data and the report layout implies that the developer would need to be familiar with both the development aspect of obtaining the database data and the design aspect of the report layout.

# Summary

In this chapter, we demonstrated the use of the Oracle Enterprise Pack for Eclipse's integrated support for WebLogic server to deploy and run any web application that requires an application server. First, we configured a datasource JNDI in WebLogic Server. We created and deployed a web application for JasperReports to the WebLogic Server, and subsequently ran the web application to create PDF and Excel reports.

In the next chapter, we shall create a JSF data table using the JavaServer Faces project facet.

# 4
# Creating a JSF Data Table

**JavaServer Faces (JSF)** offers a set of components for implementing a **user interface (UI)** for a web application (refer to `http://jcp.org/aboutJava/ communityprocess/final/jsr252/index.html` for more information on JSF). A JSF data table is one such component. A data table consists of a grid of rows and columns. The header row includes the column headers. The column detail may either be static data or data generated dynamically from **expression language (EL)** value expressions (refer to `http://today.java.net/pub/a/today/2006/03/07/ unified-jsp-jsf-expression-language.html`). Data may be retrieved from a database table and added to the JSF data table using any of the database persistence technologies such as JDBC and EJB. For using JSF with EJB refer the book, *EJB 3.0 Database Persistence with Oracle Fusion Middleware 11g, Deepak Vohra, Packt Publishing*. JSF data tables may be bound to a managed bean. In this chapter we shall create a data table from a database table using a SQL query input in an input text field. This chapter has the following sections:

- Setting the environment
- Creating a web project
- Creating a managed bean
    - Constructing the managed bean class
    - The managed bean class
- Creating a JSF page
    - Adding components to the JSF page
    - The JSF page
- Running the JSF page

# Setting the environment

For setting the environment, install Oracle Enterprise Pack for Eclipse 12*c*. Create a domain in WebLogic Server 12*c*. We also need to install Oracle Database 11*g* XE. Using SQL Command Line, create a database table—`Catalog`—with the following SQL script:

```
CREATE TABLE OE.Catalog(CatalogId INTEGER PRIMARY KEY, Journal
VARCHAR(25), Publisher VARCHAR(25),Edition VARCHAR(25), Title
Varchar(45), Author Varchar(25));
INSERT INTO OE.Catalog VALUES('1', 'Oracle Magazine',  'Oracle
Publishing', 'Nov-Dec 2004', 'Database Resource  Manager', 'Kimberly
Floss');
INSERT INTO OE.Catalog VALUES('2', 'Oracle Magazine',   'Oracle
Publishing', 'Nov-Dec 2004', 'From ADF UIX to JSF',  'Jonas Jacobi');
INSERT INTO OE.Catalog VALUES('3', 'Oracle Magazine',   'Oracle
Publishing', 'March-April 2005', 'Starting with  Oracle ADF ', 'Steve
Muench');
```

# Creating a web project

In this section we will create a web project in Eclipse for the JSF web application. We shall be using JSF 1.2 version in this chapter; we will use Version 2.0 in the next chapter. To create a web project select **File | New | Other**. In the **New** wizard select **Web | Dynamic Web Project**. In the **New Dynamic Web Project** window click on **New Runtime...** to configure a new runtime for Oracle WebLogic Server 12*c* as discussed in *Chapter 1, EJB 3.0 Database Persistence*. Select **2.5** as **Dynamic web module version** and select **JavaServer Faces v1.2 Project** as **Configuration**. Click on **Next**, as shown in the following screenshot:

Select the default Java settings of source folders on build path as `src`, and default output folder as `build/classes`. Click on **Next**. Select **JSFDataTable** as **Context root** and **WebContent** as **Content directory**, and click on **Next**. In **JSF Capabilities** select the default settings and click on **Finish**, as follows:

A **JSFDataTable** web project gets created, as shown in the **Project Explorer** tab:

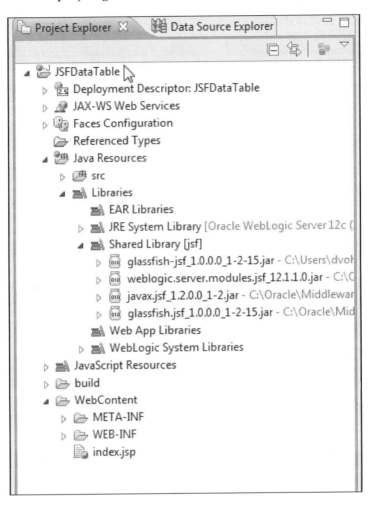

Right-click on the project node and select **Properties**. Select **Project Facets**. The **JavaServer Faces** facet with **1.2** as **Version** should be shown as selected. A project facet adds the required libraries, and configuration for the selected technology.

**Project Facets**

Configuration: &lt;custom&gt;

| Project Facet | Version | |
|---|---|---|
| ▷ ☐ Apache XMLBeans | | |
| ▷ ☐ Axis2 Web Services | | |
| ☐ CXF 2.x Web Services | 1.0 | |
| ☑ Dynamic Web Module | 2.5 | ▾ |
| ☑ Java | 1.5 | ▾ |
| ☐ Java Annotation Processing Support | 5.0 | |
| ☑ JavaScript | 1.0 | |
| ☑ JavaServer Faces | 1.2 | ▾ |
| ☐ JAX-RS (REST Web Services) | 1.1 | ▾ |
| ☐ JAXB | 2.1 | ▾ |
| ☐ JPA | 2.0 | ▾ |
| ☐ JSTL | 1.2 | ▾ |
| ☐ Oracle Coherence | 3.7.1 | ▾ |
| ☐ Oracle WebLogic SCA | 12.1.1 | |
| ☐ Oracle WebLogic Scripting Tools (WLST) Support | 12.1.1 | ▾ |
| ☑ Oracle WebLogic Web App Extensions | 12.1.1 | ▾ |
| ☐ Oracle WebLogic Web Service Clients | 2.1 | |
| ☐ Oracle WebLogic Web Services | 2.1 | |
| ☐ Spring | 2.5 | ▾ |
| ☐ Struts | 1.3 | ▾ |
| ☐ Trinidad | 1.2 | ▾ |
| ☐ WebDoclet (XDoclet) | 1.2.3 | ▾ |

The JSFDataTable project includes a `faces-config.xml` file, which we shall discuss when we create a managed bean, and a `web.xml` file with the following configuration for a Faces servlet. The Faces servlet class — `javax.faces.webapp.FacesServlet` gets invoked with URL pattern — `/faces/*`, which is specified in the servlet mapping:

```
<servlet>
<servlet-name>Faces Servlet</servlet-name>
<servlet-class>javax.faces.webapp.FacesServlet</servlet-class>
    <load-on-startup>1</load-on-startup>
</servlet>
<servlet-mapping>
<servlet-name>Faces Servlet</servlet-name>
    <url-pattern>/faces/*</url-pattern>
</servlet-mapping>
```

# Creating a managed bean

A managed bean is just a Java bean class managed by the JSF container, the JSF managed bean facility. The JSF page UI components are bound to properties in the managed bean, which contains the business logic for the input and output to the UI components. In the **Model View Controller** (**MVC**) design pattern, the JSF page represents the view, the managed bean represents the controller, and the JDBC mapping to the database represents the model. To create a managed bean, right-click on **faces-config.xml** and select **Open With | Faces Config Editor**, as shown in the following screenshot:

In **Faces Config Editor** select the **Managed Beans** tab. The managed bean elements get listed under **Managed Bean Elements**. Select the **session** scope and click on **Add** to add a new managed bean, as shown in the following screenshot:

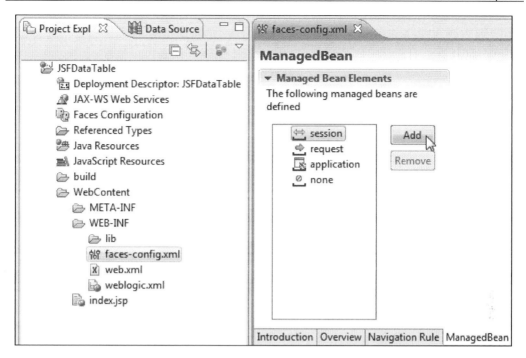

In the **New Managed Bean Wizard** window check the **Create a new Java class** checkbox and click on **Next**, as shown in the following screenshot:

In the **Java Class** dialog box specify `datatable.managed` as a package name in the **Package** field, specify `Catalog` as a class name in the **Name** field, and click on **Next**, as follows:

In the **Managed Bean Configuration** dialog box specify `catalog` as **Name**, select **session** as **Scope**, and click on **Next**, as shown in the following screenshot:

In the **Wizard Summarys** dialog box click on **Finish,** as shown in the following screenshot:

A managed bean (**catalog**) including a Java bean class—**Catalog.java**—gets added to the **JSFDataTable** application, as shown in the following screenshot:

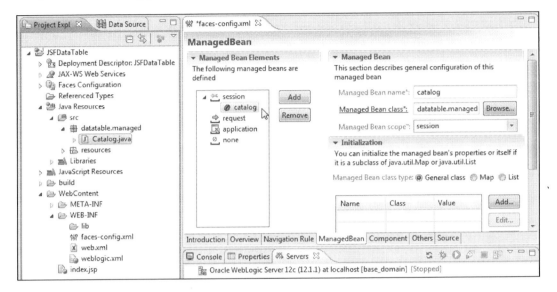

# Constructing the managed bean class

In a managed bean a data table property is represented with the `javax.faces.component.html.HtmlDataTable` class. The columns' properties are represented by the `javax.faces.component.UIColumn` class. In the managed bean class—`Catalog.java`—add the required `import` statements for the UI components. Add an `HtmlDataTable` property for a data table and add `UIColumn` properties for the data table columns. Also add properties for a form, an input text to specify a SQL query, and a command button to submit the SQL query. We shall bind the UI component properties to the JSF page when we construct the JSF page. Add getter/setter methods for the UI components' properties. Add an action method that is invoked when the command button is clicked, as follows:

```
public String commandButton1_action() { }
```

An action method must not take any arguments and must return a String. In the action method, retrieve the SQL query input in the JSF page input text field and run the SQL query using a `Statement` object to generate a result set:

```
rs = stmt.executeQuery((String) inputText1.getValue());
```

Set the border and cell padding for the data table. Set the iteration variable that represents a row of data in the data table:

```
dataTable1.setBorder(5);
dataTable1.setCellpadding("1");
dataTable1.setVar("journalcatalog");
```

Set the header values for the columns in the data table. The data table has columns corresponding to the columns in the database table. Column headers are added by creating the `HtmlOutputText` header components and setting the headers on the `UIColumn` components with the `setHeader()` method. The `HtmlOutputText` value is set using the `setValue` method. For example, the column header for the `CatalogId` column is added, as follows:

```
HtmlOutputText headerComponent = new HtmlOutputText();
headerComponent.setValue("CatalogId");
column1.setHeader(headerComponent);
```

For each of the columns in the data table, create a `HtmlOutputText` object, specify a value expression for the `HtmlOutputText` object, and add the component to the column. A `ValueExpression` object is created by first obtaining the current `FacesContext` object using a static method—`getCurrentInstance()`. Subsequently create an `ELContext` object from the `FacesContext` object using the `getELContext()` method. Create a `ExpressionFactory` object from the `FacesContext` object. Then, create a `ValueExpression` object from the `ExpressionFactory` object using the `createValueExpression()` method by providing the `ELContext` object and the EL value expression as arguments to the method. The EL expression for a column must map to the table column name. The value expression for a `HtmlOutputText` object is set using the `setValueExpression()` method. A `HtmlOutputText` component is added to a `UIColumn` component by invoking the `getChildren()` method for the column to retrieve a `List` object and subsequently invoking the `add()` method to add to the `List` object. As an example for the `CatalogId` column, a `HtmlOutputText` component is added, as follows:

```
HtmlOutputText column1Text = new HtmlOutputText();
FacesContext fCtx = FacesContext.getCurrentInstance();
ELContext elCtx = fCtx.getELContext();
ExpressionFactory ef = fCtx.getApplication().getExpressionFactory();
ValueExpression ve = ef.createValueExpression(elCtx,
        "#{catalog.catalogid}", String.class);
column1Text.setValueExpression("value", ve);
column1.getChildren().add(column1Text);
```

We use the `DataModel` instance, which represents a data collection as a collection of rows, to wrap the result set to a JSF data table. `ResultSetDataModel` is a convenient implementation of a `DataModel` instance that wraps a `ResultSet` object of Java objects. The `ResultSet` object must be scrollable. Next, create a `ResultSetDataModel` object. A `ResultSetDataModel` object is used to wrap the `ResultSet` object that we generated using the SQL query. Set the `ResultSet` object retrieved with the SQL query as the data collection for the `ResultSetDataModel` object using the `setWrappedData()` method:

```
ResultSetDataModel dataModel=new ResultSetDataModel();
dataModel.setWrappedData(rs);
```

Bind the data table with the `ResultSetDataModel` object using the `setValue()` method, as follows:

```
dataTable1.setValue(dataModel);
```

# The managed bean class

The managed bean class — `Catalog.java` — is listed, as follows:

```
package datatable.managed;

import javax.faces.component.html.HtmlCommandButton;
import javax.faces.component.html.HtmlDataTable;
import javax.faces.component.html.HtmlForm;
import javax.faces.component.html.HtmlInputText;
import javax.faces.component.UIColumn;
import javax.faces.component.html.HtmlOutputText;
import javax.faces.context.FacesContext;
import javax.el.*;
import javax.faces.model.ResultSetDataModel;
import java.sql.*;


public class Catalog {
```

First, declare the variables for the managed bean properties and connection parameters:

```
private HtmlForm form1;
private HtmlInputText inputText1;
private HtmlCommandButton commandButton1;
private HtmlDataTable dataTable1;
private UIColumn column1;
private UIColumn column2;
private UIColumn column3;
```

```
private UIColumn column4;
private UIColumn column5;
private UIColumn column6;
private Statement stmt;
private Connection connection;
private ResultSet rs;
```

Add getter/setter methods for the managed bean properties:

```
public void setForm1(HtmlForm form1) {
   this.form1 = form1;
}
public HtmlForm getForm1() {
   return form1;
}
public void setInputText1(HtmlInputText inputText1) {
   this.inputText1 = inputText1;
}
public HtmlInputText getInputText1() {
   return inputText1;
}
public void setCommandButton1(HtmlCommandButton commandButton1) {
   this.commandButton1 = commandButton1;
}
public HtmlCommandButton getCommandButton1() {
   return commandButton1;
}
public void setDataTable1(HtmlDataTable dataTable1) {
   this.dataTable1 = dataTable1;
}
public HtmlDataTable getDataTable1() {
   return dataTable1;
}
public void setColumn1(UIColumn column1) {
   this.column1 = column1;
}
public UIColumn getColumn1() {
   return column1;
}
public void setColumn2(UIColumn column2) {
   this.column2 = column2;
}
public UIColumn getColumn2() {
   return column2;
}
```

```
public void setColumn3(UIColumn column3) {
  this.column3 = column3;
}
public UIColumn getColumn3() {
  return column3;
}
public void setColumn4(UIColumn column4) {
  this.column4 = column4;
}
public UIColumn getColumn4() {
  return column4;
}
public void setColumn5(UIColumn column5) {
  this.column5 = column5;
}
public UIColumn getColumn5() {
  return column5;
}
public void setColumn6(UIColumn column6) {
  this.column6 = column6;
}
public UIColumn getColumn6() {
  return column6;
}
```

Add an action method for the command button:

```
public String commandButton1_action() {

  try {
```

Load the Oracle database driver using the `Class.forName()` method, and create a `Connection` object using the `DriverManager.getConnection()` method with connection URL for Oracle Database instance XE running on port 1521 at host— `localhost`:

```
Class.forName("oracle.jdbc.OracleDriver");
String url = "jdbc:oracle:thin:@localhost:1521:XE";
connection = DriverManager.getConnection(url, "OE", "OE");
```

Create a `Statement` object using the `createStatement()` object of the `Connection` object with scrollable `ResultSet`:

```
stmt = connection.createStatement(
    ResultSet.TYPE_SCROLL_INSENSITIVE,
    ResultSet.CONCUR_READ_ONLY);
```

Run the SQL query retrieved from the input text using the `executeQuery()` method of the `Statement` object:

```
rs = stmt.executeQuery((String) inputText1.getValue());
```

Set the border, cell padding, and iteration variable for the data table:

```
dataTable1.setBorder(5);
dataTable1.setCellpadding("1");
dataTable1.setVar("journalcatalog");
```

Add header components to the data table:

```
HtmlOutputText headerComponent = new HtmlOutputText();
headerComponent.setValue("CatalogId");
column1.setHeader(headerComponent);
headerComponent = new HtmlOutputText();
headerComponent.setValue("Journal");
column2.setHeader(headerComponent);
headerComponent = new HtmlOutputText();
headerComponent.setValue("Publisher");
column3.setHeader(headerComponent);
headerComponent = new HtmlOutputText();
headerComponent.setValue("Edition");
column4.setHeader(headerComponent);
headerComponent = new HtmlOutputText();
headerComponent.setValue("Title");
column5.setHeader(headerComponent);
headerComponent = new HtmlOutputText();
headerComponent.setValue("Author");
column6.setHeader(headerComponent);
```

Specify the value expression binding for the data table rows:

```
HtmlOutputText column1Text = new HtmlOutputText();
FacesContext fCtx = FacesContext.getCurrentInstance();
ELContext elCtx = fCtx.getELContext();
ExpressionFactory ef = fCtx.getApplication().
getExpressionFactory();
ValueExpression ve = ef.createValueExpression(elCtx,
    "#{journalcatalog.catalogid}", String.class);
column1Text.setValueExpression("value", ve);

column1.getChildren().add(column1Text);
HtmlOutputText column2Text = new HtmlOutputText();
```

```
        fCtx = FacesContext.getCurrentInstance();

        ef = fCtx.getApplication().getExpressionFactory();
        ve = ef.createValueExpression(elCtx, "#{journalcatalog.
journal}",
            String.class);
        column2Text.setValueExpression("value", ve);

        column2.getChildren().add(column2Text);
        HtmlOutputText column3Text = new HtmlOutputText();

        fCtx = FacesContext.getCurrentInstance();

        ef = fCtx.getApplication().getExpressionFactory();
        ve = ef.createValueExpression(elCtx, "#{journalcatalog.
publisher}",
            String.class);
        column3Text.setValueExpression("value", ve);

        column3.getChildren().add(column3Text);
        HtmlOutputText column4Text = new HtmlOutputText();
        fCtx = FacesContext.getCurrentInstance();

        ef = fCtx.getApplication().getExpressionFactory();
        ve = ef.createValueExpression(elCtx, "#{journalcatalog.
edition}",
            String.class);
        column4Text.setValueExpression("value", ve);

        column4.getChildren().add(column4Text);
        HtmlOutputText column5Text = new HtmlOutputText();
        fCtx = FacesContext.getCurrentInstance();

        ef = fCtx.getApplication().getExpressionFactory();
        ve = ef.createValueExpression(elCtx, "#{journalcatalog.title}",
            String.class);
        column5Text.setValueExpression("value", ve);

        column5.getChildren().add(column5Text);
        HtmlOutputText column6Text = new HtmlOutputText();
        fCtx = FacesContext.getCurrentInstance();

        ef = fCtx.getApplication().getExpressionFactory();
        ve = ef.createValueExpression(elCtx, "#{journalcatalog.author}",
```

```
            String.class);
       column6Text.setValueExpression("value", ve);


       column6.getChildren().add(column6Text);
```

Create a `ResultSetDataModel` object, set the `ResultSet` object as its data collection, and set it to the data table's value:

```
       ResultSetDataModel dataModel = new ResultSetDataModel();
       dataModel.setWrappedData(rs);
       dataTable1.setValue(dataModel)
    } catch (SQLException e) {

       System.err.println(e.getMessage());
    } catch (ClassNotFoundException e) {
       System.err.println(e.getMessage());
    } finally {

    }
    return null;
  }

}
```

The managed bean class is specified in the `faces-config.xml` file using the `managed-bean` element. `faces-config.xml` is listed, as follows:

```
<?xml version="1.0" encoding="UTF-8"?>

<faces-config
    xmlns="http://java.sun.com/xml/ns/javaee"
    xmlns:xsi="http://www.w3.org/2001/XMLSchema-instance"
    xsi:schemaLocation="http://java.sun.com/xml/ns/javaee http://java.
sun.com/xml/ns/javaee/web-facesconfig_1_2.xsd"
    version="1.2">

  <managed-bean>
    <managed-bean-name>catalog</managed-bean-name>
    <managed-bean-class>datatable.managed.Catalog</managed-bean-class>
    <managed-bean-scope>session</managed-bean-scope>
  </managed-bean>

</faces-config>
```

# Creating a JSF page

In this section we create the JSF page containing the user interface components including the data table. Subsequently, we shall bind the components to the UI component properties in the managed bean. Select **File | New | Other** and select **JSP File** under **Web** in the **New** wizard. Click on **Next**, as shown in the following screenshot:

In **New JSP File** select the **WebContent** folder and specify **catalog.jsp** as the filename in the **File name** field and click on **Next**. In **Select JSP Template** select **New JavaServer Faces (JSF) Page (html)** and click on **Finish**. Open the **catalog.jsp** JSP with the web page editor. Expand the components palette with **Show Palette**. The **JSF Core** and **JSF HTML** tag libraries are listed in the components palette. Select the **JSF HTML** tag library:

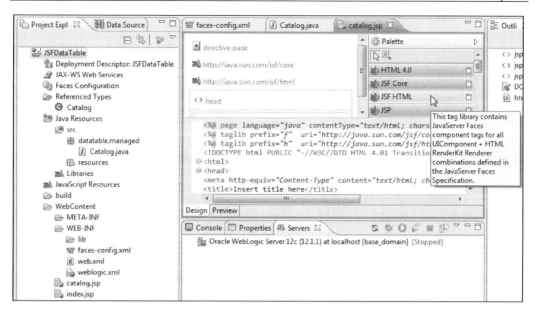

# Adding components to the JSF page

Having created a JSF page, we will add components to create a data table. We add
`h:form` for the JSF components. We shall add an input text field (`h:inputText`) to
specify a SQL query and a command button (`h:commandButton`) to submit the query.
We shall add a data table component (`h:dataTable`) to display the JSF data table.
Next, position the cursor within the `f:view` tag and select the **Form** component from
the **JSF HTML** tag library, as shown in the following screenshot:

In the **New Form** window specify an ID in the **Id** field and click on the button next to **Binding** to bind the form to managed bean property, as follows:

In the **Choose Binding** window select the **form1** property and click on **OK**, as shown in the following screenshot:

The binding EL expression for the form gets specified. Click on **Finish**:

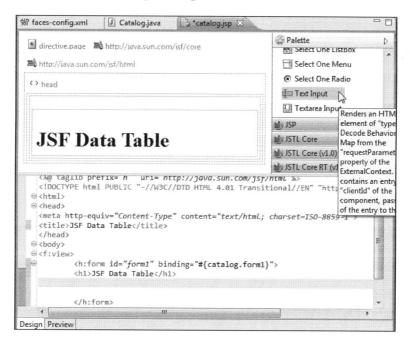

A h:form component gets added to the f:view element. Next, we shall add the JSF components including a JSF data table. We shall add an InputText component for a SQL query and CommandButton to submit the SQL query. The data table shall be generated dynamically using a SQL query specified in the input text field and submitted with a **Submit** button. Though we have used a SQL query from input, it is only to demonstrate the data table. For a production web application, SQL injection should be taken into consideration. Position the cursor within the h:form component and select **Text Input** in the component palette, as follows:

In the **New Input Text** wizard specify an ID in the **Id** field and click on the button for the value binding next to **Value**, as follows:

In the **Choose Binding** window select the **inputText1** property and click on **OK**, as shown in the following screenshot:

The binding EL expression gets specified for the **Input Text** component. Click on **Finish**:

Position the cursor after the input text field in the form and select **Command Button** in the **JSF HTML** palette, as follows:

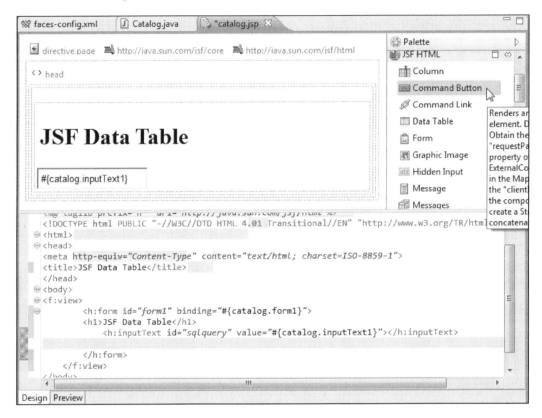

In the **New Command Button** window specify an ID in the **Id** field and click on the button next to **Action**. An action method is a method in the managed bean that returns a string and does not take any parameters. The action method is invoked when the command button is clicked on a JSF page running on the web server.

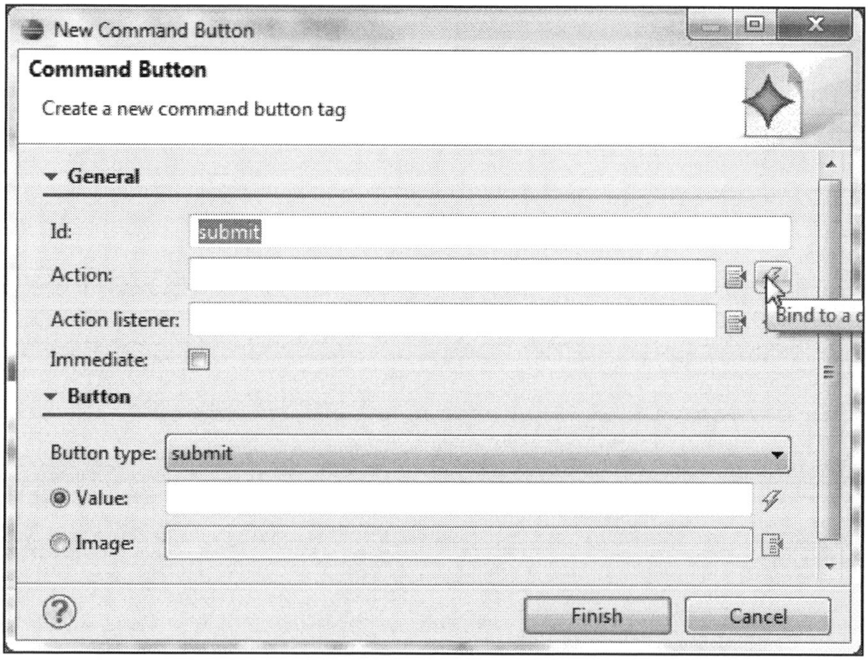

In the **Choose Method** window select the **String commandButton1_action()** method and click on **OK**, as shown in the following screenshot:

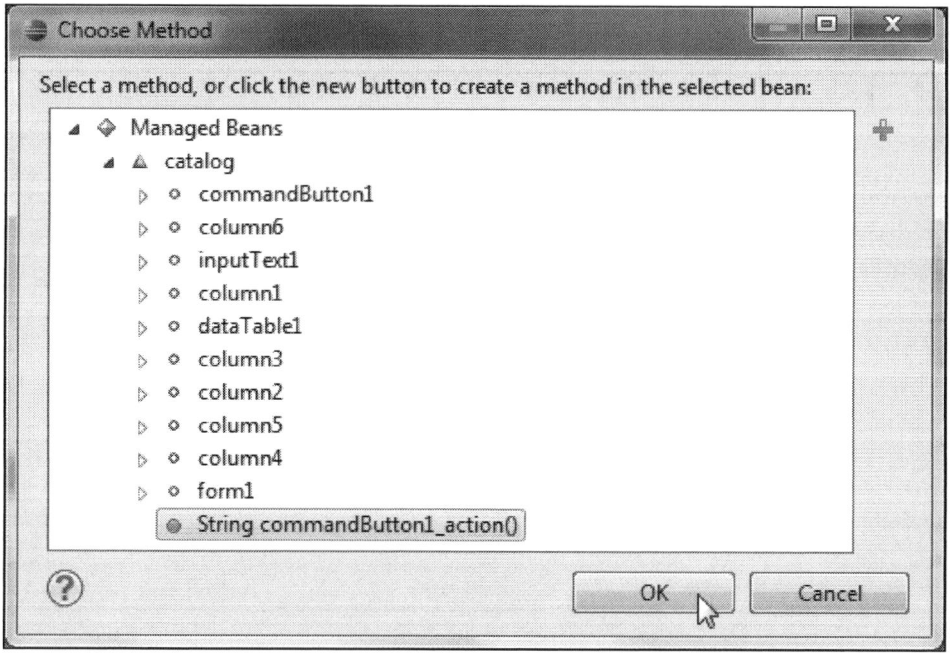

The action method EL expression for the command button gets specified. Select **submit** as **Button type** and **Submit Query** as **Value**. Click on **Finish**, as follows:

An input text and a command button get added to the JSF page. Next, position the cursor after the command button in the form and select **Data Table** in the component palette, as shown in the following screenshot:

In the **New Data Table** wizard check the **Configure a dataTable tag** checkbox, specify an ID in the **Id** field, and click on the button next to the **Binding** field to bind the data table to a dynamic managed bean property, as follows:

In the **Choose Binding** window select the **dataTable1** property and click on **OK**, as shown in the following screenshot:

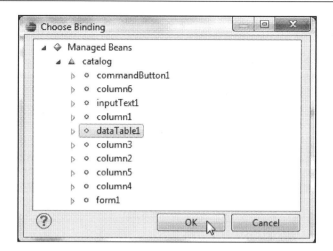

The binding EL expression for the data table gets specified. Specify a border size in the **Border size** field and click on **Finish**, as shown in the following screenshot:

A data table gets added to the JSF page. We need to add columns to the data table. Position the cursor within the `<h:dataTable>` and `</h:dataTable>` tags, and select **Column** in the component palette, as follows:

In the **New Column** window specify an ID in the **Id** field and click on the button next to the **Binding** field. In **Choose Binding** select the **column1** managed bean property and click on **OK**, as shown in the following screenshot:

The EL binding expression for the column gets specified. Click on **Finish**:

Similarly, add column binding for the other columns — `column2` to `column6`, as follows:

```
<f:view>
    <h:form id="form1" binding="#{catalog.form1}">
    <h1>JSF Data Table</h1>
        <h:inputText id="sqlquery" value="#{catalog.inputText1}"></h:inpu
        <h:commandButton id="submit"
            action="#{catalog.commandButton1_action}" value="Submit Query
        <h:dataTable id="datatable1" binding="#{catalog.dataTable1}"
            border="1">
            <h:column  id="column1" binding="#{catalog.column1}"></h:colu
            <h:column id="column2" binding="#{catalog.column2}"></h:colum
            <h:column  id="column3" binding="#{catalog.column3}"></h:colu
            <h:column id="column4" binding="#{catalog.column4}"></h:colum
            <h:column  id="column5" binding="#{catalog.column5}"></h:colu

        </h:dataTable>
```

Design | Preview

Click on the **Preview** tab to preview the data table.

# The JSF page

The `catalog.jsp` page, which has the data table component and other JSF components with binding to the managed bean, is listed as follows:

```
<%@taglib uri="http://java.sun.com/jsf/core" prefix="f"%><%@taglib
  uri="http://java.sun.com/jsf/html" prefix="h"%><%@ page
language="java" contentType="text/html; charset=ISO-8859-1"
    pageEncoding="ISO-8859-1"%>
<!DOCTYPE html PUBLIC "-//W3C//DTD HTML 4.01 Transitional//EN"
"http://www.w3.org/TR/html4/loose.dtd">
<html>
<head>
```

```
<meta http-equiv="Content-Type" content="text/html;
charset=ISO-8859-1">
<title>JSF Data Table</title>
</head>
<body>
<%
response.setHeader("Cache-Control","no-cache"); //HTTP 1.1
response.setHeader("Pragma","no-cache"); //HTTP 1.0
response.setDateHeader ("Expires", 0); //prevents caching at the proxy
server
%>
<f:view>
  <h:form binding="#{catalog.form1}">
  <h2>JSF Data Table</h2>
    <h:inputText value="#{catalog.inputText1}"  id="sqlquery"
required="true"></h:inputText>
    <h:commandButton  id="submit"
      action="#{catalog.commandButton1_action}" value="Submit Query"
binding="#{catalog.commandButton1}"/>
    <h:dataTable  id="dataTable1" binding="#{catalog.dataTable1}"
border="1" rows="5">
      <h:column id="column1" binding="#{catalog.column1}"></h:column>
      <h:column id="column2" binding="#{catalog.column2}"></h:column>
      <h:column id="column3"  binding="#{catalog.column3}"></h:column>
      <h:column id="column4"  binding="#{catalog.column4}"></h:column>
      <h:column id="column5"  binding="#{catalog.column5}"></h:column>
      <h:column id="column6"  binding="#{catalog.column6}"></h:column>
    </h:dataTable>
  </h:form>

</f:view>
</body>
</html>
```

# Running the JSF page

In this section we will run the JSF page on the WebLogic Server to create a JSF data table. We specify a SQL query and click on the **Submit Query** button to send the SQL query to the server. The managed bean on the server retrieves the SQL query and runs the query on the Oracle database. The result set generated by the SQL query is bound to the data table using value expressions. Right-click on **catalog.jsp** and select **Run As | Run on Server**, as shown in the following screenshot:

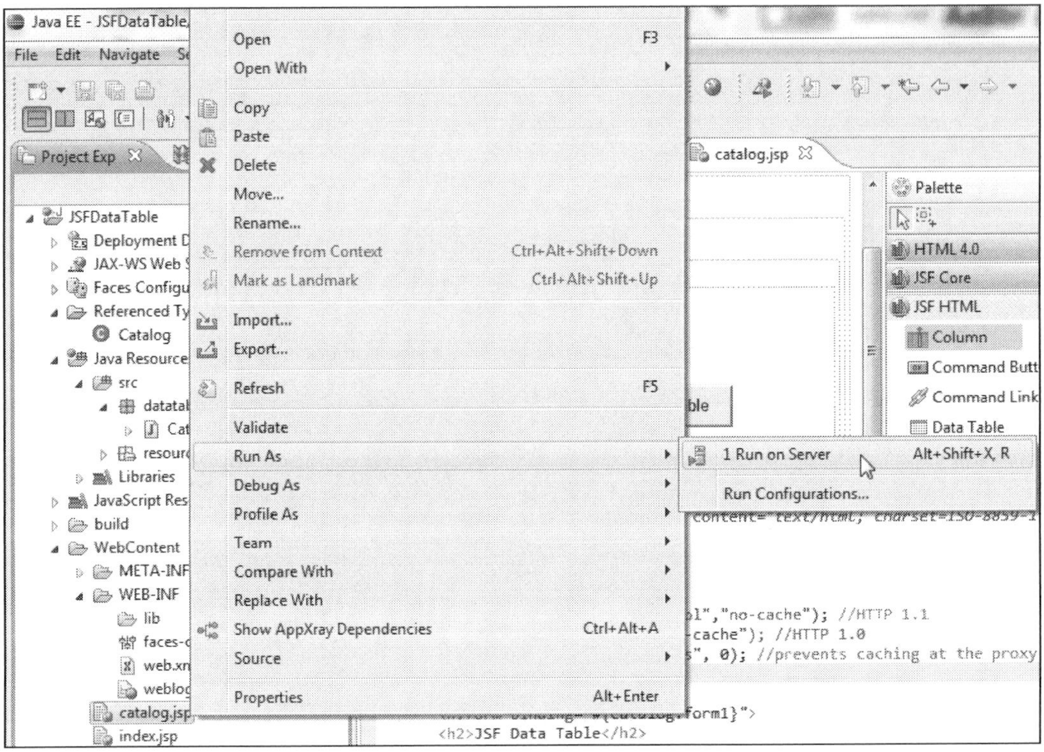

Start WebLogic Server if not already started. Select **Oracle WebLogic Server 12c (12.1.1) at localhost** and click on **Next**, as follows:

In the **Add and Remove** window add the **JSFDataTable** resource to the
**Configured** section with the **Add** button and click on **Finish**, as shown in
the following screenshot:

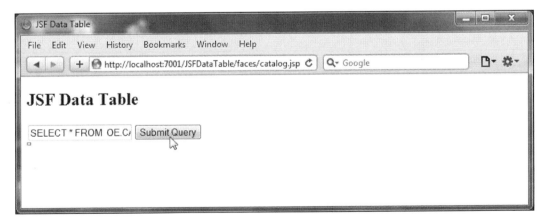

The **JSFDataTable** application gets deployed on the server.

The `catalog.jsp` JSF page may be run separately in a browser with the URL
`http://localhost:7001/JSFDataTable/faces/catalog.jsp`. Specify a SQL
query (**SELECT * FROM OE.CATALOG**) and click on **Submit Query**, as follows:

A data table for the SQL query gets generated and displayed, as shown in the following screenshot:

# Summary

In this chapter we used the JavaServer Faces project facet to create a JSF data table. First, we created a web project. Subsequently we created a managed bean, created a JSF page, added the InputText and CommandButton JSF HTML components, added a JSF DataTable JSF HTML component to the JSF page, and ran the JSF web application on the integrated WebLogic Server to create a JSF data table. We learned about a JSF component, which is a data table, that has common application in displaying database data.

In the next chapter we will carry on using the JavaServer Faces project facet, but we will use JSF Version 2.0 to create a Facelets application.

# 5
# Templating with Facelets

Facelets is the default **view declaration language (VDL)**, instead of JSP in JSF 2.0. Facelets is a Java Server Faces-centric view technology. It is is based on compositions. A composition defines a JSF `UIComponent` instance's structure in a Facelets page. A Facelets application may consist of compositions defined in different Facelets pages that are run as an application. Why use Facelets? Facelets provide templating, re-use, and ease of development in a web application. JSF validators and converters may be added to Facelets just as to any other `UIComponent`. Facelets provides complete expression language and JSTL support.

In this chapter we will develop a Facelets web application in Eclipse 3.7, **Oracle Enterprise Pack for Eclipse (OEPE)** 12*c*, and deploy the application to Oracle WebLogic Server 12*c*. The support of JSF 2.0 in WebLogic Server is available since the Version 10.3.4. Facelets application consists of an input JSF page and an output JSF page. We add an input text component to the input page. We specify a SQL query in the input page, click on the **Submit** button, and using implicit navigation, which is a new feature in JSF 2.0, navigate to the output page, which displays the JSF data table generated from the SQL query specified in the input page. We shall use Oracle Database 11*g* XE as the database. Templating is demonstrated by using a template for the graphics that get included for the header and the footer in the input and the output.

## Facelets structure

Before we develop the application we shall review the Facelets technology. Facelets provides a set of XML tags in the `http://java.sun.com/jsf/facelets` namespace. With Facelets in JSF 2.0, we don't need to configure a view handler as we needed to in JSF 1.2. Facelets tags are used with JSF Core and JSF HTML tag libraries to develop a JSF Facelets application. Some of the commonly used Facelets tags are discussed in the following table:

| Facelets tag | Description | Attributes |
|---|---|---|
| ui:composition | Defines a composition of the UIComponent instances. A composition may consist of multiple UI components. Text not within ui:composition tags is not compiled in a Facelet and is ignored; it is not included in the rendered output. | • template: This is an optional attribute. template specifies the template to use for adding the UIComponent instances within a composition. |
| ui:define | ui:define is used in a Facelet page in conjunction with the target template's ui:insert tags to add UIComponent instances within a composition. | • name: This is a required attribute. The name attribute in ui:define matches with the name attribute in ui:insert. |
| ui:decorate | ui:decorate is similar to ui:composition except that text not within the ui:decorate tags is also included in the Facelets page. | • template: This is a required attribute. The template attribute specifies the template to use for adding UIComponent instances in ui:decorate tags. |
| ui:component | ui:component is similar to ui:composition except that ui:component adds a new UIComponent as the root component in the UIComponents' structure. | • id: If id is not specified, Facelets assigns an id attribute.<br>• binding: This binds a UIComponent to a property of a JavaBean. |
| ui:fragment | ui:fragment is a non-trimming tag for ui:component, as ui:decorate is to ui:composition. | • id and binding (same as for ui:component). |

| Facelets tag | Description | Attributes |
|---|---|---|
| ui:include | The ui:include tag includes a Facelets page, which defines a composition or a component in a Facelets page or the template page. | • src: The src attribute is a required attribute. It specifies target Facelets to include with an EL expression or a string literal. |
| ui:insert | The ui:insert tag is used in a template to define the layout of a Facelets page that uses the template for defining UIComponents. A template client adds UIComponents to a Facelet with corresponding ui:define tags. If a Facelet specifies a template, and does not specify ui:define tags corresponding to ui:insert tags, the default ui:insert tags are used in the Facelet. | • name: The name attribute has a corresponding name attribute in a Facelet's ui:define tag for matching a template with a Facelet. |
| ui:param | ui:param is used to specify a variable when a Facelet is included within a template or a Facelet. | • name: This is a required attribute and specifies variable name.<br><br>• value: This is required attribute and it specifies the variable's value as an EL expression or a literal. |

Facelets' namespace tags may be used in an XHTML file. A Facelets application consists of the following configuration and templating files:

- A Facelets template page, which is a .xhtml page
- Facelets header and footer XHTML pages
- Configuration file—faces-config.xml
- Facelets composition page, which is also a .xhtml page

The template file defines the layout of a Facelets application. A template file consists of `<ui:insert/>` tags to specify the structure of a Facelets application that uses the template for defining UIComponents. The JSF configuration file is the only configuration file required; a Facelets-specific configuration file is not required. A Facelets page is an XHTML page that includes tags in the Facelets namespace. In the following section we shall create a Facelets application with Eclipse 3.7 (OEPE 12*c*), WebLogic Server 12*c*, and Oracle Database 11*g* XE.

# Setting the environment

Download and install the following software:

- Oracle WebLogic Server 12*c* (12.1.1) Installer from `http://www.oracle.com/technetwork/middleware/ias/downloads/wls-main-097127.html`.

- Eclipse 3.7 (Oracle Enterprise Pack for Eclipse 12*c* included with WebLogic Server 12*c*).

- Oracle Database 11*g* XE from `http://www.oracle.com/technetwork/database/express-edition/overview/index.html`. The Oracle Database JDBC JAR file, `ojdbc6.jar`, gets added to the runtime classpath of WebLogic Server from the `C:\Oracle\Middleware\wlserver_12.1\server\lib` directory.

- A taglib, Jakarta Standard 1.1.2 or later from `http://archive.apache.org/dist/jakarta/taglibs/standard/binaries/`.

Create a WebLogic Server domain (`base_domain`) using Configuration Wizard. Extract the Jakarta Standard taglib JAR file. Add the Jakarta taglibs standard files, `standard.jar` and `jstl.jar`, to the `\\user_projects\domains\base_domain\bin\startWebLogic` batch script to the CLASSPATH variable, as follows:

```
C:\JSTL\jakarta-taglibs-standard-1.1.2\lib\standard.jar;C:\JSTL\
jakarta-taglibs-standard-1.1.2\lib\jstl.jar
```

To generate a JSF data table we need to create a database table in Oracle Database XE. Install Oracle Database XE 11*g*. Create a user OE and create a table with the following SQL script:

```
CREATE USER OE IDENTIFIED BY OE;
GRANT CONNECT, RESOURCE to OE;

CREATE TABLE OE.Catalog(CatalogId INTEGER
PRIMARY KEY, Journal VARCHAR(25), Publisher VARCHAR(25),
 Edition VARCHAR(25), Title Varchar(45), Author Varchar(25));
INSERT INTO OE.Catalog VALUES('1', 'Oracle Magazine',
```

```
   'Oracle Publishing', 'Nov-Dec 2004', 'Database Resource
Manager', 'Kimberly Floss');
INSERT INTO OE.Catalog VALUES('2', 'Oracle Magazine',
 'Oracle Publishing', 'Nov-Dec 2004', 'From ADF UIX to JSF',
'Jonas Jacobi');
INSERT INTO OE.Catalog VALUES('3', 'Oracle Magazine',
 'Oracle Publishing', 'March-April 2005', 'Starting with
Oracle ADF ', 'Steve Muench');
```

# Configuring JSF 2.0 support in WLS

JSF 2.0 support is not configured in WLS 12*c* by default. To configure JSF 2.0
support we need to install the JSF 2.0 shared library in WebLogic Server. Start the
Admin Server Console for WebLogic Server domain—**base_domain**. Navigate to
the Admin Server Console with the URL `http://localhost:7001/console` and
select the **Deployments** node in the **base_domain** node. In the **Deployments**
table click on **Install**, as shown in the following screenshot:

Navigate to the C:\Oracle\Middleware\wlserver_12.1\common\deployable-libraries directory and select **jsf-2.0.war** and click on **Next**, as shown in the following screenshot:

**Install Application Assistant**

| Back | Next | Finish | Cancel |

**Locate deployment to install and prepare for deployment**

Select the file path that represents the application root directory, archive file, exploded archive directory, or application module descriptor directory or file in the Path field.

**Note:** Only valid file paths are displayed below. If you cannot find your deployment files, upload your file(s) and/or confirm that your appl

| **Path:** | C:\Oracle\Middleware\wlserver_12.1\common\deployable-libraries\jsf-2.0.war |
| **Recently Used Paths:** | (none) |
| **Current Location:** | dvohra-pc \ C: \ Oracle \ Middleware \ wlserver_12.1 \ common \ deployable-libraries |

- active-cache-1.0.jar
- jackson-core-asl-1.1.1.war
- jackson-jaxrs-1.1.1.war
- jackson-mapper-asl-1.1.1.war
- jersey-bundle-1.1.5.1.war
- jettison-1.1.war
- jsf-1.2.war
- ⦿ jsf-2.0.war
- jsr311-api-1.1.1.war
- jstl-1.1.2.war
- jstl-1.2.war
- pubsub-1.0.war
- rome-1.0.war
- toplink-grid-1.0.jar
- weblogic-sca-1.1.war

| Back | Next | Finish | Cancel |

In **Choose targeting style** select **Install this deployment as a library**. Click on **Next**. Select the default **Optional Settings** and click on **Next**. Click on **Finish** to complete the JSF 2.0 deployment. On the configuration screen click on **Save** to save the configuration, as follows:

**Messages**

✔ All changes have been activated. No restarts are necessary.

✔ Settings updated successfully.

**Settings for jsf(2.0,1.0.0.0_2-0-2)**

| Overview | Targets | Notes |

[ Save ]

Use this page to view, and sometimes change, general configuration information about the Java EE library, such as its name field to change the order that the library is deployed at server startup, relative to other deployments.

| **Name:** | jsf |
| **Specification Version:** | 2.0 |
| **Implementation Version:** | 1.0.0.0_2-0-2 |
| **Path:** | C:\Oracle\Middleware\wlserver_12. 1\common\deployable-libraries\jsf-2. 0. war |
| **Staging Mode:** | (not specified) |
| **Deployment Order:** | 100 |
| **Deployment Principal Name:** | |

Click on **Deployments**. A deployment configuration for JSF 2.0 is shown added under the **Deployments** section, as follows:

The JSF 2.0 shared library gets configured in the `base_domain` configuration file—C:\Oracle\Middleware\user_projects\domains\base_domain\config\config.xml.

```
<library>
    <name>jsf#2.0@1.0.0.0_2-0-2</name>
    <target>AdminServer</target>
    <module-type>war</module-type>
    <source-path>C:\Oracle\Middleware\wlserver_12.1\common\deployable-
libraries\jsf-2.0.war</source-path>
    <security-dd-model>DDOnly</security-dd-model>
</library>
```

Having installed the JSF 2.0 shared library, we shall be able to deploy and run the JSF 2.0 Facelets application in WebLogic Server.

# Creating a Facelets project

Start Eclipse 3.7 (OEPE 12*c*). Select **File** | **New** | **Other**. In the **New** wizard select
**Web** | **Dynamic Web Project**. Click on **Next**, as shown in the following screenshot:

In **Dynamic Web Project** configuration specify **Project name** (Facelets, for example) and create a new target runtime with the **New...** button under **Target Runtime**. In the **New Server Runtime Environment** configuration select **Oracle WebLogic Server 12c (12.1.1)**, check the **Create a new local server** checkbox, and click on **Next**, as follows:

In the **New Server Runtime Environment** configuration specify the WebLogic home directory in the **WebLogic home** field. The **Java home** directory gets configured to JDK 1.6. Click on **Next**, as follows:

In the server configuration select the **Local** radio button for **Server Type**, and specify `base_domain` as **Domain Directory**. Click on **Finish**. Select **2.5** as the **Dynamic Web Module** version. For Facelets support we need to add JSF 2.0 configuration. Click on the **Modify...** button for **Configuration**. Select **JavaServer Faces** as **Project Facet** and select **2.0** as **Version**. Click on **OK**, as shown in the following screenshot:

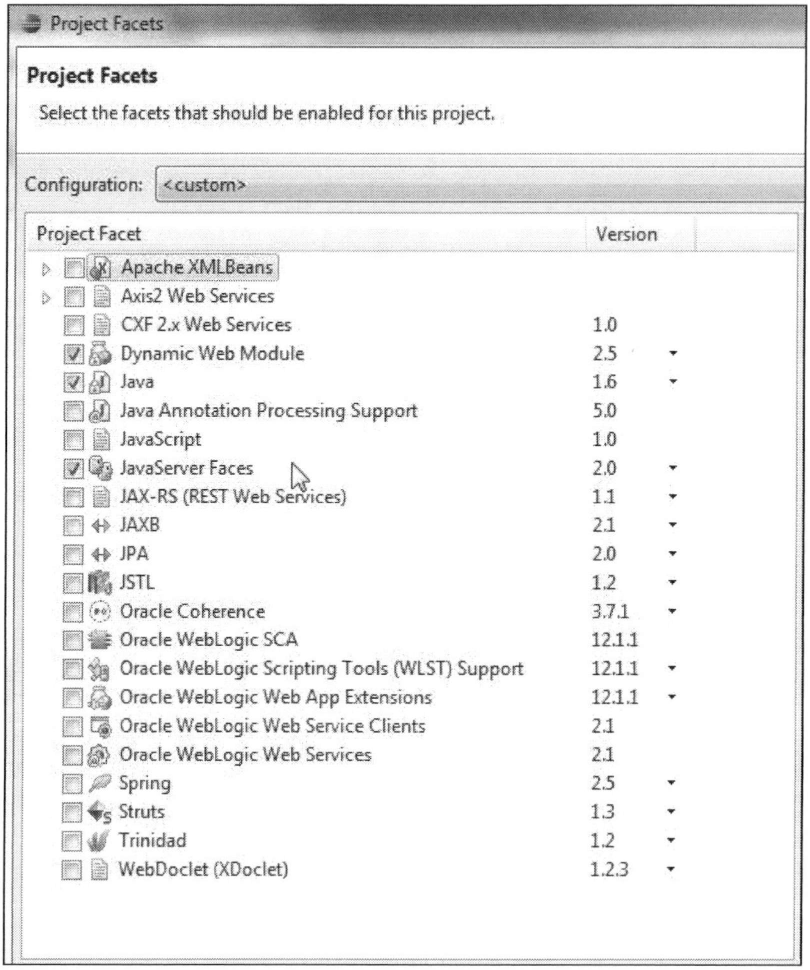

The **Configuration** field should get set to **&lt;custom&gt;**. Click on **Next**, as follows:

In the Java configuration the default output folder is set as `build/classes`.
Click on **Next**. In the **Web Module** configuration specify `Facelets` as **Context root**
and `WebContent` as **Content directory**. Check the **Generate web.xml deployment
descriptor** checkbox and click on **Next**. To configure a JSF implementation library
select **User Library** as **Type** and click on the download library button. In the
**Download Library** window select the **JSF 2.0 (Mojarra 2.0.3-FCS)** library for
**Library name** and click on **Next**, as shown in the following screenshot:

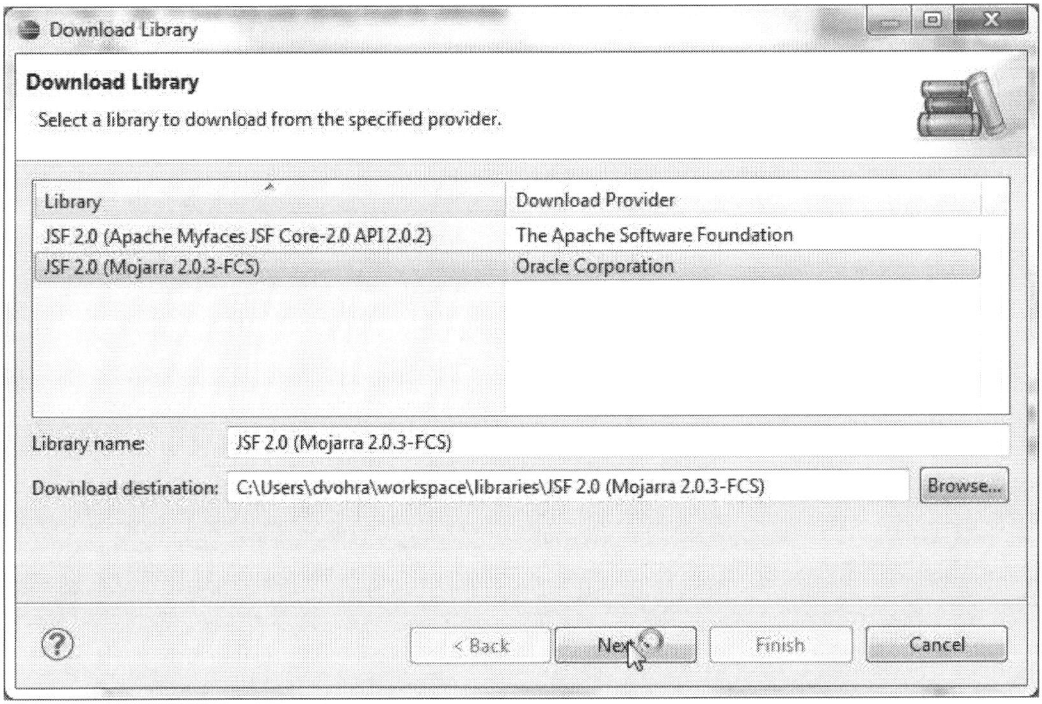

Accept the library license and click on **Finish**. A JSF implementation library gets configured. Click on **Finish**, as follows:

The **JavaServer Faces** facet gets installed. The **Facelets** project gets created, as follows:

Next specify some application configuration parameters, which are specified in web. xml, to differentiate between JSF pages and Facelets from other pages. Add javax. faces.DEFAULT_SUFFIX to web.xml. The javax.faces.DEFAULT_SUFFIX context-param defines the default suffix for view pages with JSF components, as follows:

```
<context-param>
    <param-name> javax.faces.DEFAULT_SUFFIX </param-name>
    <param-value>.xhtml</param-value>
</context-param>
```

The default suffix for a Facelets page is `.xhtml`. Another suffix may be specified as the default for Facelets-based XHTML pages with `javax.faces.FACELETS_SUFFIX` as `context-param` in `web.xml`, as follows:

```
<context-param>
<param-name>javax.faces.FACELETS_SUFFIX</param-name>
<param-value>.xhtml</param-value>
</context-param>
```

A set of view pages may be specified to be interpreted as using Facelets regardless of their extensions using `javax.faces.FACELETS_VIEW_MAPPING` as `context-param`. Each entry is either a file extension or a resource prefix starting with "/" and relative to the web application root, as follows:

```
<context-param>
<param-name> javax.faces.FACELETS_VIEW_MAPPINGS</param-name>
<param-value>*.jspx;/facelets/*</param-value>
</context-param>
```

The configuration parameters that specify the default suffix, the Facelets suffix, and the Facelets view mappings are set with the following static string fields (constants) from the `javax.faces.application.ViewHandler` class:

| Constant | Description |
| --- | --- |
| DEFAULT_SUFFIX_PARAM_NAME | This specifies the param name for the default suffix for JSF pages. Value is `javax.faces.DEFAULT_SUFFIX`. |
| FACELETS_SUFFIX_PARAM_NAME | This specifies the param name for the Facelets suffix. Value is `javax.faces.FACELETS_SUFFIX`. |
| FACELETS_VIEW_MAPPINGS_PARAM_NAME | This specifies the param name for the Facelets view mappings. Value is `javax.faces.FACELETS_VIEW_MAPPINGS`. |

Application configuration parameters supported by all JSF implementations are specified in the application configuration parameters section of the JSF 2.0 specification. Mojarra supports some additional initialization (configuration) parameters (`http://javaserverfaces.java.net/nonav/rlnotes/2.0.3/whatsnew.html`). `Faces Servlet` and the servlet mapping are configured by default in `web.xml` when the JSF project facet is selected. The **web.xml** file is shown in the following screenshot:

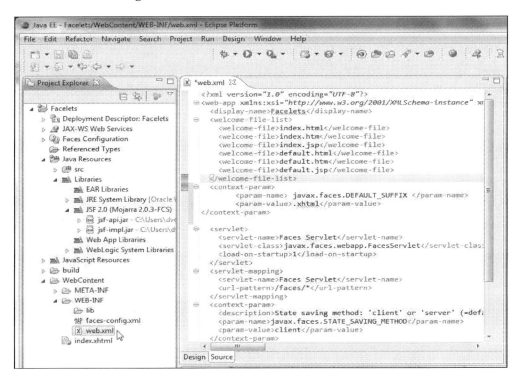

Next add the `weblogic.xml` deployment descriptor to the `WEB-INF` directory. Select **File | New**. In the **New** wizard select **WebLogic | Configuration | Oracle WebLogic Web Module Descriptor** and click on **Next**, as shown in the following screenshot:

In the **New WebLogic Web Module Descriptor** wizard select the **WEB-INF** folder under **WebContents** and specify `weblogic.xml` as **File name**. Click on **Finish**, as follows:

The `weblogic.xml` deployment descriptor gets added to the `WEB-INF` directory. Add a reference to the JSF 2.0 shared library module that we installed earlier to `weblogic.xml`. A library reference indicates that a library shall be used as a web application library in the web application and it is added with the `library-ref` element. The `exact-match` element indicates if an exact match between the library reference specification and implementation versions, and the actual shared library versions is required.

```
<wls:library-ref>
   <wls:library-name>jsf</wls:library-name>
   <wls:specification-version>2.0</wls:specification-version>
   <wls:implementation-version>1.0.0.0_2-0-2</wls:implementation-
version>
   <wls:exact-match>true</wls:exact-match>
</wls:library-ref>
```

# Creating a managed bean

To create a managed bean for the Facelets, right-click on **WebContent/WEB-INF/ faces-config.xml** and select **Open With | Faces Config Editor**, as shown in the following screenshot:

Select the **ManagedBean** tab. Click on **Add** to add a managed bean, as follows:

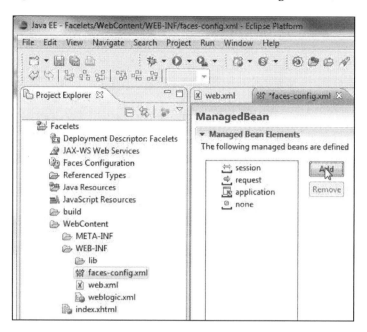

In the **New Managed Bean Wizard** dialog box select **Create a new Java class** and click on **Next**. Select **Facelets/src** as **Source folder**, and **catalog.backing** as **Package**. Specify the Java class name as `Catalog` in the **Name** field and click on **Next**, as shown in the following screenshot:

Specify `catalog` as **Managed Bean name**, set **session** as **Managed Bean Scope**, and click on **Next**. In **Wizard Summarys** click on **Finish**. A managed bean gets added.

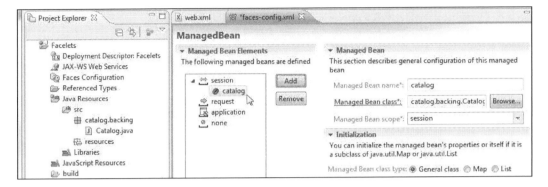

In `Catalog.java`, which is the Java class for the managed bean, add the required `import` statements for the HTML and UI components. Add managed bean properties for the various components used in the application. Add a bean property for an `HtmlDataTable` type component for a data table and add bean properties of the `UIColumn` type for the data table columns. Also add bean properties for an `HTMLInputText` type component for an input text to specify a SQL query, and an `HTMLCommandButton` type component for a command button to submit the SQL query. We shall bind the managed bean properties to Facelets' composition pages when we construct the Facelets pages.

```
private HtmlDataTable dataTable1;
   private UIColumn column1;
   private UIColumn column2;
   private UIColumn column3;
   private UIColumn column4;
   private UIColumn column5;
   private UIColumn column6;
```

The `UIColumn` type bean properties may also be declared as an array. Add getter/setter methods for the managed bean properties. Add an action method that is invoked when the command button is clicked, as follows:

```
public String commandButton1_action() { }
```

Retrieve the SQL query input in the JSF input text field and run the SQL query to generate a result set in the command button action method, as follows:

```
rs = stmt.executeQuery((String) inputText1.getValue());
```

Practical considerations such as SQL injection and erroneous SQL statements should be included when designing a production application. For example, instead of a complete SQL statement in the input, a parameter may be specified that is used in conjunction with a prepared statement in the managed bean. Set a border for the data table using the `setBorder()` method and the cell padding using the `setCellPadding()` method. Using the `setVar()` method set the variable that represents a row of data in the data table, as follows:

```
dataTable1.setBorder(5);
dataTable1.setCellpadding("1");
dataTable1.setVar("catalog");
```

In the data table set the header values for the columns. The data table has columns corresponding to each of the columns in the database table—`Catalog`. Add column headers by creating the `HtmlOutputText` header components and setting the headers on the `UIColumn` components using the `setHeader` method. Set the `HtmlOutputText` value using the `setValue` method. For example, add the column header for the `CatalogId` column, as follows:

```
HtmlOutputText headerComponent = new HtmlOutputText();
headerComponent.setValue("CatalogId");
column1.setHeader(headerComponent);
```

Create an `HtmlOutputText` component using the class constructor for each of the columns in the data table. Specify a value expression for the `HtmlOutputText` component and subsequently add the component to the header column. Set the value on an `HtmlOutputText` object, as follows:

1. Create a `FacesContext` object using the static method—`getCurrentInstance()`.
2. Create a `ELContext` object using the `getELContext()` method on the `FacesContext` object.
3. Create an `ExpressionFactory` object from the `FacesContext` object using the `getApplication()` and `getExpressionFactory()` methods in a sequence.
4. Create a `ValueExpression` object from the `ExpressionFactory` object using the `createValueExpression()` method.
5. Set the `ValueExpression` object on the `HtmlOutputText` object using the `setValueExpression()` method.

Add the `HtmlOutputText` object to the header column by obtaining `List` of subcolumns with the `getChildren()` method and adding it to the list with the `add()` method.

For example, for the `CatalogId` column an `HtmlOutputText` component is added, as follows:

```
HtmlOutputText column1Text = new HtmlOutputText();
FacesContext fCtx = FacesContext.getCurrentInstance();
ELContext elCtx = fCtx.getELContext();
ExpressionFactory ef = fCtx.getApplication().getExpressionFactory();
ValueExpression ve = ef.createValueExpression(elCtx,
        "#{catalog.catalogid}", String.class);
column1Text.setValueExpression("value", ve);
column1.getChildren().add(column1Text);
```

Next create a `ResultSetDataModel` object to wrap a `ResultSet` object, which is required to be scrollable. Set the `ResultSet` object retrieved with the SQL query as the data for the `ResultSetDataModel` object using the `setWrappedData()` method, as follows:

```
ResultSetDataModel dataModel=new ResultSetDataModel();
dataModel.setWrappedData(rs);
```

Bind the data table with the `ResultSetDataModel` object using the `setValue` method, as follows:

```
dataTable1.setValue(dataModel);
```

The managed bean Java class, `Catalog.java`, is listed as follows:

```
package catalog.backing;

import javax.faces.bean.ManagedBean;
import javax.faces.component.html.HtmlCommandButton;
import javax.faces.component.html.HtmlDataTable;
import javax.faces.component.html.HtmlForm;
import javax.faces.component.html.HtmlInputText;
import javax.faces.component.html.HtmlOutputLabel;
import javax.faces.component.UIColumn;
import javax.faces.component.html.HtmlOutputText;
import javax.faces.context.FacesContext;
import javax.faces.model.ResultSetDataModel;
import javax.el.ELContext;
import javax.el.ExpressionFactory;
import javax.el.ValueExpression;
import java.sql.*;
```

Annotate the Java class with `@ManagedBean` to make it a managed bean. Declare variables for bean properties and connection parameters, as follows:

```
@ManagedBean(name="catalog")
public class Catalog {
  private HtmlForm form1;
  private HtmlInputText inputText1;
  private HtmlOutputLabel outputLabel1;
  private HtmlCommandButton commandButton1;
  private HtmlDataTable dataTable1;
  private UIColumn column1;
  private UIColumn column2;
  private UIColumn column3;
  private UIColumn column4;
  private UIColumn column5;
  private UIColumn column6;
  private Statement stmt;
  private Connection connection;
  private ResultSet rs;
```

Add getter/setter methods for bean properties, as follows:

```
public void setForm1(HtmlForm form1) {
  this.form1 = form1;
}

public HtmlForm getForm1() {
  return form1;
}

public void setInputText1(HtmlInputText inputText1) {
  this.inputText1 = inputText1;
}

public HtmlInputText getInputText1() {
  return inputText1;
}

public void setOutputLabel1(HtmlOutputLabel outputLabel1) {
  this.outputLabel1 = outputLabel1;
}

public HtmlOutputLabel getOutputLabel1() {
  return outputLabel1;
}

public void setCommandButton1(HtmlCommandButton commandButton1) {
  this.commandButton1 = commandButton1;
}
```

```java
    public HtmlCommandButton getCommandButton1() {
      return commandButton1;
    }

    public void setDataTable1(HtmlDataTable dataTable1) {
      this.dataTable1 = dataTable1;
    }

    public HtmlDataTable getDataTable1() {
      return dataTable1;
    }

    public void setColumn1(UIColumn column1) {
      this.column1 = column1;
    }

    public UIColumn getColumn1() {
      return column1;
    }

    public void setColumn2(UIColumn column2) {
      this.column2 = column2;
    }

    public UIColumn getColumn2() {
      return column2;
    }

    public void setColumn3(UIColumn column3) {
      this.column3 = column3;
    }

    public UIColumn getColumn3() {
      return column3;
    }

    public void setColumn4(UIColumn column4) {
      this.column4 = column4;
    }

    public UIColumn getColumn4() {
      return column4;
    }
```

```
public void setColumn5(UIColumn column5) {
  this.column5 = column5;
}

public UIColumn getColumn5() {
  return column5;
}

public void setColumn6(UIColumn column6) {
  this.column6 = column6;
}

public UIColumn getColumn6() {
  return column6;
}
```

Add an action method to be invoked by the command button in input.xhtml. The procedure to run a SQL query and construct a data table was discussed in detail in *Chapter 4, Creating a JSF Data Table*.

```
public String commandButton1_action() {

  try {

    Class.forName("oracle.jdbc.OracleDriver");

    String url = "jdbc:oracle:thin:@localhost:1521:XE";

    connection = DriverManager.getConnection(url, "OE", "pw");

    stmt = connection.createStatement(
        ResultSet.TYPE_SCROLL_INSENSITIVE,
        ResultSet.CONCUR_READ_ONLY);

    rs = stmt.executeQuery((String) inputText1.getValue());

    HtmlDataTable dataTable1 = new HtmlDataTable();
    dataTable1.setBorder(5);
    dataTable1.setCellpadding("1");
    dataTable1.setVar("journalcatalog");
    ResultSetDataModel dataModel = new ResultSetDataModel();

    dataModel.setWrappedData(rs);

    this.setDataTable1(dataTable1);
```

```
UIColumn column1 = new UIColumn();
UIColumn column2 = new UIColumn();
UIColumn column3 = new UIColumn();
UIColumn column4 = new UIColumn();
UIColumn column5 = new UIColumn();
UIColumn column6 = new UIColumn();

this.setColumn1(column1);
this.setColumn2(column2);
this.setColumn3(column3);
this.setColumn4(column4);
this.setColumn5(column5);
this.setColumn6(column6);

HtmlOutputText headerComponent = new HtmlOutputText();
headerComponent.setValue("CatalogId");
column1.setHeader(headerComponent);
headerComponent = new HtmlOutputText();
headerComponent.setValue("Journal");
column2.setHeader(headerComponent);
headerComponent = new HtmlOutputText();
headerComponent.setValue("Publisher");
column3.setHeader(headerComponent);
headerComponent = new HtmlOutputText();
headerComponent.setValue("Edition");
column4.setHeader(headerComponent);
headerComponent = new HtmlOutputText();
headerComponent.setValue("Title");
column5.setHeader(headerComponent);
headerComponent = new HtmlOutputText();
headerComponent.setValue("Author");
column6.setHeader(headerComponent);

HtmlOutputText column1Text = new HtmlOutputText();

FacesContext fCtx = FacesContext.getCurrentInstance();
ELContext elCtx = fCtx.getELContext();
ExpressionFactory ef = fCtx.getApplication().
getExpressionFactory();
ValueExpression ve = ef.createValueExpression(elCtx,
    "#{journalcatalog.catalogid}", String.class);

column1Text.setValueExpression("value", ve);

column1.getChildren().add(column1Text);
```

```
        HtmlOutputText column2Text = new HtmlOutputText();


      ve = ef.createValueExpression(elCtx, "#{journalcatalog.
journal}",
           String.class);
      column2Text.setValueExpression("value", ve);

      column2.getChildren().add(column2Text);
      HtmlOutputText column3Text = new HtmlOutputText();


      ve = ef.createValueExpression(elCtx, "#{journalcatalog.
publisher}",
           String.class);
      column3Text.setValueExpression("value", ve);

      column3.getChildren().add(column3Text);
      HtmlOutputText column4Text = new HtmlOutputText();


      ve = ef.createValueExpression(elCtx, "#{journalcatalog.
edition}",
           String.class);
      column4Text.setValueExpression("value", ve);

      column4.getChildren().add(column4Text);
      HtmlOutputText column5Text = new HtmlOutputText();

      ve = ef.createValueExpression(elCtx, "#{journalcatalog.title}",
           String.class);
      column5Text.setValueExpression("value", ve);

      column5.getChildren().add(column5Text);
      HtmlOutputText column6Text = new HtmlOutputText();

      ve = ef.createValueExpression(elCtx, "#{journalcatalog.author}",
           String.class);
      column6Text.setValueExpression("value", ve);

      column6.getChildren().add(column6Text);

      dataTable1.setValue(dataModel);

    } catch (SQLException e) {
      System.out.println(e.getMessage());
      return "error";
```

```
    } catch (ClassNotFoundException e) {
      System.out.println(e.getMessage());
      return "error";
    } finally {

    }
    return "output";
  }
}
```

The managed bean class, `Catalog.java`, is shown, as follows:

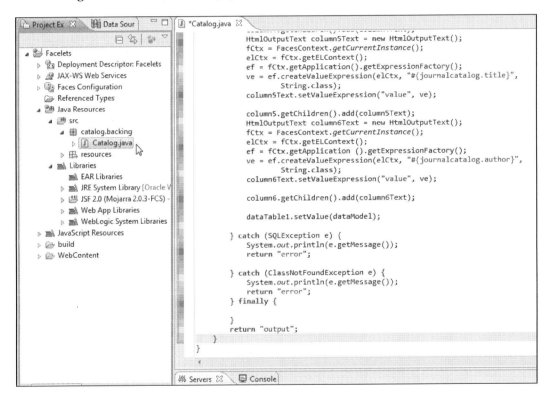

# Creating a Facelets template

First create a `templates` directory in the `WEB-INF` directory. Right-click on the **WEB-INF** directory and select **New | Folder**. In the **New Folder** wizard select the **WEB-INF** directory to add the `templates` folder to. Specify `templates` as **Folder name** and click on **Finish**. Next add an XHTML page for the Facelets template file to the `templates` directory. Right-click on the **WebContent** folder and select **New | Other**. In the **New** wizard select **XHTML Page** under **GlassFish** and click on **Next**, as shown in the following screenshot:

In the **New XHTML File** wizard specify `BasicTemplate.xhtml` as **File name** and click on **Next**, as shown in the following screenshot:

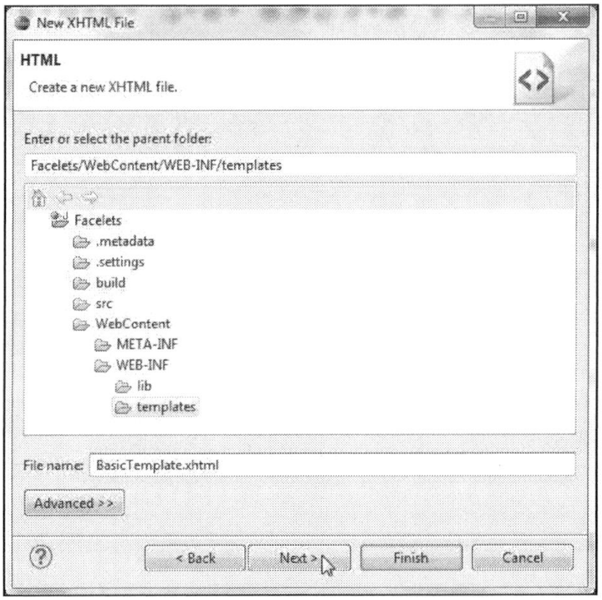

Select **New Facelet Template** and click on **Finish**, as follows:

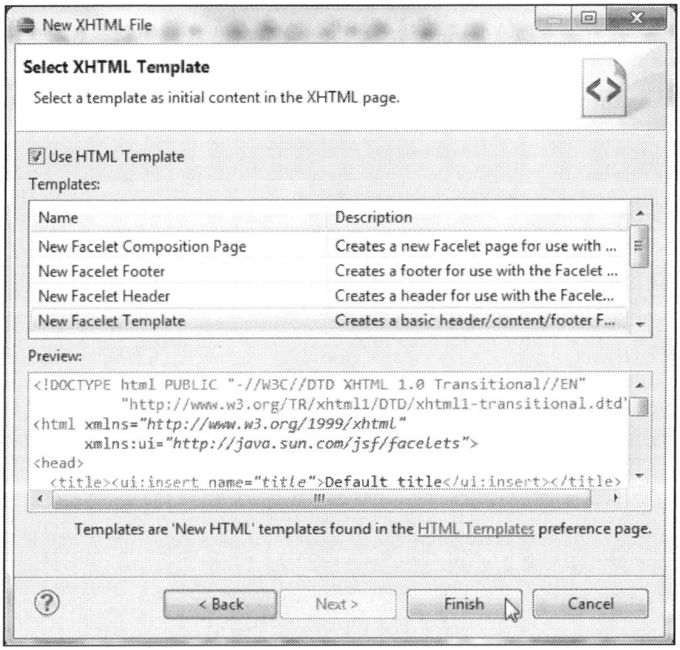

A **BasicTemplate.xhtml** template with a header, content, and footer gets added to the **templates** folder, as shown in the following screenshot:

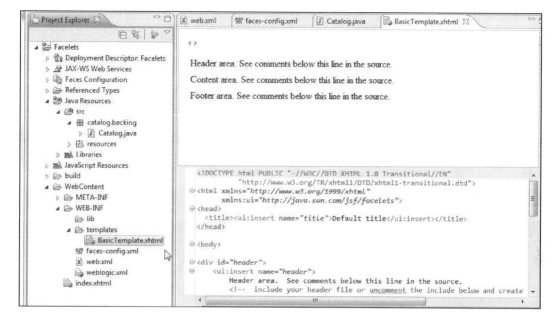

The root element of the template is `html`, which includes the namespace declaration for the Facelets namespace. Add `ui:insert` tags enclosed in the `<div/>` tags to the template for the different sections of a Facelets composition—title, header, content, and footer. Specify the relative path to the `header.xhtml` and `footer.xhtml` Facelets pages using the `ui:include` tag. The `BasicTemplate.xhtml` template is listed, as follows:

```
<!DOCTYPE html PUBLIC "-//W3C//DTD XHTML 1.0 Transitional//EN"
          "http://www.w3.org/TR/xhtml1/DTD/xhtml1-transitional.dtd">
<html xmlns="http://www.w3.org/1999/xhtml"
  xmlns:ui="http://java.sun.com/jsf/facelets">
<head>
<title><ui:insert name="title">JSF Facelets</ui:insert></title>
</head>
<body>
<div id="header">
    <ui:insert name="header">
        <ui:include src="/WEB-INF/templates/header.xhtml" />
    </ui:insert>
</div>
<div id="content">
    <ui:insert name="content">
```

```
        </ui:insert>
    </div>
    <div id="footer">
        <ui:insert name="footer">
      <ui:include src="/WEB-INF/templates/footer.xhtml" />
        </ui:insert></div>
    </body>
    </html>
```

# Creating Facelets

Similar to `BasicTemplate.xhtml` add the following XHTML pages:

- `header.xhtml` for a common header section to the `WEB-INF/templates` directory. For `header.xhtml` select the **New Facelet Header** template.

- `footer.xhtml` for a common footer section to the `WEB-INF/templates` directory. For `footer.xhtml` select the **New Facelet Footer** template.

- An input Facelets composition page (`input.xhtml`) to the `WebContent` directory. For `input.xhtml` select the **New Facelet Composition Page** template.

- An output Facelets composition page (`output.xhtml`) to the `WebContent` directory. For `output.xhtml` select the **New Facelet Composition Page** template.

The XHTML pages based on different types of templates are shown in the Facelets application, as follows:

In the `header.xhtml` page specify a JPEG for the header with the `h:graphicImage` tag. The `header.xhtml` page is listed, as follows:

```
<?xml version="1.0" encoding="ISO-8859-1" ?>
<!DOCTYPE html PUBLIC "-//W3C//DTD XHTML 1.0 Transitional//EN"
"http://www.w3.org/TR/xhtml1/DTD/xhtml1-transitional.dtd">
<html xmlns="http://www.w3.org/1999/xhtml"
    xmlns:ui="http://java.sun.com/jsf/facelets"
    xmlns:h="http://java.sun.com/jsf/html"
    xmlns:f="http://java.sun.com/jsf/core">
<f:view>
        <h:form>
            <h:panelGrid columns="1">
        <h:graphicImage value="FaceletsHeader.jpg" />
   </h:panelGrid>
    </h:form>
    </f:view>
</html>
```

In the `footer.xhtml` page specify a JPEG for the footer using the `h:graphicImage` tag enclosed in an `h:panelGrid` tag. The `footer.xhtml` page is listed, as follows:

```
<?xml version="1.0" encoding="ISO-8859-1" ?>
<!DOCTYPE html PUBLIC "-//W3C//DTD XHTML 1.0 Transitional//EN"
"http://www.w3.org/TR/xhtml1/DTD/xhtml1-transitional.dtd">
<html xmlns="http://www.w3.org/1999/xhtml"
    xmlns:ui="http://java.sun.com/jsf/facelets"
    xmlns:h="http://java.sun.com/jsf/html"
    xmlns:f="http://java.sun.com/jsf/core">

<f:view>
        <h:form>
            <h:panelGrid columns="1">
        <h:graphicImage value="FaceletsFooter.jpg" />
   </h:panelGrid>
    </h:form>
    </f:view>
</html>
```

The example JPEGs, `FaceletsHeader.jpg` and `FaceletsFooter.jpg`, are included with the source code ZIP file, but any JPEGs may be used. Copy the header and footer JPEGs to the `WebContent` directory, which is the same directory which has the composition pages `input.xhtml` and `output.xhtml`.

Next construct the `input.xhtml` Facelets composition page that has an input field
(`h:inputText` tag) for input text and an `h:commandButton` tag for submitting
the input in the content section. The `h:commandButton` tag is bound to the
`commandButton1` bean property in the managed bean catalog using an **expression
language (EL)** expression. The `action` attribute of the command button has binding
to the `catalog.commandButton1_action` action method in the managed bean.

The `input.xhtml` Facelets page consists of a `ui:composition` tag for defining the
composition of the Facelets page, and `ui:define` tags within the `ui:composition`
tag for the different sections of the Facelets composition such as header, content,
and footer. The template name is specified in the `template` attribute of the
`ui:composition` tag. The `ui:define` tags correspond to the `ui:insert` tags in the
template. If a `ui:define` tag is not specified corresponding to a `ui:insert` tag, the
default `ui:insert` tag in the `BasicTemplate.xhtml` page is used in the Facelets
composition page. Only the `ui:define` tag for the content is defined in the `input.
xhtml` page; the header and footer JPEGs specified in `header.xhtml` and `output.
xhtml` and included in `BasicTemplate.xhtml` with `ui:insert` / `ui:include`,
are used for the header and footer sections.

```
<!DOCTYPE html PUBLIC "-//W3C//DTD XHTML 1.0 Transitional//EN"
    "http://www.w3.org/TR/xhtml1/DTD/xhtml1-transitional.dtd">
<html xmlns="http://www.w3.org/1999/xhtml"
    xmlns:ui="http://java.sun.com/jsf/facelets"
    xmlns:h="http://java.sun.com/jsf/html"
    xmlns:f="http://java.sun.com/jsf/core">
<ui:composition template="/WEB-INF/templates/BasicTemplate.xhtml">
    <ui:define name="content">
        <h:form>
      <h:panelGrid columns="2">
        <h:outputLabel binding="#{catalog.outputLabel1}" value="SQL
Query:" />
        <h:inputText binding="#{catalog.inputText1}" />
        <h:commandButton value="Submit" binding="#{catalog.
commandButton1}"
          action="#{catalog.commandButton1_action}" />
      </h:panelGrid>
    </h:form>
    </ui:define>
</ui:composition>
</html>
```

The `output.xhtml` Facelets composition page consists of an `h:dataTable` tag in the content section to output the JSF data table generated in the managed bean from the SQL query specified in the `input.xhtml` Facelets composition page. The `ui:define` tag for content defines the composition of the Facelets page. The `h:dataTable` tag has binding to the `dataTable1` bean property in the managed bean and the `h:column` tags have binding to the `column1`, `column2`, `column3`, `column4`, `column5`, and `column6` properties in the managed bean. The Facelets composition page, `output.xhtml`, is listed as follows:

```
<!DOCTYPE html PUBLIC "-//W3C//DTD XHTML 1.0 Transitional//EN"
    "http://www.w3.org/TR/xhtml1/DTD/xhtml1-transitional.dtd">
<html xmlns="http://www.w3.org/1999/xhtml"
    xmlns:ui="http://java.sun.com/jsf/facelets"
    xmlns:h="http://java.sun.com/jsf/html"
    xmlns:f="http://java.sun.com/jsf/core">
<ui:composition template="/WEB-INF/templates/BasicTemplate.xhtml">
    <ui:define name="content">
        <h:form>
        <h:dataTable  binding="#{catalog.dataTable1}" border="1"
rows="5">
        <h:column binding="#{catalog.column1}"></h:column>
        <h:column binding="#{catalog.column2}"></h:column>
        <h:column binding="#{catalog.column3}"></h:column>
        <h:column binding="#{catalog.column4}"></h:column>
        <h:column binding="#{catalog.column5}"></h:column>
        <h:column binding="#{catalog.column6}"></h:column>
    </h:dataTable>
    </h:form>
    </ui:define>
</ui:composition>
</html>
```

# Creating navigation

Next we shall discuss navigation in the Facelets application. Add a Facelets composition page, `error.xhtml`, for navigating to if an error is generated.

If the outcome from `input.xhtml` is "output", navigate to `output.xhtml`. If the outcome is "error", navigate to `error.xhtml`. The outcome is the value returned by the action method—`commandButton1_action`. We have used the implicit navigation provided by JSF 2.0 in which the navigation controller navigates to the Facelets page with the same name as the outcome of an action.

We have also used the @ManagedBean annotation to declare a managed bean. faces-config.xml becomes essentially an empty file with JSF 2.0 implicit navigation and the @ManagedBean annotation specified in the managed bean.

```xml
<?xml version="1.0" encoding="UTF-8"?>
<faces-config
    xmlns="http://java.sun.com/xml/ns/javaee"
    xmlns:xsi="http://www.w3.org/2001/XMLSchema-instance"
    xsi:schemaLocation="http://java.sun.com/xml/ns/javaee http://java.sun.com/xml/ns/javaee/web-facesconfig_2_0.xsd"
    version="2.0">


</faces-config>
```

The managed bean section implementing the implicit navigation is listed, as follows:

```java
@ManagedBean(name="catalog")
public class Catalog {

try{
...
...
    dataTable1.setValue(dataModel);

} catch (SQLException e) {
  System.out.println(e.getMessage());
  return "error";

} catch (ClassNotFoundException e) {
  System.out.println(e.getMessage());
  return "error";
} finally {

}
return "output";
}
```

# Running the Facelets application

We need to specify some factory implementation classes for the Facelets application. Add a WEB-INF/classes/META-INF/services directory. In the services directory create the following factory files with the corresponding factory implementation classes specified in the factory files; factory filenames are to be specified without an extension.

| Filename | Class to be specified in the file |
|---|---|
| `javax.faces.application.ApplicationFactory` | `com.sun.faces.application.ApplicationFactoryImpl` |
| `javax.faces.context.FacesContextFactory` | `com.sun.faces.context.FacesContextFactoryImpl` |
| `javax.faces.lifecycle.LifecycleFactory` | `com.sun.faces.lifecycle.LifecycleFactoryImpl` |
| `javax.faces.render.RenderKitFactory` | `com.sun.faces.renderkit.RenderKitFactoryImpl` |

The directory structure of the Facelets application including the factory files is shown in the following screenshot:

Start the WebLogic Server if not already started. To run the Facelets application, right-click on **input.xhtml** and select **Run As | Run on Server**, as shown in the following screenshot:

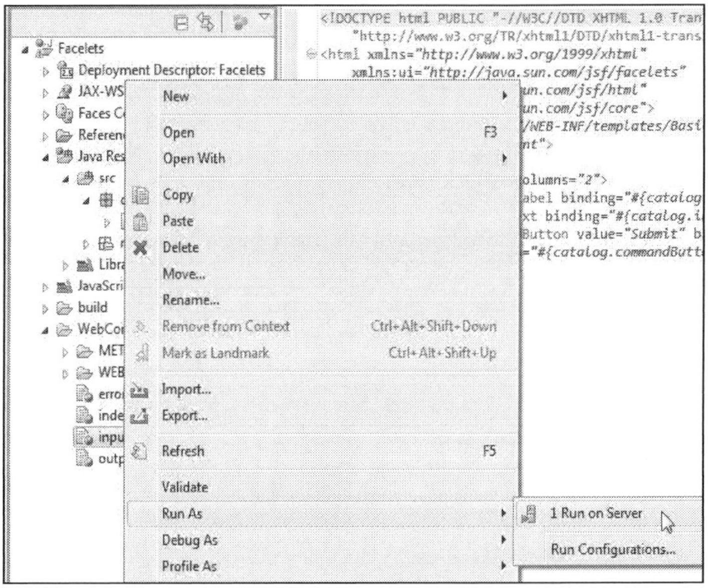

Select the server to run the application. Click on **Next**, as follows:

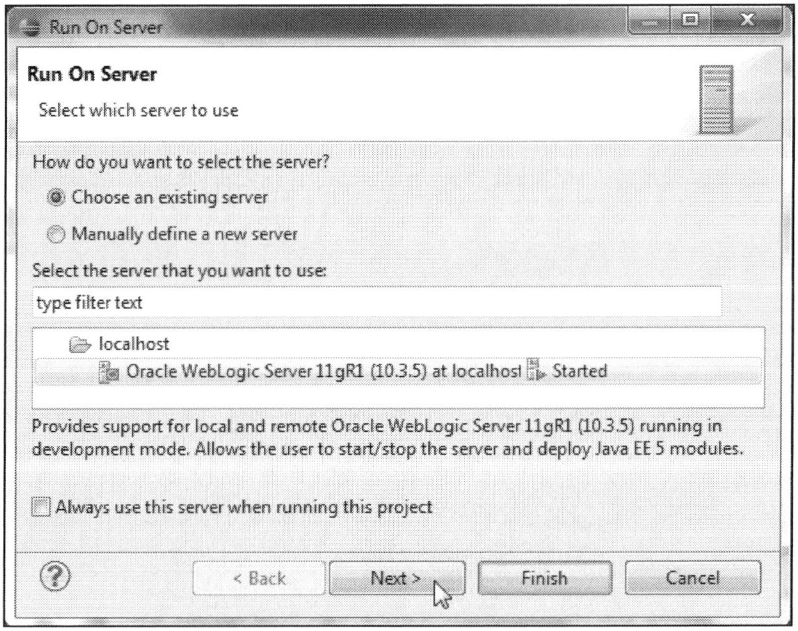

Select default settings and click on **Next**. Click on **Finish**. An ear application gets created and gets deployed to the WebLogic Server, as shown in the following screenshot:

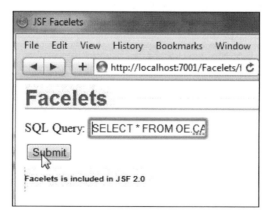

Run the `input.xhtml` Facelets composition page on the WebLogic Server in a browser with the URL `http://localhost:7001/Facelets/faces/input.xhtml`. The three sections of the input Facelets page, header, content, and footer, get rendered. The header and footer from the `BasicTemplate.xhtml` template get included in the composition. Specify a SQL query such as `SELECT * FROM OE.CATALOG` to create a data table from and click on **Submit**, as shown in the following screenshot:

The `output.xhtml` Facelets composition page gets rendered with a JSF data table generated for the SQL query. Templating is demonstrated with the common header and footer in the composition page; the same header and footer JPEGs get displayed, as follows:

# Summary

Facelets is an integrated feature of JSF 2.0. In this chapter we discussed templating with Facelets. WebLogic Server includes a shared library for JSF 2.0, which we configured first. We added the 2.0 version of the JavaServer Faces project facet. We created a web project for Facelets, and created a managed bean to create a JSF data table. For templating we added a Facelets template in which we configured the default sections of a Facelets page such as header, content, and footer. We added Facelets pages for a SQL query input and a JSF data table output. We added implicit navigation to the JSF pages. We ran the Facelets application to demonstrate templating by including the same header and footer images in the input and output pages.

Having introduced creating a JSF data table in *Chapter 4, Creating a JSF Data Table*, and templating with Facelets in JSF 2.0 in this chapter, in the next chapter we shall discuss the Apache MyFaces Trinidad, which is a JSF framework.

# 6
# Creating Apache Trinidad User Interfaces

Apache MyFaces Trinidad (referred to as "Trinidad" in this chapter) is a JSF framework that provides a component library suitable for an enterprise-level application. Trinidad is supported in **Oracle Enterprise Pack for Eclipse** (**OEPE**) 12*c* as a project facet. In this chapter we shall create a Trinidad project in OEPE 12*c* and run a web application consisting of Trinidad user interfaces on Oracle WebLogic Server. The web application is run to create and find a catalog entry in Oracle database.

In this chapter we shall learn the following:

- Configuring Trinidad in OEPE 12*c*
- Adding Trinidad components to a JSF page
- Value binding Trinidad components to a managed bean
- Creating and finding a database table row from Trinidad UIs
- Accessing Oracle database from the managed bean
- Running the Trinidad UIs on WebLogic Server

# Configuring Trinidad

Trinidad may be configured in any Java EE application server. Installing and using Trinidad in a JSF page requires the following setup:

1. Install JSF (JSF 1.1.01 reference implementation or later version). Register the Faces servlet in `web.xml` and specify its servlet mapping.

2. Install the Trinidad libraries and dependencies. We shall install the Trinidad libraries using the Trinidad project facet in OEPE 12c.

3. Register the Trinidad filter in `web.xml` and specify the filter mapping to the Faces servlet.

4. Register the Apache Trinidad RenderKit in `faces-config.xml` so that JSF uses the Trinidad render kit.

5. Register `ResourceServlet` in `web.xml` to serve web application resources such as styles, images, and JavaScript.

# Setting the environment

We shall use an Oracle database table to add and find a table row from Trinidad user interfaces. Install Oracle Enterprise Pack for Eclipse 12c, and install the Oracle Database 11g XE. We shall be creating a catalog entry in an Oracle database table with user input from a Trinidad components-based user interface. For that create a database table— `JournalCatalog`— and add some table rows with the following SQL script:

```
CREATE TABLE JournalCatalog(CatalogId VARCHAR(255) PRIMARY KEY,
Journal VARCHAR(255), Publisher Varchar(255), Edition VARCHAR(255),
Title Varchar(255), Author Varchar(255));
INSERT INTO JournalCatalog VALUES('catalog1', 'Oracle Magazine',
'Oracle Publishing', 'September-October 2010', 'Using Oracle Essbase
Release 11.1.2 Aggregate Storage Option Databases', 'Mark Rittman and
Venkatakrishnan Janakiraman');
INSERT INTO JournalCatalog VALUES('catalog2', 'Oracle Magazine',
'Oracle Publishing', 'July-August 2010', 'Infrastructure Software and
Virtualization', 'David Baum');
```

We also need to create a WebLogic Server data source with the JNDI name `jdbc/OracleDS`, as discussed in *Chapter 1, EJB 3.0 Database Persistence*.

# Creating a Trinidad project

In this section we shall create a web project in OEPE 12*c* for the Trinidad application. Select **File | New | Other**. In the **New** wizard select **Web | Dynamic Web Project** and click on **Next**. Specify the project name as `TrinidadEclipse` in the **Project name** field and configure a new runtime for **Oracle WebLogic Server 12c (12.1.1)**, which was discussed in *Chapter 1, EJB 3.x Database Persistence*. Select **2.5** as **Dynamic web module version** and **JavaServer Faces v1.2 Project** as **Configuration**, as shown in the following screenshot. Click on **Next**, as follows:

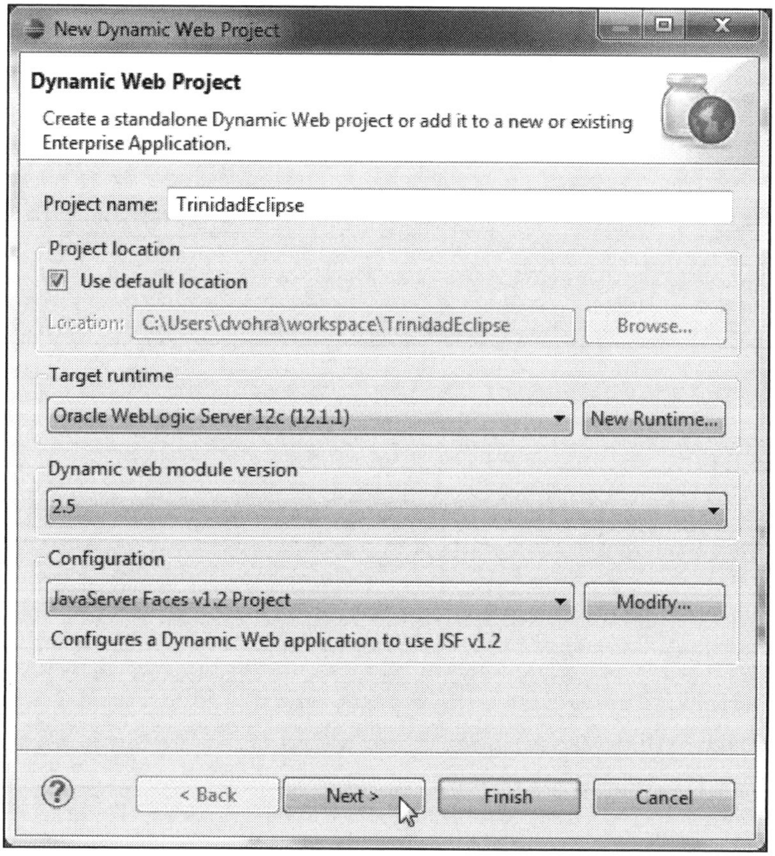

Select the default Java settings with source folders on the build path as `src`, and default output folder as `build/classes` and click on **Next**. In the **Web Module** settings window, specify **TrinidadEclipse** as **Context root** and **WebContent** as **Content directory**, and check the **Generate web.xml deployment descriptor** checkbox. Click on **Next**. In the **JSF Capabilities** window select **WebLogic Shared Library** as **Type, jsf** as **Library name**, and **1.2** as **Version** under the **JSF Implementation Library** section. Check the **Configure JSF servlet in deployment descriptor** checkbox. The **JSF Configuration File** field specifies the **/WEB-INF/faces-config.xml** configuration file. The **JSF Servlet Name** field specifies **Faces Servlet**. The **JSF Servlet Class Name** field specifies the **javax.faces.webapp. FacesServlet** class. The **URL Mapping Patterns** field specifies the URL pattern to include in a URL for a Trinidad UI to invoke the Faces servlet. Click on **Finish**:

If the Java EE perspective is not already selected, a dialog message gets initiated to prompt if the Java EE perspective should be opened. Click on **Yes**. A web project gets created. OEPE 12*c* provides the Trinidad project facet to create Trinidad components-based UIs. We need to add the Trinidad project facet to the web project. Right-click on the project and select **Properties**. In **Properties** select the **Trinidad** project facet with **1.2** as **Version**. The **Trinidad** project facet version should correspond with the JSF version. Click on **Further configuration required...**, as follows:

**Project Facets**

Configuration: `<custom>`

| Project Facet | Version |
| --- | --- |
| ▷ ☐ Apache XMLBeans | |
| ▷ ☐ Axis2 Web Services | |
| ☐ CXF 2.x Web Services | 1.0 |
| ☑ Dynamic Web Module | 2.5 |
| ☑ Java | 1.5 |
| ☐ Java Annotation Processing Support | 5.0 |
| ☑ JavaScript | 1.0 |
| ☑ JavaServer Faces | 1.2 |
| ☐ JAX-RS (REST Web Services) | 1.1 |
| ☐ JAXB | 2.1 |
| ☐ JPA | 2.0 |
| ☐ JSTL | 1.2 |
| ☐ Oracle Coherence | 3.7.1 |
| ☐ Oracle WebLogic SCA | 12.1.1 |
| ☐ Oracle WebLogic Scripting Tools (WLST) Support | 12.1.1 |
| ☑ Oracle WebLogic Web App Extensions | 10.3.5 |
| ☐ Oracle WebLogic Web Service Clients | 2.1 |
| ☐ Oracle WebLogic Web Services | 2.1 |
| ☐ Spring | 2.5 |
| ☐ Struts | 1.3 |
| ☑ Trinidad | 1.2 |
| ☐ WebDoclet (XDoclet) | 1.2.3 |

❸ Further configuration required...

Select **User Library** as **Type** under the **Library** section and click on the **Download Library** button, as shown in the following screenshot:

In the **Download Library** window select the **Trinidad 1.2 (Apache MyFaces Trinidad API1.2.13)** library and click on **Next**, as follows:

Select **Library License** and click on **Finish**. For Apache Trinidad Software licensing information refer to `http://myfaces.apache.org/trinidad/license.html`. The **Trinidad 1.2 (Apache MyFaces Trinidad API1.2.13)** library gets configured. Click on **OK**:

Click on **Apply**, go to **Properties | Project Facets**, and click on **OK**. The **Oracle WebLogic Server 12c** target runtime gets configured with the **Trinidad** project facet. The Trinidad JAR files get added to the project. The Trinidad filter and Trinidad servlet get configured in **web.xml**, as follows:

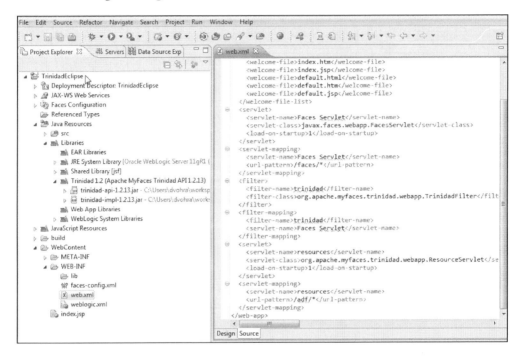

The Trinidad filter is a servlet filter used to initialize Trinidad by establishing a `RequestContext` object. We will use `RequestContext` in this chapter to create a `pageFlowScope` instance. The Trinidad filter may be applied to only certain types of requests with the `dispatcher` subelements in the `filter-mapping` element. We have set the Trinidad filter to be applied only to requests originating from the client or forwarded to a component with the FORWARD and REQUEST dispatchers. A servlet —`org.apache.myfaces.trinidad.webapp.ResourceServlet`— used to serve web application resources is configured in `web.xml`. `FacesServlet` is specified for JSF. The servlet mappings for `ResourceServlet` and `FacesServlet` are also specified. Save the state of a JSF page view on the client by setting the `javax.faces.STATE_SAVING_METHOD` parameter to `client`. Trinidad provides an improved version of client-side state saving. The `org.apache.myfaces.trinidad.CHECK_FILE_MODIFICATION` parameter, which checks whether the JSF files have been modified and discards saved states when JSF files have been modified, is set to `false` to save an overhead. For some of the other Trinidad configuration parameters that may be configured in `web.xml` refer to `http://myfaces.apache.org/trinidad/devguide/configuration.html#web.xml`. The `web.xml` configuration file is listed, as follows:

```xml
<?xml version = '1.0' encoding = 'windows-1252'?>
<web-app xmlns:xsi="http://www.w3.org/2001/XMLSchema-instance"
  xsi:schemaLocation="http://java.sun.com/xml/ns/javaee http://java.
sun.com/xml/ns/javaee/web-app_2_5.xsd"
  version="2.5" xmlns="http://java.sun.com/xml/ns/javaee">
  <context-param>
    <param-name>javax.faces.STATE_SAVING_METHOD</param-name>
    <param-value>client</param-value>
  </context-param>
  <context-param>
    <param-name>org.apache.myfaces.trinidad.CHECK_FILE_MODIFICATION</
param-name>
    <param-value>false</param-value>
  </context-param>

  <filter>
    <filter-name>trinidad</filter-name>
    <filter-class>org.apache.myfaces.trinidad.webapp.TrinidadFilter</
filter-class>
  </filter>

  <filter-mapping>
    <filter-name>trinidad</filter-name>
    <servlet-name>Faces Servlet</servlet-name>
    <dispatcher>FORWARD</dispatcher>
    <dispatcher>REQUEST</dispatcher>
  </filter-mapping>
  <servlet>
    <servlet-name>Faces Servlet</servlet-name>
    <servlet-class>javax.faces.webapp.FacesServlet</servlet-class>
    <load-on-startup>1</load-on-startup>
  </servlet>
  <servlet>
    <servlet-name>resources</servlet-name>
    <servlet-class>org.apache.myfaces.trinidad.webapp.
ResourceServlet</servlet-class>
  </servlet>
  <servlet-mapping>
    <servlet-name>Faces Servlet</servlet-name>
    <url-pattern>/faces/*</url-pattern>
  </servlet-mapping>
```

```
<servlet-mapping>
  <servlet-name>resources</servlet-name>
  <url-pattern>/adf/*</url-pattern>
</servlet-mapping>
<servlet-mapping>
  <servlet-name>resources</servlet-name>
  <url-pattern>/afr/*</url-pattern>
</servlet-mapping>
</web-app>
```

The default `render-kit` gets configured in `faces-config.xml` to the Trinidad render kit—`org.apache.myfaces.Trinidad.core`.

In the next section we will develop the Trinidad web application to create and find a catalog entry.

# Creating Trinidad UIs

In this section we will discuss the following:

- Creating JSF pages to create and retrieve a catalog entry in an Oracle database table that we created earlier
- Adding Trinidad components in the JSF pages instead of adding the standard JSF components
- Value binding the Trinidad components to managed bean properties
- Access Oracle database from the managed bean

Select **File | New | Other**. In the **New** wizard select **JSP File** under **Web** and click on **Next**. Select the `WebContent` folder, and specify **create.jsp** as **File name**. Click on **Next**. Select the default **New JavaServer Faces (JSF) Page (html)** template and click on **Finish**. Similarly add the **find.jsp** JSF page to find a catalog entry, **catalogentry.jsp** to display a catalog entry, and **error.jsp** to be used when an error is generated. The directory structure of the **TrinidadEclipse** application is shown, as follows:

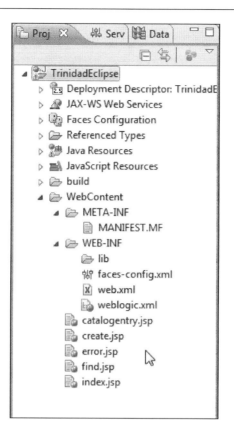

# Creating a managed bean

Trinidad has a dependency on JSF 1.1 or later reference implementation. Alternatively MyFaces 1.0.8 may be used, but we are using JSF 1.2. Typically, JSF is used with managed beans, which are JavaBeans components that are managed using the managed bean facility. The managed bean facility instantiates the beans and stores them in the scope. Managed beans are specified using the `managed-bean` element in the application configuration resource file— `faces-config.xml`— in pre JSF 2.x, or the `@ManagedBean` annotation in the bean in JSF Version 2.x. JSF pages may have value binding or component binding to a managed bean. Unless the components are required to be programmatically modified in the managed bean, it is a best practice to use value binding.

Backing beans are managed beans that are associated with UI components on a particular page. Backing beans are typically used to manage the "view" facet of a MVC design pattern with getters/setters for the view properties. Controller managed beans are managed beans that are used for the "controller" facet of the MVC design pattern for using business logic on input values and returning a navigation outcome to the navigation handler. The difference between a controller managed bean and a backing bean is that a controller managed bean typically consists of action methods that are invoked from a JSF page, with a command button for example, and has value binding with view properties, while a backing bean is used to manage view properties, in a Facelets page for example, and has component binding with view properties. As we shall be using more than one JSF UI page and shall be using navigation between the JSF pages in addition to applying business logic on input values, we shall be using a (controller) managed bean. To create a managed bean right-click on `faces-config.xml` and select **Open With | Faces Config Editor**, as shown in the following screenshot:

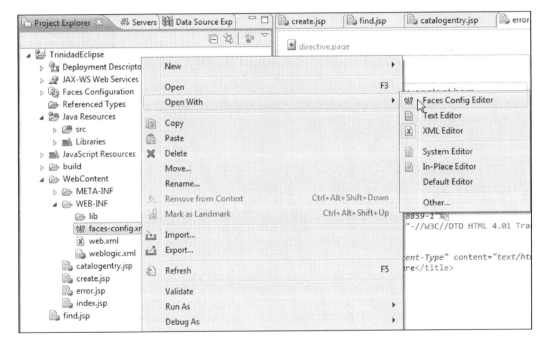

In **Faces Config Editor** select the **Managed Beans** tab. The managed beans get listed. Click on **Add** to add a managed bean, as follows:

In the **Managed Bean** wizard specify a Java class source folder (`TrinidadEclipse/src`), package (`catalog.managed`), and name (`Catalog`). Click on **Next**. In **Java Class Selection** select **Create a new Java class** and click on **Next**. In **Managed Bean Configuration** specify a managed bean name in the **Managed Bean name** field and select a scope in the **Managed Bean scope** field (**session**). A managed bean gets created.

The managed bean class, **catalog.managed.Catalog,** gets created at the location Java Resources/src.

```
Proj     Serv  Data                error.jsp    faces-config.xml    Catalog.java      5

                                   package catalog.managed;

TrinidadEclipse                    import javax.naming.InitialContext;
  Deployment Descriptor: TrinidadE import javax.naming.NamingException;
  JAX-WS Web Services              import java.sql.*;
  Faces Configuration             import org.apache.myfaces.trinidad.context.RequestContext;
  Referenced Types
  Java Resources                  import org.apache.myfaces.trinidad.component.*;
    src
      catalog.managed             public class Catalog {
        Catalog.java                  private UIXForm form1;
      resources                       private UIXDocument document1;
  Libraries                           private UIXPanel panel1;
                                      private UIXInput input1;
                                      private UIXInput input2;
```

In Catalog.java import the Trinidad components package org.apache.myfaces. trinidad.component and the RequestContext class, as follows:

```
import org.apache.myfaces.trinidad.context.RequestContext;
import org.apache.myfaces.trinidad.component.*;
```

Catalog.java is the managed bean for two JSF pages—create.jsp to create a catalog entry and find.jsp to find a catalog entry. The create.jsp page has six Trinidad input fields to create a catalog entry. In Catalog.java, specify properties of component type UIXInput and getter/setter methods for the properties, which shall have value binding with tr:inputText components on create.jsp. The CoreInputText class may be used for an input field, but using the UIXInput class instead of a more specific class adds the flexibility to use a different component from the component group by modifying only the JSF page(s). Using a subclass has the advantage of providing more component-specific methods. Specify a property and getter/setter methods for a Catalog object. Specify the catalogId, journal, publisher, edition, title, and author properties and getters/setters for the properties. Specify action methods cb1_action() and cb2_action1() for the command buttons; one on create.jsp and another on find.jsp. In cb1_action1() retrieve the input field values from create.jsp, obtain a connection with the database using the JNDI configured in WebLogic Server and create a catalog entry using the Catalog constructor, and the JDBC API. In cb2_action1() retrieve the Catalog Id value from find.jsp. Retrieve the catalog entry from the Oracle database using the JDBC API. We shall be displaying the catalog entry retrieved on another JSF page—catalogentry.jsp. As we are taking search criteria from one page (create.jsp) and showing the result on the second page (catalogentry.jsp), we are communicating values between pages.

Trinidad provides `pageFlowScope` for communicating values between pages. Values in `pageFlowScope` are available as the user navigates from one page to another in the current page flow. To add values to `pageFlowScope` obtain a `RequestContext` object using the static method `getCurrentInstance()`. Obtain `Map` of objects at the `pageFlowScope` scope using the `getPageFlowScope()` method of the `RequestContext` object and add values to `Map` using the `put(String, Object)` method. For example, the `catalogId` value is added, as follows:

```
RequestContext requestContext = RequestContext.getCurrentInstance();
requestContext.getPageFlowScope().put("catalogId", catalogId);
```

Similarly add values for the `journal`, `publisher`, `edition`, `title`, and `author` properties to `pageFlowScope`. As we will be displaying catalog entry properties on a JSF page, we also need labels for the properties. The labels are added as string values either on the JSF page or to `pageFlowScope`. The `Catalog.java` class is listed with additional discussion, as follows:

```
package catalog.managed;

import javax.naming.InitialContext;
import javax.naming.NamingException;
import java.sql.*;
import org.apache.myfaces.trinidad.context.RequestContext;

import org.apache.myfaces.trinidad.component.*;

public class Catalog {
```

Declare the bean properties for components that have corresponding components on the JSF pages:

```
private UIXForm f1;
private UIXDocument d1;
private UIXPanel pfl1;
private UIXInput input1;
private UIXInput input2;
private UIXGroup g1;
private UIXInput input3;
private UIXInput input4;
private UIXInput input5;
private UIXInput input6;
private UIXInput input7;
private UIXCommand cb1;
private UIXCommand cb2;
```

Declare the properties for fields of a catalog entry:

```
private Catalog catalog;
  private String catalogId;
  private String journal;
  private String publisher;
  private String edition;
  private String title;
  private String author;
```

Declare variables for connection parameters:

```
private java.sql.Connection conn;
private Statement stmt;
private ResultSet rs;
```

Declare getter/setter methods for the bean properties:

```
public void setF1(UIXForm f1) {
  this.f1 = f1;
}

public UIXForm getF1() {
  return f1;
}

public void setD1(UIXDocument d1) {
  this.d1 = d1;
}

public UIXDocument getD1() {
  return d1;
}

public void setPfl1(UIXPanel pfl1) {
  this.pfl1 = pfl1;
}

public UIXPanel getPfl1() {
  return pfl1;
}

public void setInput1(UIXInput input1) {
  this.input1 = input1;
}
```

```
public UIXInput getInput1() {
  return input1;
}

public void setInput2(UIXInput input2) {
  this.input2 = input2;
}

public UIXInput getInput2() {
  return input2;
}

public void setG1(UIXGroup g1) {
  this.g1 = g1;
}

public UIXGroup getG1() {
  return g1;
}

public void setInput3(UIXInput input3) {
  this.input3 = input3;
}

public UIXInput getInput3() {
  return input3;
}

public void setInput4(UIXInput input4) {
  this.input4 = input4;
}

public UIXInput getInput4() {
  return input4;
}

public void setInput5(UIXInput input5) {
  this.input5 = input5;
}

public UIXInput getInput5() {
  return input5;
}
```

```
public void setInput6(UIXInput input6) {
  this.input6 = input6;
}

public UIXInput getInput6() {
  return input6;
}

public void setInput7(UIXInput input7) {
  this.input7 = input7;
}

public UIXInput getInput7() {
  return input7;
}

public void setCb1(UIXCommand cb1) {
  this.cb1 = cb1;
}

public UIXCommand getCb1() {
  return cb1;
}

public void setCb2(UIXCommand cb2) {
  this.cb2 = cb2;
}


public UIXCommand getCb2() {
  return cb2;
}
```

Add an action method to create a catalog entry in the Oracle database. The input values are retrieved from create.jsp using the getValue() method. The data source JNDI created in WebLogic Server is used to obtain a Connection object using JNDI lookup with InitialContext. Create a Statement object to construct the SQL to insert a database table row. Alternatively, a PreparedStatement object may be used. Close the Statement and Connection objects in finally. The action method returns **persisted** if a catalog entry gets created without an error. The navigation rule for getting **persisted** as an outcome is to navigate to the index.jsp JSF page. If the outcome is **error**, the navigation handler navigates to error.jsp.

```
public String cb1_action() {
  try {

    catalogId = (String) input1.getValue();

    journal = (String) input2.getValue();

    publisher = (String) input3.getValue();

    edition = (String) input4.getValue();

    title = (String) (input5.getValue());

    author = (String) (input6.getValue());

    InitialContext initialContext = new InitialContext();
    javax.sql.DataSource ds = (javax.sql.DataSource) initialContext
        .lookup("jdbc/OracleDS");
    conn = ds.getConnection();

    stmt = conn.createStatement();
    String sql = "INSERT INTO JournalCatalog VALUES(" + "\'"
        + catalogId + "\'" + "," + "\'" + journal + "\'" + ","
        + "\'" + publisher + "\'" + "," + "\'" + edition + "\'"
        + "," + "\'" + title + "\'" + "," + "\'" + author + "\'"
        + ")";

    stmt.execute(sql);

  } catch (NamingException e) {
    System.err.println(e.getMessage());
    return "error";
  } catch (SQLException e) {
    System.err.println(e.getMessage());
    return "error";
  } finally {
    try {

      stmt.close();
      conn.close();
    } catch (SQLException e) {
      System.err.println(e.getMessage());
          return "error";
    }
  }

  return "persisted";
}
```

Add an action method to retrieve a catalog entry result set from the Oracle database for a catalog ID specified on the find.jsp JSF page. As in the previous action method a Connection object was obtained using JNDI lookup and a SQL statement run using a Statement object. The catalog entry result set field values are added to pageFlowScope. The method returns **catalogentry** for which the navigation rule is to navigate to the index.jsp page. If an error is generated the outcome is **error**, which navigates to the error.jsp page.

```
public String cb2_action1() {

    RequestContext requestContext = RequestContext.
getCurrentInstance();
    try {

        InitialContext initialContext = new InitialContext();
        javax.sql.DataSource ds = (javax.sql.DataSource) initialContext
            .lookup("jdbc/OracleDS");
        conn = ds.getConnection();
        String catalogId = (String) input7.getValue();
        System.out.println(catalogId);
        stmt = conn.createStatement();
        // Obtain result set

        String query = "SELECT * from JournalCatalog WHERE CATALOGID="
            + "'" + catalogId + "'";
        rs = stmt.executeQuery(query);

        rs.next();
        requestContext.getPageFlowScope().put("CatalogIdLabel", "Catalog
ID:");
        requestContext.getPageFlowScope().put("JournalLabel",
"Journal:");
        requestContext.getPageFlowScope().put("PublisherLabel",
"Publisher:");
        requestContext.getPageFlowScope().put("EditionLabel",
"Edition:");
        requestContext.getPageFlowScope().put("TitleLabel", "Title:");
        requestContext.getPageFlowScope().put("AuthorLabel", "Author:");

        catalogId = rs.getString("CATALOGID");
```

```
            requestContext.getPageFlowScope().put("catalogId", catalogId);

            journal = rs.getString("JOURNAL");

            requestContext.getPageFlowScope().put("journal", journal);

            publisher = rs.getString("PUBLISHER");

            requestContext.getPageFlowScope().put("publisher", publisher);

            edition = rs.getString("EDITION");
            requestContext.getPageFlowScope().put("edition", edition);

            title = rs.getString("TITLE");
            requestContext.getPageFlowScope().put("title", title);

            author = rs.getString("AUTHOR");
            requestContext.getPageFlowScope().put("author", author);

        } catch (NamingException e) {
          System.err.println(e.getMessage());
          return "error";
        } catch (SQLException e) {
          System.err.println(e.getMessage());
          return "error";
        } finally {
          try {

            stmt.close();
            conn.close();
          } catch (SQLException e) {
            System.err.println(e.getMessage());
          }
        }
        return "catalogentry";
    }
}
```

As we created a managed bean, the following `managed-bean` declaration gets added to `faces-config.xml`:

```
<managed-bean>
<managed-bean-name>catalog</managed-bean-name><managed-bean-
class>catalog.managed.Catalog</managed-bean-class><managed-bean-
scope>request</managed-bean-scope>
</managed-bean>
```

In **Properties** the **Java Build Path** section should include the Trinidad libraries, as shown in the following screenshot:

In the next section we will add Trinidad components to the application.

# Adding Trinidad components

In this section we shall add Trinidad components to the index.jsp, create.jsp, find.jsp, and catalogentry.jsp pages. We shall use the panel form layout component tr:panelFormLayout, which is suitable for input form components because it aligns the labels and fields vertically. First, create index.jsp, which has the command links for create.jsp and find.jsp. In index.jsp the root element is an f:view element, which provides a container component for all JSF and Trinidad components. Add the taglib declaration for the Trinidad tag library, as follows:

```
<%@ taglib uri="http://myfaces.apache.org/trinidad" prefix="tr"%>
```

First, add the tr:document tag, which represents the CoreDocument class and adds root elements for an HTML construct. To add the tr:document tag, add < and select **tr:document** from the pop-up menu, as shown in the following screenshot:

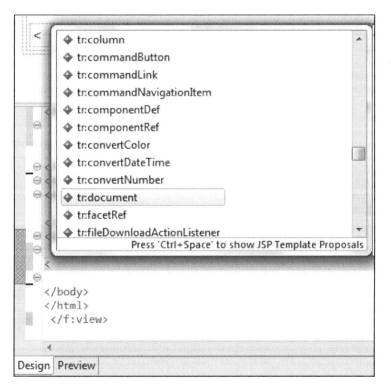

In **Properties** specify the ID in the **Id** field for the `tr:document` element. Within the `tr:document` tag, add the **tr:form** tag, as shown in the following screenshot. The `tr:form` tag represents the `UIXForm` class and adds a `<form>` element for adding `tr:inputText` tags for user input:

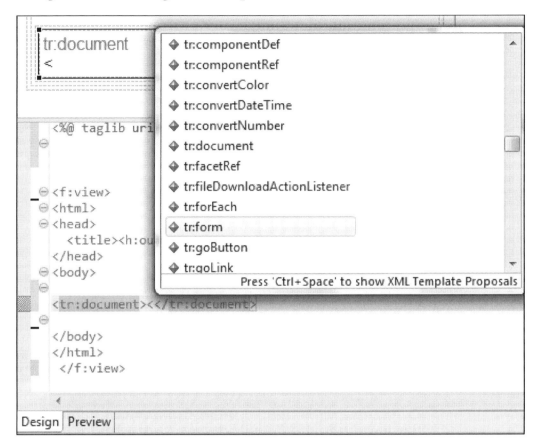

Next, add a **tr:commandLink** tag, which is a link representation of UIXCommand, as shown in the following screenshot:

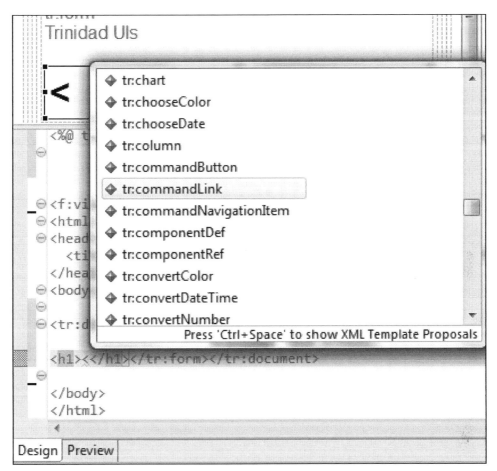

The `tr:commandLink` tag is added to invoke the `create.jsp` JSF page for creating a catalog entry. The static outcome for the `tr:commandLink` tag is specified using the `action` property. To add a property click within the `tr:commandLink` tag and add a space to display the pop-up menu. Select **Properties** from the pop-up menu, as shown in the following screenshot:

In the **Properties** tab add the value for the `action` property in the **Value** column, as shown in the following screenshot. The **action** property is set to **create**, which is an outcome for the `tr:commandLink` component and has a navigation rule specified in `faces-config.xml` to navigate to `create.jsp`.

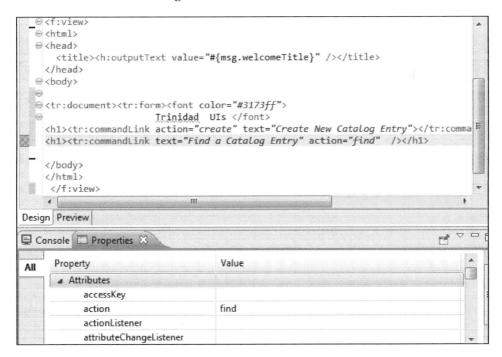

Similarly, add a `tr:commandLink` tag to find a catalog entry with **action** property set to **find**, as shown in the following screenshot. The **find** outcome has a navigation rule in `faces-config.xml` to navigate to `find.jsp`.

`index.jsp` is listed, as follows:

```
<!DOCTYPE HTML PUBLIC "-//W3C//DTD HTML 4.01 Transitional//EN"
"http://www.w3.org/TR/html4/loose.dtd">
<%@ page contentType="text/html;charset=windows-1252"%>
<%@ taglib
uri="http://java.sun.com/jsf/core" prefix="f"%>
<%@ taglib
uri="http://java.sun.com/jsf/html" prefix="h"%>
<%@ taglib
uri="http://myfaces.apache.org/trinidad" prefix="tr"%>
<html>
<head>
<meta http-equiv="Content-Type" content="text/html;
charset=ISO-8859-1">
<title>Trinidad UIs</title>
</head>
<body>
<f:view locale="en_US">
  <tr:document id="d1">
    <tr:form id="f1"><h1>
        <font color="#3173ff">
          Trinidad  UIs </font>
      </h1><h1><tr:commandLink text="Create New Catalog Entry"
          action="create" id="cl1" /></h1><h1>
<tr:commandLink text="Find a Catalog Entry" action="find"
        id="cl2" /></h1></tr:form>
  </tr:document>
</f:view>
</body>
</html>
```

In create.jsp we shall add Trinidad components in a panel form layout. To the f:view element on create.jsp add the tr:document and tr:form elements, as discussed for index.jsp. To the tr:form element add the tr:panelFormLayout element, also discussed previously. Add a f:facet element within the tr:panelFormLayout element; the f:facet component represents a named facet (section) within the enclosing tag. Add a tr:group tag within the f:facet element. The tr:group tag just aggregates semantically-related components and has no corresponding client representation. Within the tr:group element add tr:inputText tags for catalog entry properties—catalogid, journal, publisher, edition, title, and author. The tr:inputText tag creates an input text widget in the browser. Specify value binding in the tr:inputText components to the corresponding UIXInput properties in the managed bean. If the EL binding for the "value" points to a bean property with a getter but no setter, and this is an editable component, the component will be rendered in a read-only mode. We have specified both getter/setter methods which makes the components rendered as editable. Add a tr:commandButton tag, which is a button representation of a UIXCommand object to submit the form. The Trinidad components are added, as discussed for index.jsp. First, add < to display the pop-up menu. From the pop-up menu select the component to add. create.jsp is listed, as follows:

```
<!DOCTYPE HTML PUBLIC "-//W3C//DTD HTML 4.01 Transitional//EN"
"http://www.w3.org/TR/html4/loose.dtd">
<%@ page contentType="text/html;charset=windows-1252"%>
<%@ taglib uri="http://java.sun.com/jsf/core" prefix="f"%>
<%@ taglib uri="http://java.sun.com/jsf/html" prefix="h"%>
<%@ taglib
uri="http://myfaces.apache.org/trinidad" prefix="tr"%>
<html>
<head>
<meta http-equiv="Content-Type" content="text/html;
charset=ISO-8859-1">
<title>Create a Catalog Entry</title>
</head>
<body>
<f:view>
  <tr:document id="d1" binding="#{catalog.d1}">
    <tr:form id="f1" binding="#{catalog.f1}">
```

```
      <h1>
        <font color="#6363ff" face="Verdana">
          Create a Catalog Entry
        </font>
         
      </h1>
        <h1>
        <tr:panelFormLayout binding="#{catalog.pfl1}" id="pfl1">
          <f:facet name="footer">
            <tr:group binding="#{catalog.g1}" id="g1">
<tr:inputText label="Catalog Id" binding="#{catalog.input1}"
                      id="it1"/>
<tr:inputText label="Journal" binding="#{catalog.input2}"
                      id="it2"/>
<tr:inputText label="Publisher" binding="#{catalog.input3}"
                      id="it3"/>
<tr:inputText label="Edition" binding="#{catalog.input4}"
                      id="it4"/>
<tr:inputText label="Title" binding="#{catalog.input5}"
                      id="it5"/>
<tr:inputText label="Author" binding="#{catalog.input6}"
                      id="it6"/>
            <tr:commandButton text="Create"
                              binding="#{catalog.cb1}" id="cb1"
                              action="#{catalog.cb1_action}"/>
          </tr:group>
        </f:facet>

      </tr:panelFormLayout>
      </h1></tr:form>
  </tr:document>
</f:view>
</body>
</html>
```

In `find.jsp` add the `tr:inputText` and `tr:commandButton` elements in a
`tr:panelFormLayout` element. The input text widget is for specifying the
catalog ID for which the catalog entry is to be retrieved and displayed. We
shall demonstrate the use of the JSF pages in the next section. `find.jsp` is
listed, as follows:

```
<!DOCTYPE HTML PUBLIC "-//W3C//DTD HTML 4.01 Transitional//EN"
"http://www.w3.org/TR/html4/loose.dtd">
<%@ page contentType="text/html;charset=windows-1252"%>
<%@ taglib uri="http://java.sun.com/jsf/core" prefix="f"%>
<%@ taglib uri="http://java.sun.com/jsf/html" prefix="h"%>
<%@ taglib
uri="http://myfaces.apache.org/trinidad" prefix="tr"%>
<html>
<head>
<meta http-equiv="Content-Type" content="text/html;
charset=ISO-8859-1">
<title>Find a Catalog Entry</title>
</head>
<body>
<f:view>
   <tr:document title="find" id="d1">
     <tr:form id="f1">
       <h1>
         <font color="#5252ff">
           Find a Catalog Entry
         </font>
       </h1>
       <h1>
         <tr:panelFormLayout id="pfl1">
           <f:facet name="footer" />
           <tr:inputText label="Catalog Id" id="it7"
             binding="#{catalog.input7}" />
           <tr:commandButton text="Find" id="cb2"
binding="#{catalog.cb2}" action="#{catalog.cb2_action1}" />
         </tr:panelFormLayout>
       </h1>
     </tr:form>
   </tr:document>
</f:view>
</body>
</html>
```

We have used the `tr:panelFormLayout` element in all the JSF pages and its use becomes apparent in the JSF page to display a catalog entry. A panel form layout displays a set of components in rows and columns. The number of rows is specified using the rows attribute of `tr:panelFormLayout`. The maximum number of columns is specified using the `maxColumns` attribute. The number of actual columns is based on the number of components in the grid, the number of rows in the grid, and the maximum number of columns. The components in a panel layout are added to the specified number of rows starting with the first column. A new panel column is started after the specified number of rows in a column have been allocated. For example, if the specified number of rows in a `panelFormLayout` is three and the number of components to be added to the panel is 10, and the maximum number of columns is four, the first three components are added to the first column; the next three to the second column. Another three components are added to the third column and the fourth column has one component.

In `catalogentry.jsp` add six `tr:outputLabel` tags for a `Catalog` entry properties' labels and six `tr:outputText` tags for a `Catalog` entry properties' values. Specify rows as 6 and `maxColumns` as 2. The `tr:outputLabel` and `tr:outputText` components have value binding with the corresponding values added to `pageFlowScope` previously. `catalogentry.jsp` just displays a catalog entry for the catalog ID specified in `find.jsp` and doesn't invoke any managed bean action methods. `catalogentry.jsp` is listed, as follows:

```
<!DOCTYPE HTML PUBLIC "-//W3C//DTD HTML 4.01 Transitional//EN"
"http://www.w3.org/TR/html4/loose.dtd">
<%@ page contentType="text/html;charset=windows-1252 "%>
<%@ taglib uri="http://java.sun.com/jsf/core" prefix="f"%>
<%@ taglib uri="http://java.sun.com/jsf/html" prefix="h"%>
<%@ taglib uri="http://myfaces.apache.org/trinidad" prefix="tr"%>
<html>
<head>
<meta http-equiv="Content-Type" content="text/html;
charset=ISO-8859-1">
<title>Catalog Entry</title>
</head>
<body>
  <f:view>
    <tr:document title="catalogentry" id="d1">
      <tr:form id="f1">
        <h1>
          <font face="Verdana" color="#5252ff"> Catalog Entry </font>
        </h1>
```

```
          <h1>
            <tr:panelFormLayout rows="6" maxColumns="2" id="pfl1">
              <tr:outputLabel value="#{pageFlowScope.CatalogIdLabel}"
id="ol1"/>
              <tr:outputLabel value="#{pageFlowScope.JournalLabel}"
id="ol2" />
              <tr:outputLabel value="#{pageFlowScope.PublisherLabel}"
id="ol3" />
              <tr:outputLabel value="#{pageFlowScope.EditionLabel}"
id="ol4" />
              <tr:outputLabel value="#{pageFlowScope.TitleLabel}"
id="ol5" />
              <tr:outputLabel value="#{pageFlowScope.AuthorLabel}"
id="ol6" />
              <tr:outputText value="#{pageFlowScope.catalogId}" />
              <tr:outputText value="#{pageFlowScope.journal}" />
              <tr:outputText value="#{pageFlowScope.publisher}" />
              <tr:outputText value="#{pageFlowScope.edition}" />
              <tr:outputText value="#{pageFlowScope.title}" />
              <tr:outputText value="#{pageFlowScope.author}" />
            </tr:panelFormLayout>
          </h1>
        </tr:form>
      </tr:document>
    </f:view>

</body>
</html>
```

We also need to create an error.jsp page to navigate to, if an error is generated while creating or finding a catalog entry. An outcome of **error** is generated if an error occurs. A navigation rule for the **error** outcome is specified in faces-config.xml to navigate to error.jsp. The error.jsp page just has a tr:outputText element for the error message, and is listed as follows:

```
<!DOCTYPE HTML PUBLIC "-//W3C//DTD HTML 4.01 Transitional//EN"
"http://www.w3.org/TR/html4/loose.dtd">
<%@ page contentType="text/html;charset=windows-1252"%>
```

```
<%@ taglib uri="http://java.sun.com/jsf/core" prefix="f"%>
<%@ taglib uri="http://java.sun.com/jsf/html" prefix="h"%>
<%@ taglib
uri="http://myfaces.apache.org/trinidad" prefix="tr"%>
<html>
<head>
<meta http-equiv="Content-Type" content="text/html;
charset=ISO-8859-1">
<title>Error Page</title>
</head>
<body>
<f:view>
  <tr:document id="d1">
    <tr:form id="f1">
      <tr:outputText value="Error Generated" id="ot1" />
    </tr:form>
  </tr:document>
</f:view>
</body>
</html>
```

The navigation rules between the JSPs are defined in `faces-config.xml`, which we have referred to throughout this chapter, and is listed as follows:

```
<?xml version="1.0" encoding="UTF-8"?>
<faces-config xmlns="http://java.sun.com/xml/ns/javaee"
  xmlns:xsi="http://www.w3.org/2001/XMLSchema-instance"
  xsi:schemaLocation="http://java.sun.com/xml/ns/javaee http://java.
sun.com/xml/ns/javaee/web-facesconfig_1_2.xsd"
  version="1.2">
  <application>
    <message-bundle>resources.application</message-bundle>
    <locale-config>
      <default-locale>en</default-locale>
    </locale-config>
  </application>
  <application>
    <default-render-kit-id>org.apache.myfaces.trinidad.core</default-
render-kit-id>
  </application>
  <managed-bean>
```

```
      <managed-bean-name>managed_catalog</managed-bean-name>
      <managed-bean-class>catalog.managed.Catalog</managed-bean-class>
      <managed-bean-scope>request</managed-bean-scope>
   </managed-bean>
<navigation-rule>
    <navigation-case>
      <from-outcome>create</from-outcome>
      <to-view-id>/create.jsp</to-view-id>
    </navigation-case>
  </navigation-rule>
  <navigation-rule>
    <navigation-case>
      <from-outcome>catalogentry</from-outcome>
      <to-view-id>/catalogentry.jsp</to-view-id>
    </navigation-case>
  </navigation-rule>
  <navigation-rule>
    <navigation-case>
      <from-outcome>persisted</from-outcome>
      <to-view-id>/index.jsp</to-view-id>
    </navigation-case>
  </navigation-rule>
  <navigation-rule>
    <navigation-case>
      <from-outcome>error</from-outcome>
      <to-view-id>/error.jsp</to-view-id>
    </navigation-case>
  </navigation-rule>
  <navigation-rule>
    <navigation-case>
      <from-outcome>find</from-outcome>
      <to-view-id>/find.jsp</to-view-id>
    </navigation-case>
  </navigation-rule>

</faces-config>
```

A diagram to illustrate the navigation rules, the outcomes, and the JSF pages navigated to is shown in the following screenshot:

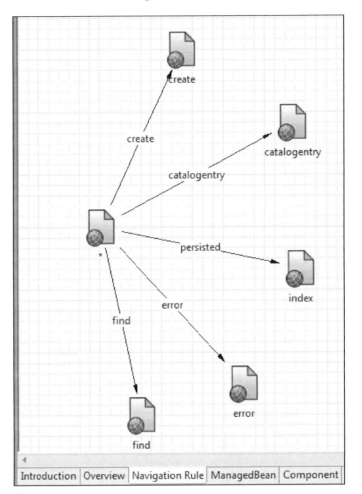

# Running the Trinidad application

Having created the Trinidad UIs, the managed bean, and the configuration files, in this section we shall deploy and run the Trinidad application on WebLogic Server. Next, deploy the Trinidad application onto the WebLogic Server. Right-click on **index.jsp** and select **Run As | Run on Server**, as shown in the following screenshot:

In the **Run On Server** window select **Oracle WebLogic Server 12c (12.1.1) at localhost** and click on **Finish**, as follows:

An autogenerated EAR module gets built and deployed to WebLogic Server. Run the `index.jsp` page in a separate browser with the URL `http://localhost:7001/TrinidadEclipse/faces/index.jsp`. Click on **Create New Catalog Entry** to create a catalog entry, as shown in the following screenshot:

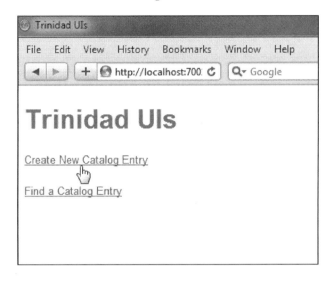

In `catalog.jsp` specify the catalog entry field values as follows, and click on **Create**:

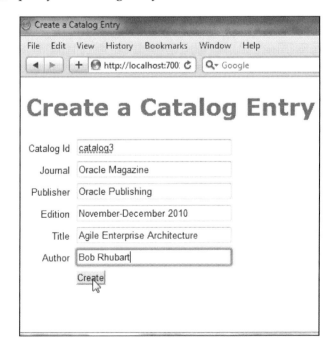

A catalog entry gets created in the Oracle database table, `JournalCatalog`, and may be retrieved with a SQL query from SQL Command Line. The outcome from the action method is **persisted**, which has a navigation rule in `faces-config.xml` to navigate to `index.jsp`. To find a catalog entry click on **Find a Catalog Entry** in `index.jsp`, as follows:

Specify a catalog ID in the **Catalog Id** field and click on **Find**. Specify **catalog3** as **Catalog Id**, for which we created a catalog entry using `create.jsp`:

The catalog entry gets displayed in `catalogentry.jsp`. We used the `tr:outputText` component to display the catalog entry values. The `tr:outputText` component supporting styled text and the output in the following screenshot is with the default style:

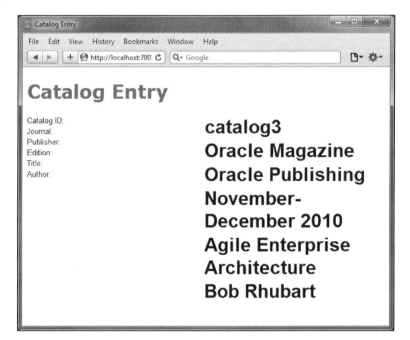

# Summary

In this chapter we discussed the Trinidad project facet. First, we created a web project and added the Trinidad project facet to it. Subsequently, we created JSF pages to create and find a catalog entry. We added Trinidad components to the JSF pages. Then, we ran the Trinidad application on the WebLogic Server.

In the next chapter we will discuss creating an AJAX web application. Asynchronous JavaScript for XML is a JavaScript-based web technique to send an asynchronous request to a web server.

# Creating an AJAX Application

Asynchronous JavaScript and XML (AJAX) is a technique for asynchronous transfer of data between a browser and a server. AJAX is implemented using JavaScript, **Document Object Model (DOM)** and XMLHttpRequest technologies. The JavaScript project facet is enabled in Oracle Enterprise Pack for Eclipse by default for a web project. **Asynchronous** implies that the processing of a webpage continues while data is transferred between a browser client and a server. AJAX provides dynamic interaction between a client and a server and has various applications, such as:

- **Dynamic Form Data Validation**: Some forms such as a login form require validation of a unique identifier field. Without AJAX, a user would need to submit the form with the submit button to find if the unique identifier is valid. With AJAX, the unique identifier gets validated as a user fills in a unique identifier in a field; the input field data is validated without the form being submitted.

- **Autocompletion**: An example of autocompletion is Google Suggest. As a user types some term to search in a search field, a list of suggestions get displayed to autocomplete the field.

- **Refreshing data on a page**: Some web pages require data to be refreshed periodically. Using AJAX, a web page polls the server for the latest data periodically and refreshes the web page content without reloading the entire page. An example is the Google Weather Module - AJAX version.

In this chapter, we shall develop an AJAX application in OEPE 12*c*. We shall develop an input form to create a catalog entry. We shall validate the catalog ID for a catalog entry using AJAX; the form is not required to be submitted to validate the form data. Catalog entries are stored in an Oracle database and catalog entry data is retrieved dynamically for form validation. We shall also demonstrate autocompletion with AJAX; a form field shall be autocompleted when a catalog ID for which a catalog entry is already created in the database is specified. In this chapter, we shall see the following sections:

- Setting the environment
- Creating a Dynamic Web project
- Creating a web application for AJAX
- Creating a servlet
- Developing the AJAX web application
- Packaging the web application
- Deploying the web application
- Running the web application

# Setting the environment

First, install Oracle Database 11g XE (`http://www.oracle.com/technetwork/products/express-edition/overview/index.html`). In this section, we shall create a database table in Oracle database 11g XE. Run the following SQL script in the SQL command line to create a database table `Catalog`. The `Catalog` database table contains `Catalog` entries for a journal as follows:

```
CREATE TABLE Catalog(CatalogId VARCHAR(255), Journal VARCHAR(255),
Publisher Varchar(255), Edition VARCHAR(255), Title Varchar(255),
Author Varchar(255));

INSERT INTO Catalog VALUES('catalog1', 'Oracle Magazine', 'Oracle
Publishing', 'September-October 2010', 'Using Oracle Essbase Release
11.1.2 Aggregate Storage Option Databases', 'Mark Rittman and
VenkatakrishnanJanakiraman');

INSERT INTO Catalog VALUES('catalog2', 'Oracle Magazine', 'Oracle
Publishing', 'July-August 2010', 'Infrastructure Software and
Virtualization', 'David Baum');
```

Install Oracle Enterprise Pack for Eclipse 12*c* using Installers with Oracle WebLogic Server, Oracle Coherence, and Oracle Enterprise Pack for Eclipse (`http://www.oracle.com/technetwork/middleware/ias/downloads/wls-main-097127.html`), if not already installed. We also need to configure a data source with JNDI name `jdbc/OracleDS` in WebLogic Server as discussed in *Chapter 1, EJB 3.0 Database Persistence*. The data source is shown in the Oracle WebLogic Server administration console.

# Creating a Dynamic Web project

In this section, we shall create a web project in Eclipse. Go to **File | New | Other** and in the **New** wizard, expand **Web** and select **Dynamic Web Project**. Click on **Next**. Specify a **Project Name** (for example, `EclipseAjax`) and configure a **Target Runtime** for **Oracle WebLogic Server 12c** as discussed in *Chapter 1, EJB 3.0 Database Persistence*. Select the **Dynamic web module version** as **2.5** and click on **Next** as shown in the following screenshot:

In **Java** Settings, select **Source folders on build path** as **src**, and the default output folder as `build/classes` and click on **Next**. In **Web Module** specify the **Context Root** as **EclipseAjax**, specify the **ContentDirectory** as **WebContent** and select the checkbox **Generate web.xml deployment descriptor** and click on **Finish**. A Dynamic Web project for AJAX gets created and gets added to the **Project Explorer** as shown in the following screenshot:

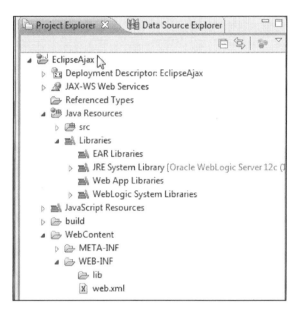

As JavaScript is used in sending an AJAX request and processing the AJAX response, the JavaScript project facet is required to be enabled, which it is by default in a dynamic web project. In the next section, we shall create a web application for an AJAX request.

# Creating a web application for AJAX

In this section, we shall create a JSP or an HTML page for sending an AJAX request and receiving an AJAX response. Go to **File | New | Other**, expand **Web,** and select **JSP File** in **New**. In **New JSP File**, select the **WebContent** folder, specify **File name** as `AjaxCatalog.jsp` and click on **Finish** as shown in the following screenshot:

A JSP file **AjaxCatalog.jsp** gets added to the project. Similarly, also add the JSPs
`catalogentrycreated.jsp` and `error.jsp` to navigate to if a catalog entry
gets created or if an error gets generated, as shown in the following screenshot:

We shall construct the JSP page, but before we can do so we also need a servlet
to process the AJAX request.

# Creating a servlet

In this section, we shall create a servlet to process the AJAX request and send a server response. A servlet represents the Controller facet of the **Model View Controller (MVC)** design pattern; the JSP page represents the View facet. Go to **File | New | Other** and in the **New** wizard, expand **Web** and select **Servlet**. Click on **Next** as shown in the following screenshot:

In **Create Servlet**, select the project **EclipseAjax** in which you want to create a servlet, select the **Source folder** as /EclipseAjax/src, specify a **Java package** name as ajax.servlet and a **Class name** as FormServlet. A servlet extends the javax.servlet.http.HttpServlet class. Click on **Next** as shown in the following screenshot:

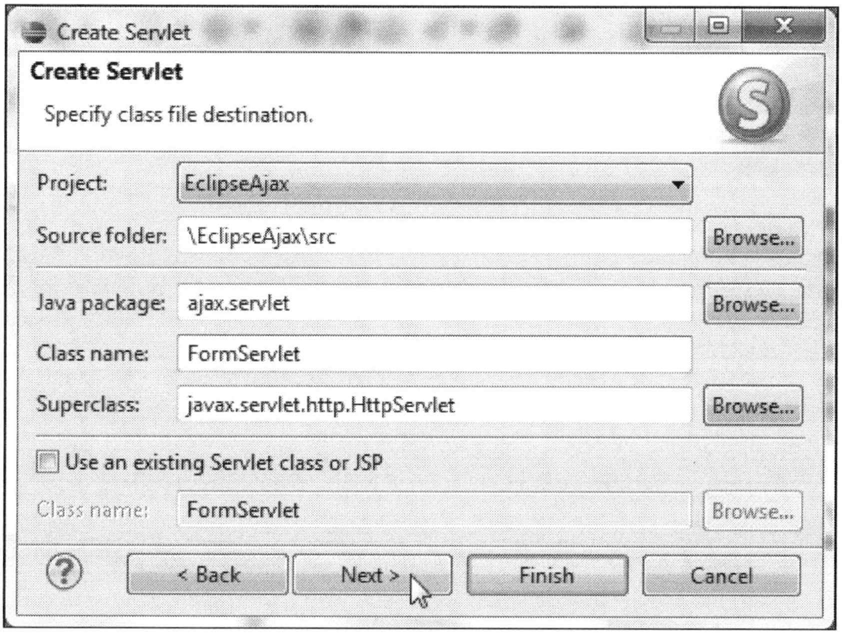

The **URL mappings** get specified as **/FormServlet**, which is based on the servlet name. Click on **Next** as shown in the following screenshot:

Select the default **Modifiers, Interfaces,** and **method stubs**, which include the **doGet** and **doPost** by default. Click on **Finish** as shown in the following screenshot:

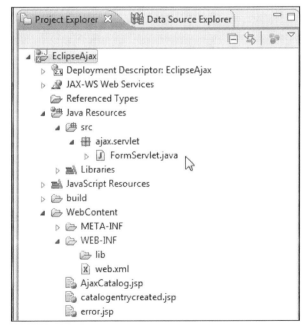

A servlet gets added to the **EclipseAjax** project as shown in the following screenshot:

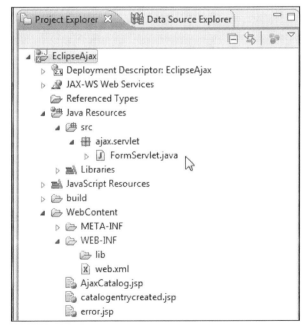

In `web.xml`, the servlet and the servlet mapping for the servlet gets added. The servlet name is specified with the `servlet-name` element and the servlet class is specified with the `servlet-class` element. The servlet mapping is specified with the `servlet-mapping` element in which the URL pattern that would invoke the servlet is specified with the `url-pattern` element as follows:

```
<servlet>
<description></description>
<display-name>FormServlet</display-name>
<servlet-name>FormServlet</servlet-name>
<servlet-class>ajax.servlet.FormServlet</servlet-class>
</servlet>
<servlet-mapping>
<servlet-name>FormServlet</servlet-name>
<url-pattern>/FormServlet</url-pattern>
</servlet-mapping>
```

When a web application is packaged and deployed to a web server a servlet is required to be packaged into the `WEB-INF/classes` directory. Create a **classes** folder in the `WEB-INF` directory by going to the **File | New | Folder** option.

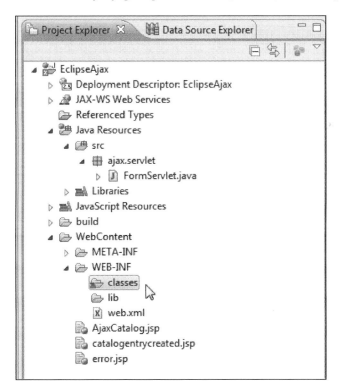

# Developing the AJAX web application

In this section, we shall construct a **Model View Controller (MVC)** web application for AJAX. The View facet is the `AjaxCatalog.jsp` file and the Model and Controller facets are provided by `FormServlet.java`. The view `AjaxCatalog.jsp` consists of an input form with fields to create a catalog entry. The catalog ID field requires a unique field value. Without AJAX, we would need to specify a `Catalog ID` value and the other field values and submit the form. By using a business logic to validate the catalog ID in the servlet, you would be able to create a new catalog entry, but if the validation for the catalog ID fails, you would get a message that the `Catalog ID` value is invalid and you would have to fill out and resubmit the entire form. With AJAX, the `Catalog ID` value may be validated dynamically at the time the value is specified in the catalog entry form, thus not having to submit/resubmit the form.

The example AJAX web application in this chapter validates data input in an HTML form using business logic that the catalog ID to create the catalog entry must be unique. The input `CatalogId` for a new catalog entry is validated against the Oracle database to find if it already exists in the database. The complete form does not have to be filled to find if a new catalog ID is valid; the catalog ID added to the JSP form is sent to the server as the `Catalog Id` value is added (not when the form is completed) using an AJAX request and the HTTP servlet immediately returns an XML response that contains information about the validity of the input catalog ID.

In the `AjaxCatalog.jsp` view facet, the `XMLHttpRequest` response from the server is processed and if the response indicates that the `Catalog Id` input is valid, a **Catalog Id is Valid** message is displayed so that the complete form may be filled and submitted to create a new catalog entry. An `XMLHttpRequest` request shall be sent to the server and a response is received with each character added to the catalog ID field. The sequence to send an `XMLHttpRequest` request involves the following:

1. Invoke a JavaScript function from an HTML event such as `onkeyup`.

2. In the invoked JavaScript function create a new `XMLHttpRequest` object.

3. Open an `XMLHttpRequest` request (AJAX request) using the URL for the server to send the request to an HTTP method.

4. In the JavaScript function, register a callback event handler that gets invoked when the request is complete with the `XMLHttpRequest` object.

5. Send the `XMLHttpRequest` request to the server asynchronously.

6. Receive the XML response from the server and update the HTML page.

Next, create a JavaScript function `validateCatalogId` in the `AjaxCatalog.jsp` file and register the function with the `onkeyup` event in the `Catalog Id` field. With each new character added to the `Catalog Id` field the `onkeyup` event is generated and the `validateCatalogId` function is invoked, and an AJAX request is sent to the server.

```
<form name="FormServlet" action="FormServlet" method="post">
<table>
<tr><td>Catalog Id:</td><td><input      type="text"
size="20"
id="catalogId"
name="catalogId"
onkeyup="validateCatalogId()"></td>
<td><div id="validationMessage"></div></td>
</tr>
</table></form>
```

A different event handler may be used instead of `onkeyup`. In the `validateCatalogId()` JavaScript function, create a new `XMLHttpRequest` object. If a browser supports the `XMLHttpRequest` object as an ActiveX object (as in IE 6), the procedure to create an `XMLHttpRequest` object is different than if the `XMLHttpRequest` object is a `window` object property (as in IE 7, Safari, or Mozilla Firefox). Create an `init()` function within the `validateCatalogId` function and create an `XMLHttpRequest` object for both types for browsers (those supporting/not supporting `XMLHttpRequest` as a `window` object) as follows:

```
function validateCatalogId(){
var xmlHttpRequest=init();
functioninit(){

if (window.XMLHttpRequest) {
return new XMLHttpRequest();
        } else if (window.ActiveXObject) {

return new ActiveXObject("Microsoft.XMLHTTP");
        }
}
```

Having created an `XMLHttpRequest` object, construct the server URL to which the request is to be sent. In the example web application, we invoke a servlet, `FormServlet`, which is mapped to the servlet URL `FormServlet` as specified in `web.xml`. Therefore, the URL consists of the servlet mapping URL and a `catalogId` parameter that specifies the value of `CatalogId`. The `encodeURIComponent(string)` method is used to encode the `CatalogId` value. The HTTP method specified is GET as follows:

```
var catalogId=document.getElementById("catalogId");
xmlHttpRequest.open("GET", "validateForm?catalogId="+
encodeURIComponent(catalogId.value), true);
```

Register a callback event handler with the `XMLHttpRequest` object using the `onreadystatechange` property. The `readyState` property indicates the current state of the request. Whenever the `readyState` changes, the callback method gets invoked. In the example web application, the callback method is the JavaScript function `processRequest`, which gets invoked whenever the value of the `readyState` property changes, as follows:

```
xmlHttpRequest.onreadystatechange=processRequest;
```

Send a AJAX request to the server using the `send()` method. As the HTTP method is GET, data sent with the `send()` method is set to `null` as follows:

```
xmlHttpRequest.send(null);
```

Create a JavaScript function to process the response called `processResponse()`. The callback event handler `processRequest` function gets invoked each time the value of the `readyState` property changes. In the `processRequest` function, retrieve the `readyState` property value. When the request has loaded completely, corresponding to `readyState` value 4, and HTTP status is OK, invoke the `processResponse` JavaScript function to process the response from the server as follows:

```
Function processRequest(){
if(xmlHttpRequest.readyState==4){
if(xmlHttpRequest.status==200){
processResponse();
    }
  }
}
```

Next, we shall discuss the server-side processing of the `XMLHttpRequest` request. The `XMLHttpRequest` is sent to the URL `FormServlet`, which has servlet mapping specified to the `FormServlet` servlet and therefore invokes the `FormServlet` servlet. As the `XMLHttpRequest` HTTP method is GET, the `doGet()` method of the servlet is invoked. In the `doGet` method, retrieve the value of the `catalogId` parameter as follows:

```
String catalogId = request.getParameter("catalogId");
```

Next, we shall validate the `CatalogID` value using the business logic that if the `catalogId` does not already exist in the database the `CatalogId` value is valid. Create a `Connection` object and using the `CatalogId` value specified in the input form, construct a SQL query to run on the database. Run the SQL query using the `executeQuery(String)` method, which generates a `ResultSet` object. If the `ResultSet` object is empty it implies that the `CatalogId` field value does not already exist in the database table `Catalog` and therefore the `CatalogId` field value is valid. If the `ResultSet` object is not empty it implies that the `CatalogId` value already exists in the database and therefore the `CatalogId` field value is not valid.

Construct an XML response to send back to the server. If the `CatalogId` value is not valid, construct an XML string that includes the different field values for the catalog entry. The XML string has a root element, which is `catalog` in the example application. The XML string includes a `<valid></valid>` element that specifies the validity of the `CatalogId` field value with a value of `true` or `false` as shown in the following code snippet (the variable `rs` represents `ResultSet`):

```
if (rs.next()) {
out.println("<catalog>" + "<valid>false</valid>" + "<journal>" +
rs.getString(2) + "</journal>" + "<publisher>" +
rs.getString(3) + "</publisher>" + "<edition>" +
rs.getString(4) + "</edition>" + "<title>" +
rs.getString(5) + "</title>" + "<author>" +
rs.getString(6) + "</author>" + "</catalog>");
            } else {
out.println("<valid>true</valid>");
            }
```

The `FormServlet` servlet sends a response back to the `AjaxCatalog.jsp` in the form of an XML string. Set the content type of the `HttpServletResponse` to `text/xml` because the response to an AJAX request is in XML format, and set the `Cache-Control` header to `no-cache` to prevent JSPs and servlets from being cached; if caching is used the server response gets cached and does not get updated with each AJAX request. As an AJAX response is updated with each request, caching is disabled to prevent an AJAX response from being re-served as follows:

```
response.setContentType("text/xml");
response.setHeader("Cache-Control", "no-cache");
```

As the AJAX response is required to be XML, we construct an XML DOM object that contains instructions about the validity of the `CatalogId` field value in the element `<valid/>`. If the `CatalogId` field value does not already exist in the database, submit the input form using the HTTP POST method. In the `doPost()` method in the servlet, create a JDBC connection to the Oracle database and add a catalog entry with the `INSERT SQL` statement. In the `processRequest()` JavaScript function, invoke the `processResponse()` JavaScript function when the HTTP request has loaded completely, which corresponds to the `readyState` property value `4`, and the HTTP status is OK, which corresponds to the status property value `200`. In the `processResponse()` function, obtain the value of the `responseXML` property, which contains the XML string returned by the server as set in the `doGet()` method of `FormServlet`.

```
var xmlMessage=xmlHttpRequest.responseXML;
```

The `responseXML` property contains instructions about the validity of the `CatalogId` value specified in the input form in the `<valid/>` element. Obtain the value of the `<valid/>` element using the `getElementsByTagName(string)` method as follows:

```
var
valid=xmlMessage.getElementsByTagName("valid")[0].firstChild.
nodeValue;
```

If the `<valid/>` element value is `true`, set the HTML `validationMessage` div to `Catalog Id is Valid` and enable the submit button in the input form. Also set the value of the form fields to an empty string so that new field values may be specified as follows:

```
if(valid=="true"){
varvalidationMessage=document.getElementById("validationMessage");
validationMessage.innerHTML = "Catalog Id is Valid";
document.getElementById("submitForm").disabled = false;
}
```

If the `<valid/>` element value is `false`, set the HTML of `validationMessage` div to `Catalog Id is not Valid`, and disable the submit button. Set the values of other input fields to corresponding catalog entry values for the `catalogId` value as shown for the `journal` field below; setting the values of the other fields is an example of autocompletion with AJAX as follows:

```
if(valid=="false"){

var validationMessage=document.getElementById("validationMessage");
validationMessage.innerHTML = "Catalog Id is not Valid";
document.getElementById("submitForm").disabled = true;
```

```
var journal=xmlMessage.getElementsByTagName("journal")[0].firstChild.
nodeValue;
...
var journalElement=document.getElementById("journal");
journalElement.value = journal;
    }
```

The `AjaxCatalog.jsp` file is listed as follows:

```
<html>
<head>
<script type="text/javascript">
```

Specify a JavaScript method to validate Catalog Id.

```
function validateCatalogId(){

var xmlHttpRequest=init();
```

The `init()` function initializes the `XMLHttpRequest` object as follows:

```
function init(){

if (window.XMLHttpRequest) {
return new XMLHttpRequest();
        } else if (window.ActiveXObject) {

return new ActiveXObject("Microsoft.XMLHTTP");
        }
}
```

Retrieve the `catalogId` value and construct a `XMLHttpRequest` object using the GET HTTP method and send an AJAX request using the `send()` method as follows:

```
var catalogId=document.getElementById("catalogId");
xmlHttpRequest.open("GET", "FormServlet?catalogId="+
encodeURIComponent(catalogId.value), true);
xmlHttpRequest.onreadystatechange=processRequest;
xmlHttpRequest.send(null);
```

The following code snippet specifies a function to process the AJAX request:

```
function processRequest(){

if(xmlHttpRequest.readyState==4){
if(xmlHttpRequest.status==200){
```

```
processResponse();


    }
  }
}
```

The following code snippet specifies a function to process the AJAX response:

```
function processResponse(){
var xmlMessage=xmlHttpRequest.responseXML;
var valid=xmlMessage.getElementsByTagName("valid")[0].firstChild.
nodeValue;
if(valid=="true"){

var validationMessage=document.getElementById("validationMessage");
validationMessage.innerHTML = "Catalog Id is Valid";
document.getElementById("submitForm").disabled = false;

var journalElement=document.getElementById("journal");
journalElement.value = "";

var publisherElement=document.getElementById("publisher");
publisherElement.value = "";

var editionElement=document.getElementById("edition");
editionElement.value = "";

var titleElement=document.getElementById("title");
titleElement.value = "";

var authorElement=document.getElementById("author");
authorElement.value = "";
}
if(valid=="false"){

var validationMessage=document.getElementById("validationMessage");
validationMessage.innerHTML = "Catalog Id is not Valid";
document.getElementById("submitForm").disabled = true;

var journal=xmlMessage.getElementsByTagName("journal")[0].firstChild.
nodeValue;
var publisher=xmlMessage.getElementsByTagName("publisher")[0].
firstChild.nodeValue;
var edition=xmlMessage.getElementsByTagName("edition")[0].firstChild.
nodeValue;
```

```
var title=xmlMessage.getElementsByTagName("title")[0].firstChild.
nodeValue;
var author=xmlMessage.getElementsByTagName("author")[0].firstChild.
nodeValue;

var journalElement=document.getElementById("journal");
journalElement.value = journal;

var publisherElement=document.getElementById("publisher");
publisherElement.value = publisher;

var editionElement=document.getElementById("edition");
editionElement.value = edition;

var titleElement=document.getElementById("title");
titleElement.value = title;

var authorElement=document.getElementById("author");
authorElement.value = author;
  }
 }
}

</script>
```

The following code snippet specifies a form with input fields for a form entry:

```
</head>
<body>
<h1>Form for Catalog Entry</h1>
<form name="FormServlet" action="FormServlet" method="post">
<table>
<tr><td>Catalog Id:</td><td><input    type="text"
size="20"
id="catalogId"
name="catalogId"
onkeyup="validateCatalogId()"></td>
<td><div id="validationMessage"></div></td>
</tr>


<tr><td>Journal:</td><td><input    type="text"
size="20"
id="journal"
name="journal"></td>
```

```
</tr>

<tr><td>Publisher:</td><td><input     type="text"
size="20"
id="publisher"
name="publisher"></td>
</tr>

<tr><td>Edition:</td><td><input     type="text"
size="20"
id="edition"
name="edition"></td>
</tr>
<tr><td>Title:</td><td><input     type="text"
size="20"
id="title"
name="title"></td>
</tr>

<tr><td>Author:</td><td><input     type="text"
size="20"
id="author"
name="author"></td>
</tr>

<tr><td><input     type="submit"
value="Create Catalog"
id="submitForm"
name="submitForm"></td>
</tr>
</table>
</form>

</body>
</html>
```

The FormServlet.java file is listed as follows:

```
package servlet;

import java.io.*;
import java.sql.*;
import javax.naming.InitialContext;
import javax.servlet.ServletException;
import javax.servlet.http.HttpServlet;
```

```
import javax.servlet.http.HttpServletRequest;
import javax.servlet.http.HttpServletResponse;

/**
 * Servlet implementation class FormServlet
 */
public class FormServlet extends HttpServlet {
```

The doGet method is used to validate the catalog Id input sent in an AJAX request and send an AJAX response back to the browser. First, an InitialContext object is created. Create a DataSource object with the InitialContext object using the JNDI lookup on the WebLogic Server data source. Create a Connection object from the DataSource object using the getConnection() method. Create a Statement object from the Connection object using the createStatement() method. Create a SQL query using the Catalog Id input in the form. Run the SQL query using executeQuery() to obtain a ResultSet object. Set headers for the HttpServletResponse object and create a PrintWriter object from the HttpServletResponse object. Construct an output of an XML response as follows:

```
    public void doGet(HttpServletRequest request, HttpServletResponse
response)
        throwsServletException, IOException {
    try {
        // Obtain value of Catalog Id field to ve validated.
        String catalogId = request.getParameter("catalogId");

        // Obtain Connection
        InitialContext initialContext = new InitialContext();
        DataSource ds = (DataSource) initialContext.lookup("jdbc/
OracleDS");
        java.sql.Connection conn = ds.getConnection();

        // Obtain result set
        Statement stmt = conn.createStatement();
        String query = "SELECT * from Catalog WHERE catalogId=" + "'"
            + catalogId + "'";
        ResultSet rs = stmt.executeQuery(query);

        // set headers before accessing the Writer
        response.setContentType("text/xml");
        response.setHeader("Cache-Control", "no-cache");

        PrintWriter out = response.getWriter();

        // then send the response
```

```
      // If result set is empty set valid element to true
      if (rs.next()) {
      out.println("<catalog>" + "<valid>false</valid>" + "<journal>"
          + rs.getString(2) + "</journal>" + "<publisher>"
          + rs.getString(3) + "</publisher>" + "<edition>"
          + rs.getString(4) + "</edition>" + "<title>"
          + rs.getString(5) + "</title>" + "<author>"
          + rs.getString(6) + "</author>" + "</catalog>");
      } else {
        out.println("<valid>true</valid>");
      }

      rs.close();
      stmt.close();
      conn.close();

    } catch (javax.naming.NamingException e) {System.err.out(e.
getMessage());
      } catch (SQLException e) {System.err.println(e.getMessage());
      }
    }
```

The doPost() method is used to create a new catalog entry. First, create an
InitialContext object. The data source configured in WebLogic Server is
used with the JNDI lookup to create a DataSource object. A Connection object
is obtained from the DataSource object using the getConnection() method.
A Statement object is created using the createStatement() method of the
Connection class. A PreparedStatement may be used instead of Statement.
A SQL string is created from values retrieved from the input form. The SQL
statement is run using the execute() method. If the SQL statement runs
without error the response is redirected to catalogentrycreated.jsp. If
an error is generated the response is redirected to error.jsp as follows:

```
    public void doPost(HttpServletRequest request, HttpServletResponse
response)
        throwsServletException, IOException {
    try {
        // Obtain Connection
        InitialContextinitialContext = new InitialContext();
        javax.sql.DataSource ds = (javax.sql.DataSource) initialContext
            .lookup("jdbc/OracleDS");
        java.sql.Connection conn = ds.getConnection();

        String catalogId = request.getParameter("catalogId");
        String journal = request.getParameter("journal");
        String publisher = request.getParameter("publisher");
        String edition = request.getParameter("edition");
        String title = request.getParameter("title");
        String author = request.getParameter("author");

        Statement stmt = conn.createStatement();
        String sql = "INSERT INTO Catalog VALUES(" + "\'" + catalogId
            + "\'" + "," + "\'" + journal + "\'" + "," + "\'"
            + publisher + "\'" + "," + "\'" + edition + "\'" + ","
            + "\'" + title + "\'" + "," + "\'" + author + "\'" + ")";

        stmt.execute(sql);

        response.sendRedirect("catalogentrycreated.jsp");

        stmt.close();
        conn.close();

    } catch (javax.naming.NamingException e) {
        response.sendRedirect("error.jsp");
    } catch (SQLException e) {
        response.sendRedirect("error.jsp");
    }
  }
}
```

# Packaging the web application

In this section, we shall package and deploy the web application to WebLogic Server using a `build.xml` script. Select the project folder in `Project Explorer` and go to **File | New | Other**. In **New**, expand the **XML** and select the **XML File** option and click on **Next**. Select the project folder, specify **File name** as `build.xml`, and click on **Finish** as shown in the following screenshot:

In `build.xml`, add the properties listed in the following table:

| Property | Value | Description |
| --- | --- | --- |
| src.dir | ${basedir}/src | Source directory |
| web.module | ${basedir}/WebContent | Web Module directory |
| weblogic.home | C:/Oracle/Middleware | WebLogic home directory |
| weblogic.server | ${weblogic.home}/ wlserver_12.1 /server | WebLogic server directory |
| build.dir | ${basedir}/build | Build directory |
| weblogic. domain.dir | ${weblogic.home}/user_ projects/ domains/base_domain | WebLogic domain directory |
| deploy.dir | ${weblogic.domain.dir}/ autodeploy | WebLogic server deploy directory |

Add a `path` element for `classpath` and add the `modules` directory, the WebLogic Server `lib` directory, and the domain `lib` directory. Add the targets listed in the following table:

| Target | Description |
| --- | --- |
| prepare | Make the required directories |
| compile | Compile the servlet |
| war | Create a WAR archive from the servlet, web.xml, and the JSPs |
| deploy | Deploy the web archive to the WebLogic server |
| clean | Delete directories and archive file |

The `build.xml` file is listed as follows:

```xml
<?xml version="1.0" encoding="UTF-8"?>
  <!--
    WebLogic build file
  -->
<project name="AjaxForm" default="deploy" basedir=".">
<property name="src.dir" value="${basedir}/src" />
  <property name="web.module" value="${basedir}/WebContent" />
  <property name="weblogic.home" value="C:/Oracle/Middleware" />
  <property name="weblogic.server" value="${weblogic.home}/
wlserver_12.1/server" />
  <property name="build.dir" value="${basedir}/build" />
  <property name="weblogic.domain.dir"
    value="${weblogic.home}/user_projects/domains/base_domain" />
  <property name="deploy.dir"
    value="${weblogic.domain.dir}/autodeploy" />

  <path id="classpath">
    <filesetdir="${weblogic.home}/modules">
      <include name="*.jar" />
    </fileset>
    <filesetdir="${weblogic.server}/lib">
      <include name="*.jar" />
    </fileset>
<filesetdir="${weblogic.domain.dir}/lib">
      <include name="*.jar" />
    </fileset>
```

```
      <pathelement location="${build.dir}" />
   </path>

   <property name="build.classpath" refid="classpath" />
   <target name="prepare">
      <mkdirdir="${build.dir}" />
<mkdirdir="${web.module}/WEB-INF/classes" />
   </target>
   <target name="compile" depends="prepare">
      <javacsrcdir="${src.dir}" destdir="${web.module}/WEB-INF/classes"
debug="on"
        includes="**/*.java">
        <classpathrefid="classpath" />
      </javac>
   </target>
   <target name="war" depends="compile">
      <warwarfile="${build.dir}/ajaxform.war">
        <filesetdir="WebContent">
          <include name="*.jsp" />
        </fileset>

        <filesetdir="${web.module}">
          <include name="WEB-INF/web.xml" />
        </fileset>
        <filesetdir="${web.module}">
          <include name="WEB-INF/classes/**/*.class" />
        </fileset>
      </war>
   </target>

   <target name="deploy" depends="war">
      <copy file="${build.dir}/ajaxform.war" todir="${deploy.dir}" />
   </target>
   <target name="clean">
      <delete file="${build.dir}/ajaxform.war" />
      <deletedir="${build.dir}" />
      <deletedir="${web.module}/WEB-INF/classes" />
   </target>

</project>
```

# Deploying the web application

In this section, we shall run the `build.xml` file to package and deploy the web application to WebLogic Server 12*c*. Right-click on **build.xml** and select **Run As | 3 Ant Build** as shown in the following screenshot:

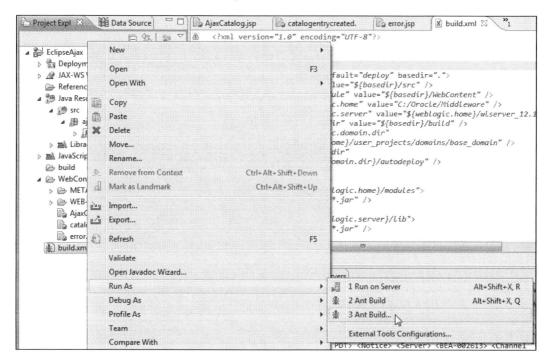

Select the **deploy** target, which has dependence on the preceding targets and click on **Run** as shown in the following screenshot:

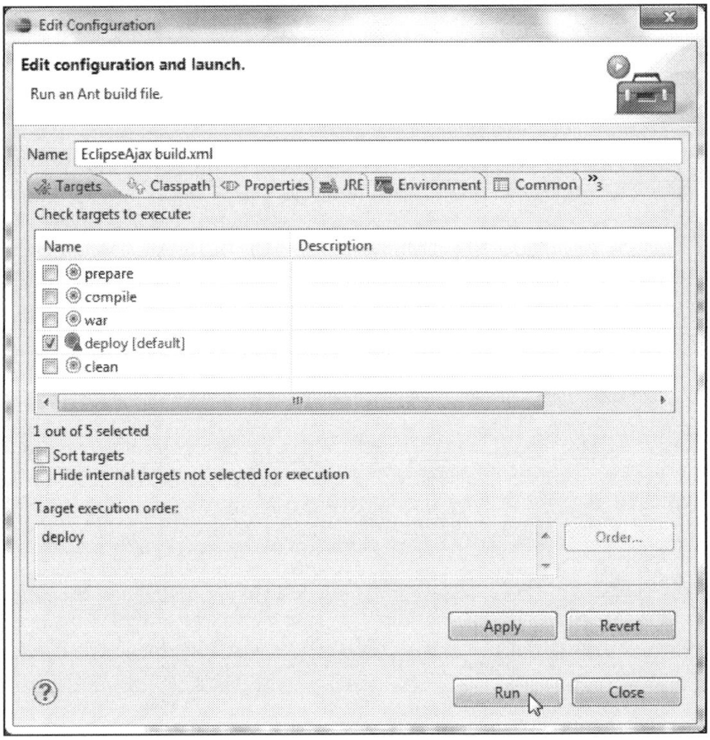

The `deploy` target and all the preceding targets get run as the `deploy` target has dependence on the preceding targets. The web application gets packaged and deployed to WebLogic Server in the `build.xml` output as shown in the following screenshot:

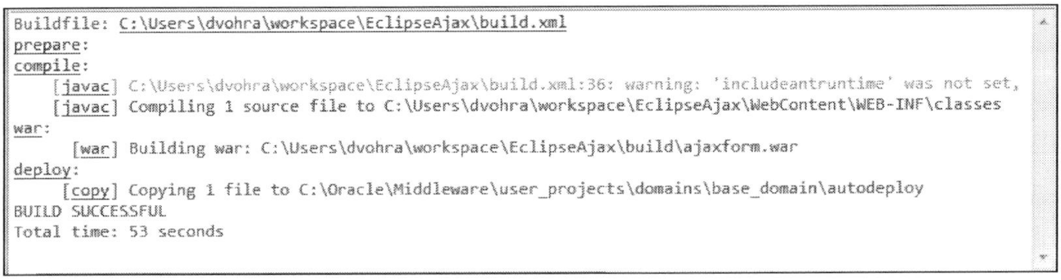

```
Buildfile: C:\Users\dvohra\workspace\EclipseAjax\build.xml
prepare:
compile:
    [javac] C:\Users\dvohra\workspace\EclipseAjax\build.xml:36: warning: 'includeantruntime' was not set,
    [javac] Compiling 1 source file to C:\Users\dvohra\workspace\EclipseAjax\WebContent\WEB-INF\classes
war:
    [war] Building war: C:\Users\dvohra\workspace\EclipseAjax\build\ajaxform.war
deploy:
    [copy] Copying 1 file to C:\Oracle\Middleware\user_projects\domains\base_domain\autodeploy
BUILD SUCCESSFUL
Total time: 53 seconds
```

In the WebLogic Server admin console, the WAR archive is displayed as deployed as shown in the following screenshot:

# Running the web application

In this section, we shall run the AjaxCatalog.jsp file to demonstrate AJAX. Run the AjaxCatalog.jsp with the URL http://localhost:7001/ajaxform/AjaxCatalog. jsp. Start to specify a catalog ID. The validation message indicates if the **Catalog Id** is valid. We created only two catalog entries in the Catalog database; catalog1 and catalog2. The business logic used to find the validity of a catalog ID is that if a catalog ID other than the two catalog IDs is specified, then the catalog ID is valid and a **Catalog Id is Valid** message gets displayed. The business logic to ascertain the validity of a catalog ID may be modified in the FormServlet servlet. An AJAX request is sent with each modification.

Specify a **Catalog Id** that already exists, such as `catalog1`. A message indicates
the catalog ID is not valid. The form fields get filled with the catalog entry values,
which is an example of autocompletion (see the following screenshot for reference).

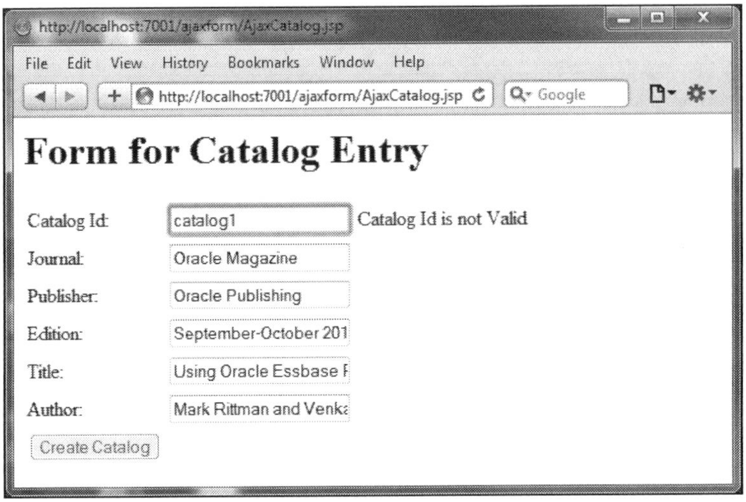

Similarly, for `catalog2` catalog ID the validation message indicates that the
catalog ID is not valid. Specify a catalog ID for which a catalog ID does not exist,
`catalog3` for example. The validation message indicates the **Catalog Id** is valid.
Specify values for the catalog entry fields and click on **Create Catalog** as shown
in the following screenshot:

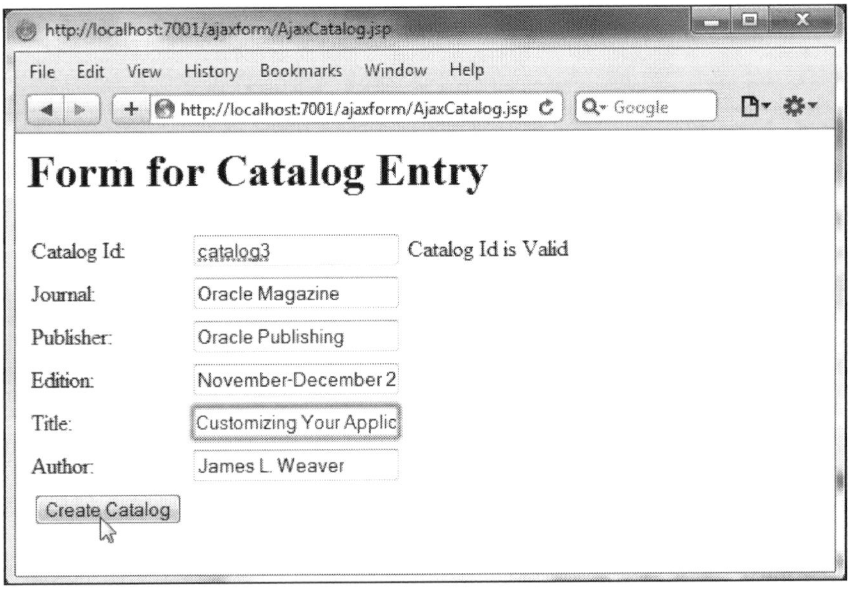

The catalog entry gets created and the response gets redirected to `catalogentrycreated.jsp` as specified in the `FormServlet` servlet. The **Catalog entry created** message indicates a catalog entry has been created as shown in the following screenshot:

If the **catalog3** is respecified as the **Catalog Id** the validation message indicates the **Catalog Id is not valid** because we just created a catalog entry with **catalog3** (see the following screenshot for reference).

The `build.xml` includes a `clean` target that may be run if the application is required to be repackaged and redeployed. Right-click on `build.xml` and select **Run As | 3 Ant Build**. In **Edit Configuration**, launch select the `clean` target and click on **Run**. The directories and WAR archive file get deleted as indicated by the build output as shown in the following screenshot:

```
Buildfile: C:\Users\dvohra\workspace\EclipseAjax\build.xml
clean:
    [delete] Deleting: C:\Users\dvohra\workspace\EclipseAjax\build\ajaxform.war
    [delete] Deleting directory C:\Users\dvohra\workspace\EclipseAjax\build
    [delete] Deleting directory C:\Users\dvohra\workspace\EclipseAjax\WebContent\WEB-INF\classes
BUILD SUCCESSFUL
Total time: 534 milliseconds
```

# Summary

In this chapter, we developed an AJAX application to send an asynchronous request to the server, process the request on the server, send a response back to the browser, and process the response from the server. The AJAX application is used to create a catalog entry by validating a catalog ID using AJAX. The application is packaged, deployed, and run on the WebLogic Server 12*c*.

In the next chapter, we shall develop a WebLogic web service using the Oracle WebLogic web services project facet.

# 8
# Creating a JAX-WS Web Service

XML is a widely used data exchange and data storage format on the Web, and off the Web as well. Because of its simplicity and flexibility XML has been included in other web standards. Java API for XML-based web services (JAX-WS) (`http://jcp.org/aboutJava/communityprocess/mrel/jsr224/index2.html`) is a technology for developing web services and clients that communicate using XML over HTTP protocol. A **web service** provides operations (methods) that may be invoked by a client. A user invokes a web service operation, optionally including request parameters, and the web service optionally returns a value. JAX-WS web services and clients are platform independent; JAX-WS clients may access web services not running on the Java platform and JAX-WS web services may be called by non-Java clients. JAX-WS makes use of W3C standards — HTTP (`http://www.w3.org/Protocols/`), SOAP (`http://www.w3.org/TR/soap/`), and WSDL (`http://www.w3.org/TR/wsdl`). A web services developer defines methods in a Java interface and implements the methods in one or more implementation classes. The web service client creates a proxy of the web service and invokes operations on the proxy. The web service invocations and responses conform to the SOAP specification and are transmitted using SOAP messages over HTTP. SOAP messages are simply XML files and are generated by the JAX-WS runtime. **WSDL** is an XML document that defines or describes network services as a set of endpoints operating on messages. An **endpoint** indicates a specific location represented by a URI for communicating with an instance of a service.

A JAX-WS web service essentially consists of a Java class annotated with the `javax.jws.WebService` annotation, the web service endpoint. A web service may optionally consist of a service endpoint interface that is implemented by the service endpoint implementation class. A web service implementation class must not be `abstract` or `final`. Business methods of the implementation class that are to be exposed as operations to a web service client must be `public`, must not be `static` or `final`, and must be annotated with the `@WebMethod` annotation. WebLogic Server 12*c* supports JAX-WS 2.1 and provides Apache Ant tasks, `jwsc` and `clientgen`, to create web service artifacts and to create artifacts for web service clients, respectively.

This chapter has the following sections:

- Setting the environment
- Creating a web service project
- Creating a WebLogic web service
- Running the web service on a server
- Generating a WSDL
- Testing WSDL in Web Services Explorer
- Generating a bindings file
- Creating a client class
- Creating a build file
- Testing the web service

# Setting the environment

We need to install Oracle WebLogic Server 12*c* including Oracle Enterprise Pack for Eclipse as we did for the other chapters. We also need to create a WebLogic Server domain (`base_domain`), as discussed in *Chapter 1, EJB 3.0 Database Persistence*.

# Creating a web service project

In this section we will create a WebLogic web service project, for which a template is provided in the **New** wizard. Select **File** | **New** | **Other** and in the **New** wizard select **Oracle** | **WebLogic** | **Web Services** | **Web Service Project**. Click on **Next**, as follows:

Specify a project name (`HelloWebService`) in the **Project name** field and configure a new **Target Runtime** for **Oracle WebLogic Server 12c (12.1.1)**, as discussed in *Chapter 1, EJB 3.0 Database Persistence*. Click on **Next**, as follows:

In Java settings select the source folders on the build path as `src` and the default output folder as `build/classes`. Click on **Next**. In **Web Module** settings specify the context root in the **Context root** field; the default is the same name as the project name. Then, specify the content directory in the **Content directory** field (the default is **WebContent**) and click on **Finish**. In the **Open Associated Perspective?** dialog box click on **Yes**. A web service project gets added, as shown in the following screenshot:

Right-click on the **HelloWebService** node and select **Properties**. In **Project Properties** select the **Project Facets** node. The **Oracle WebLogic Web Services** project facet should have been added to the web project, as shown in the following screenshot:

# Creating a WebLogic web service

Having created a WebLogic web service project, next, create a WebLogic web service. Select the project node in **Project Explorer** and select **File | New | Other**. In the **New** wizard select **Oracle | WebLogic | Web Services | WebLogic Web Service** and click on **Next**, as shown in the following screenshot:

In the **New Web Service** window specify a package name (hellowebservice) in the **Package** field and a web service name (HelloWS) in the **Name** field. Check the **Generate Service Endpoint Interface** checkbox and click on **Finish**, as shown in the following screenshot:

A web service implementation class (**HelloWSImpl.java**) and a service endpoint interface (**HelloWS.java**) get created, as shown in the following screenshot:

The web service implementation class—HelloWSImpl—is annotated with the @ WebService annotation and implements the HelloWS interface. The implementation class contains a hello method that takes a string parameter for name and returns a Hello message containing the name. The implementation class is listed, as follows:

```java
package hellowebservice;

import javax.jws.*;

@WebService(portName = "HelloWSPort", serviceName = "HelloWSService",
targetNamespace = "http://hellowebservice/", endpointInterface =
"hellowebservice.HelloWS")
public class HelloWSImpl implements HelloWS {

  public String hello(String name) {

    return "Hello "+name +" Welcome to Web Services!";

  }
}
```

The service endpoint interface, HelloWS, contains the hello method annotated with the @WebMethod annotation. The hello method is represented by the hello operation in the WSDL, which is discussed later.

```java
package hellowebservice;

import javax.jws.WebMethod;
import javax.jws.WebService;

@WebService(name = "HelloWS", targetNamespace = "http://
hellowebservice/")
public interface HelloWS {

  @WebMethod(operationName = "hello")
  public String hello(String name);
}
```

# Running the web service on the server

Having created a web service we need to test the web service by running it on the WebLogic Server. Right-click on the implementation class, **HelloWSImpl.java**, and select **Run As | Run on Server**, as shown in the following screenshot:

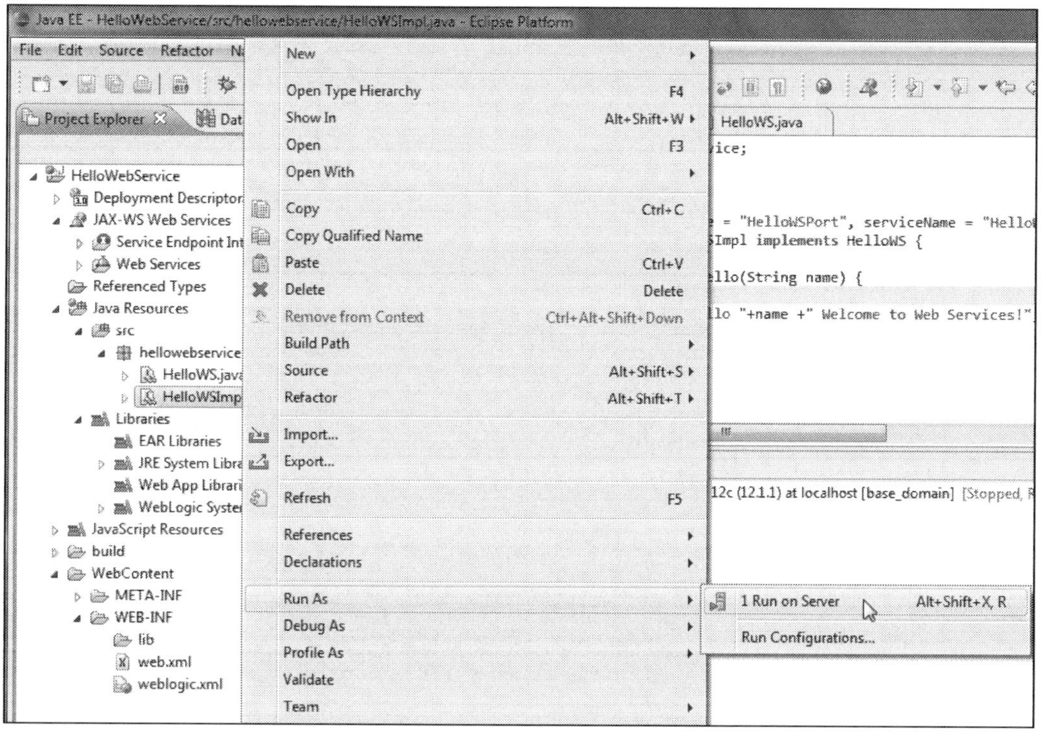

Start the Oracle WebLogic Server you have configured earlier and select the server to run the web service. Click on **Next**. In the **Run On Server** window, **HelloWebService** should be in the **Configured** section, which makes **HelloWebService** configured to run on the server. Click on **Finish**, as follows:

The WebLogic web service gets deployed on the WebLogic Server. Start the admin console for WebLogic Server with the URL `http://localhost:7001/console` and click on **Deployments**. The web service is shown deployed as an EAR application, as follows:

**WebLogic Test Client** gets started. The **Operations** section lists the **hello** operation. Specify a name in the **string arg0** field, and click on the **hello** button, as follows:

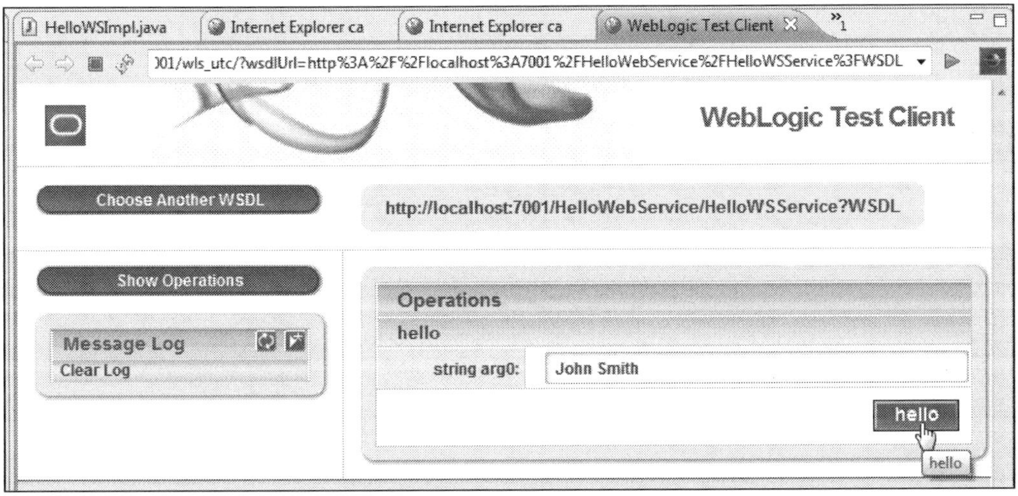

The WSDL defines an endpoint for the **hello** operation and the related SOAP messages. The SOAP request and response messages get generated. The request consists of a request argument and the response consists of a **Hello** message sent by the web service, as shown in the following screenshot:

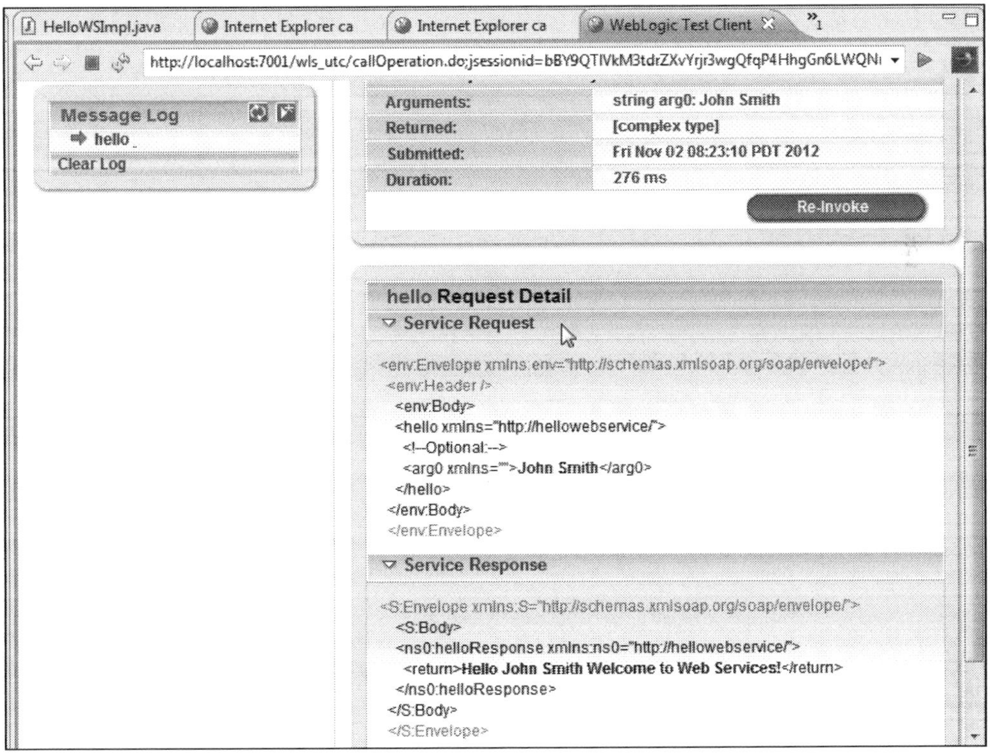

Copy the WSDL URL to be used in the WSDL, which we shall generate next.

# Generating a WSDL

A WSDL describes a service as a set of endpoints, operations, and SOAP messages, and is required to invoke a web service. Next, we shall generate a WSDL from the web service. Right-click on **HelloWSImpl.java** in **Project Explorer** and select **WebLogic Web Services | Generate WSDL**, as shown in the following screenshot:

Select the directory to generate the WSDL in the **hellowebservice** folder. Click on **OK**, as follows:

The **jwsc** task runs to generate web service artifacts, which we will discuss later.

The WSDL `HelloWSService.wsdl` gets generated. Right-click on the WSDL file and select **Open With | WSDL Editor**. The WSDL diagram is shown in the following screenshot. Copy the web service URI (`http://localhost:7001/ HelloWebService/HelloWSService?WSDL`), which we have copied earlier from the web service test client, into the **HelloWSPort** field in the **Design** view of the WSDL, as shown in the following screenshot:

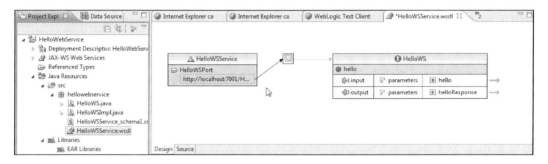

The web service URI may also be copied in the **Source** view to the `soap:address` element. The `location` attribute is marked as `REPLACE_WITH_ACTUAL_URL` in the WSDL file.

```
<service name="HelloWSService">
    <port name="HelloWSPort" binding="tns:HelloWSPortBinding">
      <soap:address location="http://localhost:7001/HelloWebService/
HelloWSService?WSDL"/>
    </port>
  </service>
```

The WSDL may be displayed in the browser using the URI `http:// localhost:7001/HelloWebService/HelloWSService?WSDL`, as follows:

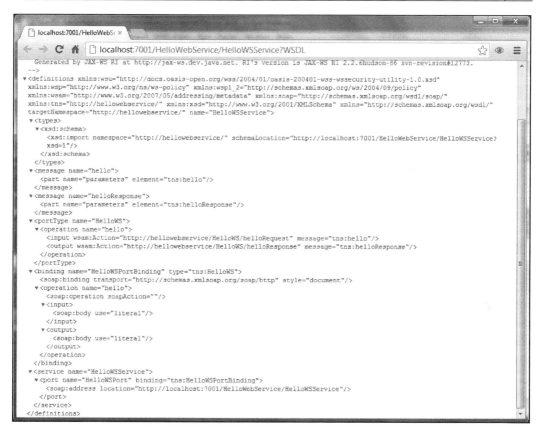

The `jwsc` **task** (`http://docs.oracle.com/cd/E11035_01/wls100/webserv_ref/anttasks.html#wp1069899`) generates all the required artifacts for a WebLogic web service. The following web service files are generated:

- A Java source file that implements a standard JSR-109 web service, the service endpoint interface `HelloWSService_HelloWSPortImpl.java`:

```
package hellowebservice;

import javax.jws.WebService;
import javax.xml.ws.BindingType;

@WebService(portName = "HelloWSPort", serviceName =
"HelloWSService", targetNamespace = "http://hellowebservice/",
wsdlLocation = "/wsdls/HelloWSService.wsdl", endpointInterface =
"hellowebservice.HelloWS")
@BindingType("http://schemas.xmlsoap.org/wsdl/soap/http")
public class HelloWSService_HelloWSPortImpl
    implements HelloWS
{
    public HelloWSService_HelloWSPortImpl() {
    }


    public String hello(String arg0) {
        //replace with your impl here
        return null;
    }

}
```

- All required deployment descriptors such as `webservices.xml` and `weblogic-webservices.xml`.

- The XML Schema representation — `HelloWSService_schema1.xsd`, of Java user-defined types used as parameters or return values to the web service methods exposed as public operations:

```
<?xml version="1.0" encoding="UTF-8"?>
<xsd:schema xmlns:ns0="http://hellowebservice/" xmlns:xsd="http://
www.w3.org/2001/XMLSchema" targetNamespace="http://
hellowebservice/">
    <xsd:complexType name="hello">
        <xsd:sequence>
            <xsd:element name="arg0" type="xsd:string"
minOccurs="0"/>
        </xsd:sequence>
    </xsd:complexType>
    <xsd:complexType name="helloResponse">
        <xsd:sequence>
            <xsd:element name="return" type="xsd:string"
minOccurs="0"/>
```

```
      </xsd:sequence>
    </xsd:complexType>
    <xsd:element name="hello" type="ns0:hello"/>
    <xsd:element name="helloResponse" type="ns0:helloResponse"/>
</xsd:schema>
```

- The WSDL file `HelloWSService.wsdl` to publicly describe the web service:

```
<?xml version="1.0" encoding="UTF-8" standalone="yes"?>
<!-- Generated by JAX-WS RI at http://jax-ws.dev.java.net. RI's
version is JAX-WS RI 2.2.6hudson-86  svn-revision#12773. -->
<definitions targetNamespace="http://hellowebservice/"
name="HelloWSService" xmlns="http://schemas.xmlsoap.org/wsdl/"
xmlns:wsp="http://www.w3.org/ns/ws-policy" xmlns:tns="http://
hellowebservice/" xmlns:xsd="http://www.w3.org/2001/
XMLSchema" xmlns:wsp1_2="http://schemas.xmlsoap.org/ws/2004/09/
policy" xmlns:soap="http://schemas.xmlsoap.org/wsdl/soap/"
xmlns:wsam="http://www.w3.org/2007/05/addressing/metadata"
xmlns:wsu="http://docs.oasis-open.org/wss/2004/01/oasis-200401-
wss-wssecurity-utility-1.0.xsd">
  <types>
    <xsd:schema>
      <xsd:import namespace="http://hellowebservice/"
schemaLocation="HelloWSService_schema1.xsd"/>
    </xsd:schema>
  </types>
  <message name="hello">
    <part name="parameters" element="tns:hello"/>
  </message>
  <message name="helloResponse">
    <part name="parameters" element="tns:helloResponse"/>
  </message>
  <portType name="HelloWS">
    <operation name="hello">
      <input wsam:Action="http://hellowebservice/HelloWS/
helloRequest" message="tns:hello"/>
      <output wsam:Action="http://hellowebservice/HelloWS/
helloResponse" message="tns:helloResponse"/>
    </operation>
  </portType>
  <binding name="HelloWSPortBinding" type="tns:HelloWS">
    <soap:binding transport="http://schemas.xmlsoap.org/soap/http"
style="document"/>
    <operation name="hello">
      <soap:operation soapAction=""/>
      <input>
        <soap:body use="literal"/>
      </input>
```

```
        <output>
          <soap:body use="literal"/>
        </output>
      </operation>
    </binding>
    <service name="HelloWSService">
      <port name="HelloWSPort" binding="tns:HelloWSPortBinding">
        <soap:address location="http://localhost:7001/
HelloWebService/HelloWSService?WSDL"/>
      </port>
    </service>
</definitions>
```

# Testing WSDL in web services explorer

Having generated a WSDL, and after adding the endpoint URI for the service to
the WSDL, next, we will test the WSDL in Web Services Explorer. Right-click on
**HelloWSService.wsdl** and select **Web Services | Test with Web Services Explorer**,
as shown in the following screenshot:

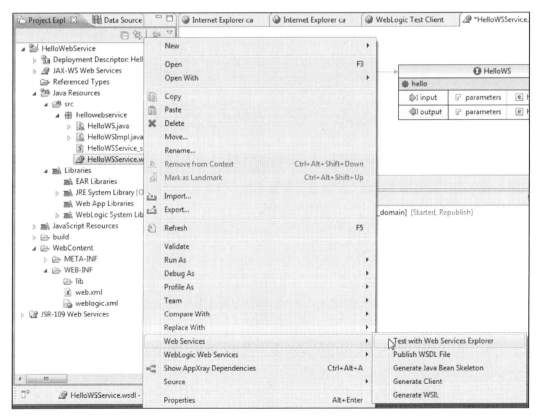

WSDL binding details get displayed. Click on the **hello** operation. Add a value (**John Smith**, for example) for **arg0** and click on **Go**, as shown in the following screenshot:

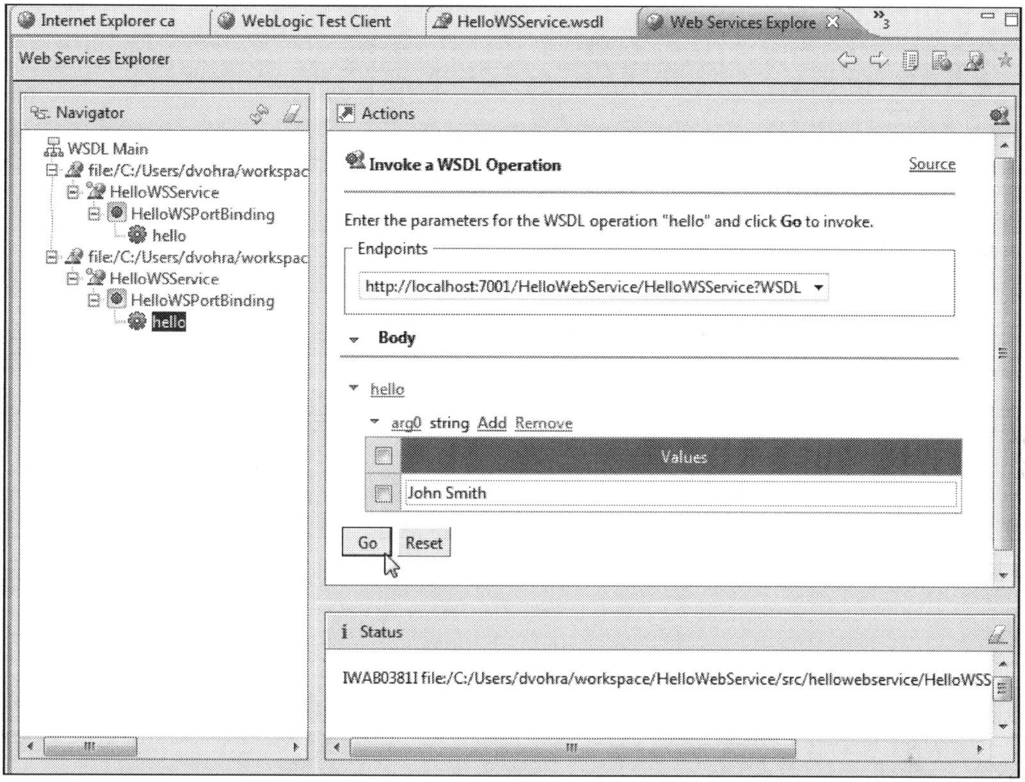

The web service response gets output. We invoked the `hello` operation of the WSDL providing a `string` argument and got a `string` response, as follows:

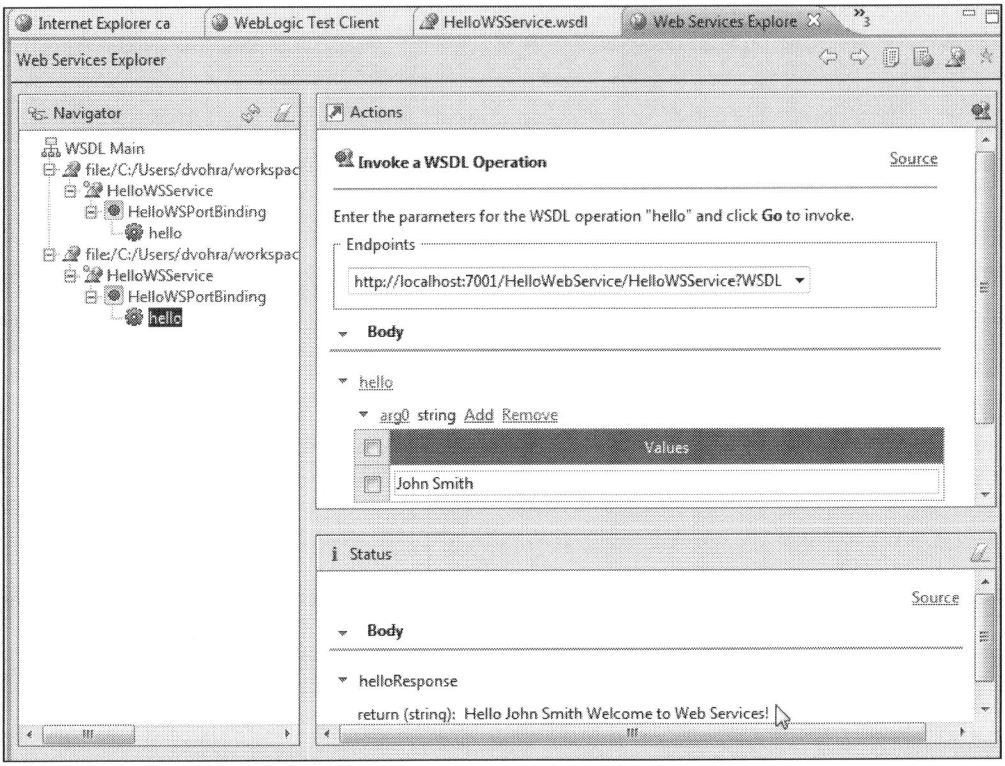

# Generating a bindings file

The JAX-WS bindings file may be used to customize the JAX-WS bindings. To generate the bindings file right-click on **HelloWSService.wsdl** and select **WebLogic Web Services | Generate JAX-WS Bindings File...**, as shown in the following screenshot:

Select the folder to generate the bindings file in and specify a filename (`jaxws-bindings.xml`) in the **File name** field and click on **Finish**, as follows:

A JAX-WS bindings file **jaxws-bindings.xml** gets generated. Some of the customizations that may be made are to the **Wrapper Style** and **Async Mapping** checkboxes, which are checked by default, as shown in the following screenshot:

We won't be using any customizations to the bindings (refer to `http://jax-ws.java.net/nonav/2.1.2/docs/customizations.html`).

# Creating a client class

Next, we shall create a web service client class, which is just a Java class. The web service client may be used to invoke the web service. In contrast to the WebLogic test client generated automatically in an earlier section, the web service invocation in the client class that we shall generate in this section is specified as required. Select the project folder and select **File | New | Other**. In the **New** wizard select **Java | Class**. In the **New Java Class** wizard specify a package name (`hellowebserviceclient`) in the **Package** field, specify a class name (`HelloWSClient`) in the **Name** field, and click on **Finish**, as shown in the following screenshot:

A web service client class `hellowebserviceclient.HelloWSClient` gets generated, as follows:

In the Java client application create an instance of the `HelloWSService` service:

```
HelloWSService service=new HelloWSService();
```

Obtain a proxy to the service from the service using the `getHelloWSPort()` method:

```
hellowebserviceclient.HelloWS port = service.getHelloWSPort();
```

Invoke the `hello(String)` method of the service:

```
String result = port.hello("John Smith.");
```

The Java client class is listed, as follows:

```
package hellowebserviceclient;

import hellowebservice.*;
import javax.xml.ws.WebServiceRef;

public class HelloWSClient {
  public static void main(String[] args) {

      HelloWSService service=new HelloWSService();

      hellowebserviceclient.HelloWS port = service.getHelloWSPort();
      String result = port.hello("John Smith");
      System.out.println(result);
    }
}
```

# Creating a build file

We compile and package the web service using the Apache Ant tasks `wsdlc` and `jwsc`. We deploy the web service to WebLogic Server. We generate web service client files using the Apache Ant task `clientgen` and subsequently test the web service using the client class. The `build.xml` file generates, packages, and deploys the web service as an EAR file to the WebLogic Server. First, we need to create the `build.xml` file. Select the project folder and select **File | New | Other**. In the **New** wizard select **XML | XML File** and click on **Next**. In the **New XML File** window specify `build.xml` as **File name** and click on **Finish**, as shown in the following screenshot:

New XML File

**XML**

Create a new XML file.

Enter or select the parent folder:

HelloWebService

HelloWebService

File name: build.xml

Advanced >>

< Back    Next >    Finish    Cancel

In the `build.xml` file add `property` elements for the properties listed in the following table:

| Property | Value | Description |
| --- | --- | --- |
| src.dir | ${basedir}/src | Source directory |
| web.module | ${basedir}/WebContent | Web module directory |
| weblogic.home | C:\Oracle\Middleware/WLS12c | WebLogic Server install directory |
| weblogic.server | ${weblogic.home}/wlserver_12.1/server | WebLogic Server directory |
| build.dir | ${basedir}/build | Build directory |
| output.dir | ${src.dir}/output | Output directory |

| Property | Value | Description |
|---|---|---|
| deploy.dir | ${weblogic.home}/user_projects/domains/base_domain/autodeploy | WebLogic Server deploy directory |
| temp.dir | ${weblogic.home}/user_projects/domains/base_domain/servers/AdminServer/tmp | Temporary directory |

In build.xml we shall specify targets for the following tasks:

- Generating JWS JAR file with the wsdlc Ant task
- Generating and packaging the web service artifacts into a WAR file with the jwsc Ant task
- Deploying web service WAR file to WebLogic Server
- Generating and packaging client artifacts with the clientgen Ant task
- Running the web service client

Specify the following targets in build.xml:

| Target | Description |
|---|---|
| prepare | Makes the required directories. |
| build | Runs the wsdlc task to generate a set of artifacts that provide a partial Java implementation of the web service. |
| build-service | Runs the jwsc task. |
| assemble-app | Generates the web service EAR file—HelloWSService_wsdl.ear. |
| deploy | Deploys the web service. |
| build-client | Runs the clientgen task to generate the client artifacts that may used to invoke the web service. Also, compiles the client Java class. |
| run | Runs the client class. |
| clean | Deletes directories and web service EAR file. |

The `build.xml` script is listed, as follows:

```xml
<?xml version="1.0" encoding="UTF-8"?>
<project name="webservices-hello" default="deploy">
```

First, specify the properties for the build file. The properties specify build parameters reused multiple times in the build file to avoid having to re-specify them at each use.

```xml
<property name="src.dir" value="${basedir}/src" />
<property name="web.module" value="${basedir}/webContent" />
<property name="weblogic.home" value="C:/Oracle/Middleware/WLS12c"
/>
<property name="weblogic.server" value="${weblogic.home}/
wlserver_12.1/server" />
<property name="build.dir" value="${basedir}/build" />
<property name="output.dir" value="${src.dir}/output" />
<property name="deploy.dir"
   value="${weblogic.home}/user_projects/domains/base_domain/
autodeploy" />
<property name="temp.dir"
   value="${weblogic.home}/user_projects/domains/base_domain/servers/
AdminServer/tmp" />
```

Specify the classpath for the build file using the `<path>` element. Specify the JAR files to include using the `<fileset>` elements with the `<include>` subelement. The JAR files required to compile the web service are in the WebLogic Server's modules directory and are `ws.api_2.0.0.0.jar`, `javax.xml.ws_2.2.0.jar`, `javax.jws_2.0.1.jar`, `javax.xml.stream_1.1.2.0.jar`, and `javax.xml. bind_2.2.3.jar`. The `weblogic.jar` file in the `lib` directory is required for the Ant tasks classes.

```xml
<path id="classpath">
  <fileset dir="${weblogic.home}/modules">
    <include name="ws.api_2.0.0.0.jar" />
    <include name="javax.xml.ws_2.2.0.jar" />
    <include name="javax.jws_2.0.1.jar" />
    <include name="javax.xml.stream_1.1.2.0.jar" />
    <include name="javax.xml.bind_2.2.3.jar" />
  </fileset>

  <fileset dir="${weblogic.server}/lib">
    <include name="weblogic.jar" />
  </fileset>
  <pathelement location="${build.dir}" />
</path>
<property name="build.classpath" refid="classpath" />
```

Create the required directories in the `prepare` target:

```
<target name="prepare">
  <mkdir dir="${build.dir}" />
  <mkdir dir="${output.dir}" />
  <mkdir dir="${output.dir}/HelloWsEar" />
  <mkdir dir="${output.dir}/compiledWsdl" />
  <mkdir dir="${output.dir}/clientclass" />
</target>
```

Next, run the `wsdlc` task (`http://docs.oracle.com/cd/E12840_01/wls/docs103/webserv_ref/anttasks.html#wp1075710`) to generate a partial Java implementation of the web service, which does not include any business logic:

```
<target name="build" depends="prepare">
  <taskdef name="wsdlc" classname="weblogic.wsee.tools.anttasks.
WsdlcTask">
    <classpath refid="classpath" />
  </taskdef>

  <wsdlc failOnError="true"
    srcWsdl="${src.dir}/hellowebservice/HelloWSService.wsdl"
destImplDir="${src.dir}"
    destJwsDir="${output.dir}/compiledWsdl"
srcPortName="HelloWSPort"
    type="JAXWS">
    <classpath refid="classpath" />
  </wsdlc>

</target>
```

Run the `jwsc` task (`http://docs.oracle.com/cd/E12840_01/wls/docs103/webserv_ref/anttasks.html#wp1069899`) to generate the complete Java implementation of the web service:

```
<taskdef name="jwsc" classname="weblogic.wsee.tools.anttasks.
JwscTask">
  <classpath refid="classpath" />
</taskdef>
<target name="build-service" depends="build">

  <jwsc srcdir="${src.dir}" destdir="${output.dir}/HelloWsEar">
    <jws file="hellowebservice/HelloWSImpl.java"
compiledWsdl="${output.dir}/compiledWsdl/HelloWSService_wsdl.jar"
      type="JAXWS" />
    <classpath refid="classpath" />
  </jwsc>

</target>
```

Assemble the web service application into an EAR file, which includes an `application.xml` application descriptor and a WAR file for the web service artifacts:

```
<target name="assemble-app" depends="build-service">
  <jar jarfile="${output.dir}/HelloWsEar/HelloWSService_wsdl.ear">
    <metainf dir="${output.dir}/HelloWsEar/META-INF">
      <include name="application.xml" />
    </metainf>
    <fileset dir="${output.dir}/HelloWsEar/hellowebservice"
      includes="HelloWSImpl.war" />
  </jar>
</target>
```

Deploy the EAR file to the WebLogic Server's `autodeployed` directory:

```
<target name="deploy" depends="assemble-app">
  <copy file="${output.dir}/HelloWsEar/HelloWSService_wsdl.ear"
    todir="${deploy.dir}" />
</target>
```

Build the web service client artifacts using the `clientgen` task (http://docs.oracle.com/cd/E12840_01/wls/docs103/webserv_ref/anttasks.html#wp1039270). Also, compile the client class `HelloWSClient.java`:

```
<target name="build-client" depends="deploy">
  <taskdef name="clientgen" classname="weblogic.wsee.tools.anttasks.
ClientGenTask">
    <classpath refid="classpath" />
  </taskdef>
  <clientgen failonerror="true" type="JAXWS"
    wsdl="http://localhost:7001/HelloWebService/HelloWSService?WSDL"
    destDir="${output.dir}/clientclass" serviceName="HelloWSService"
    copyWsdl="true" packageName="hellowebserviceclient">

    <classpath refid="classpath" />
  </clientgen>

  <javac srcdir="${output.dir}/clientclass" destdir="${output.dir}/
clientclass"
    includes="**/*.java" />
  <javac srcdir="${src.dir}" destdir="${output.dir}/clientclass"
    includes="hellowebserviceclient/HelloWSClient.java" />
</target>
<path id="client.class.path">
  <path refid="classpath" />
  <pathelement path="${output.dir}/clientclass" />
  <pathelement path="${java.class.path}" />
</path>
```

Run the client class `hellowebserviceclient.HelloWSClient` to invoke the web service:

```
<target name="run" depends="build-client">
  <java fork="true" classname="hellowebserviceclient.HelloWSClient"
    failonerror="true">
    <classpath refid="client.class.path" />
  </java>
</target>
<target name="clean">
  <delete dir="${build.dir}" />
  <delete dir="${output.dir}" />
  <delete file="${deploy.dir}/HelloWSService_wsdl.ear" />
  <delete dir="${temp.dir}" />
</target>

</project>
```

# Testing the web service

In this section we shall build and test the web service by running the `build.xml` script. We shall run the various `build.xml` targets to compile, package, and deploy the web service to WebLogic Server and subsequently invoke the web service using the client class. Right-click on **build.xml** and select **Run As | Ant Build...**, as shown in the following screenshot:

Select the **run** target and click on **Run**. The **run** target and all the preceding targets have dependence on the previous target. Thus, when the **run** target is run, all the preceding targets also run starting with the **prepare** target:

All the targets, except the **clean** target run, and the output from the web service client is shown next, as follows:

```
Servers  Console
<terminated> HelloWebService build.xml [Ant Build] C:\Oracle\Middleware\WLS12c\jdk160_29\bin\javaw.exe (2012-11-02 9:04:43 AM)
                                                                    WLST

Buildfile: C:\Users\dvohra\workspace\HelloWebService\build.xml
prepare:
    [mkdir] Created dir: C:\Users\dvohra\workspace\HelloWebService\src\output
    [mkdir] Created dir: C:\Users\dvohra\workspace\HelloWebService\src\output\HelloWsEar
    [mkdir] Created dir: C:\Users\dvohra\workspace\HelloWebService\src\output\compiledWsdl
    [mkdir] Created dir: C:\Users\dvohra\workspace\HelloWebService\src\output\clientclass
build:
    [wsdlc] Catalog dir = C:\Users\dvohra\AppData\Local\Temp\_ckr59b
    [wsdlc] Download file [HelloWSService_schema1.xsd] to C:\Users\dvohra\AppData\Local\Temp\_ckr59b
    [wsdlc] Download file [HelloWSService.wsdl] to C:\Users\dvohra\AppData\Local\Temp\_ckr59b
    [wsdlc] srcWsdl is redefined as [ C:\Users\dvohra\AppData\Local\Temp\_ckr59b\HelloWSService.wsdl ]
    [wsdlc] Consider using <depends>/<produces> so that wsimport won't do unnecessary compilation
    [wsdlc] parsing WSDL...
    [wsdlc] Generating code...
    [wsdlc] Compiling code...
[AntUtil.deleteDir] Deleting directory C:\Users\dvohra\AppData\Local\Temp\_ckr59b
build-service:
    [jwsc] warning: 'includeantruntime' was not set, defaulting to build.sysclasspath=last; set to false
    [jwsc] JWS: processing module /hellowebservice/HelloWSImpl
    [jwsc] Parsing source files
    [jwsc] Parsing source files
    [jwsc] 1 JWS files being processed for module /hellowebservice/HelloWSImpl
    [jwsc] JWS: C:\Users\dvohra\workspace\HelloWebService\src\hellowebservice\HelloWSImpl.java Validated.
    [jwsc] Processing 1 JAX-WS web services...
    [jwsc] Compiling 1 source file to C:\Users\dvohra\AppData\Local\Temp\_q5h4v7
    [jwsc] Building jar: C:\Users\dvohra\workspace\HelloWebService\src\output\HelloWsEar\hellowebservice\
    [jwsc] Created JWS deployment outputFile: C:\Users\dvohra\workspace\HelloWebService\src\output\HelloW
    [jwsc] [EarFile] Application File : C:\Users\dvohra\workspace\HelloWebService\src\output\HelloWsEar\M
[AntUtil.deleteDir] Deleting directory C:\Users\dvohra\AppData\Local\Temp\_q5h4v7
assemble-app:
    [jar] Building jar: C:\Users\dvohra\workspace\HelloWebService\src\output\HelloWsEar\HelloWSService_w
deploy:
```

The **run** target runs the client class to invoke the web service, which sends the message output in the console, as follows:

If an error is generated in the first run, run the `clean` target. The directories and files generated in the first run get deleted. Subsequently, the `run` target may be re-run.

# Summary

In this chapter we used the Java API for XML web services (JAX-WS) to create a web service. First, we created a web service project, which has the Oracle WebLogic web service project facet associated with it. We tested the web service on the server and generated a WSDL, which we tested in web explorer. We created a client class for the web service and packaged, deployed, and tested the web service on the WebLogic Server.

In the next chapter we shall discuss creating a RESTful web service using the JAX-RS project facet.

# 9
# RESTful Web Services Using the JAX-RS API

In *Chapter 8, Creating a JAX-WS Web Service*, we discussed JAX-WS API web services. In this chapter we discuss **Representational State Transfer (REST)** web services. REST is protocol independent, but we shall constrain our discussion to REST over HTTP. RESTful web services have the advantage of being simple, lightweight, and fast. A RESTful web service exposes a set of resources identified by URIs. Resources are simply **Plain Old Java Objects (POJOs)** annotated with RESTful API annotations. Two types of resource classes may be defined—root resource classes and subresource classes. Root resource classes are POJOs annotated with @PATH, and subresource classes are Java classes in which the class is not annotated with @ PATH, but one or more class methods are annotated with @PATH or resource method designators such as @GET, @PUT, @POST, and @DELETE. Resources respond to HTTP methods such as GET, POST, PUT, and DELETE (http://www.w3.org/Protocols/ HTTP/Methods.html). For example, a client may retrieve representation of resources through GET, upload a modified copy of a resource using PUT, or delete a resource using DELETE. Resources may be accessed in various formats such as HTML, plain text, XML, PDF, JPEG, and JSON among others. RESTful web services follow specific architectural principles called the RESTful principles, which are as follows:

- Every resource has a unique URI.

- Only the methods provided by the HTTP protocol may be used; the most common being GET, PUT, POST, and DELETE.

- A client interacts with a resource (service) through representations of the resource in different formats, which could be PDF for one client and XML for another.

- Stateless communication, which implies that a client session is not stored on the server. The server only stores the state of the resources. Not having to store the client session makes it easier to scale the service, as without the client session, less replication of data is required in a clustered environment.

**Java API for RESTful Web Services (JAX-RS)** is defined in JSR 311 (http://jcp. org/en/jsr/detail?id=311). Jersey is a reference implementation for JAX-RS, simplifying the process of developing RESTful web services in Java. In this chapter we shall create a RESTful web service using the Jersey implementation in Eclipse 3.7 (Oracle Enterprise Pack for Eclipse 12*c*). This chapter has the following sections:

- Setting the environment
- Creating a web project
- Creating and running a resource class
- Creating and running a test client

# Setting the environment

Download the Jersey archive jersey-archive-1.8.zip from http://download. java.net/maven/2/com/sun/jersey/jersey-archive/1.8/ to a directory, C:/ Jersey for example. jersey-archive-1.8.zip contains the Jersey JARs and core dependencies. Also, download the Jersey bundle JAR—jersey-bundle- 1.8.jar from http://download.java.net/maven/2/com/sun/jersey/jersey- bundle/1.8. As Jersey is built using JDK 6.0, we also need to install JDK 6.0; as in the other chapters we also needed to install OEPE 12*c* and WebLogic Server 12*c*. Create a WebLogic Server domain as base_domain and add the following to the set CLASSPATH declaration in the bin/startWebLogic batch file:

```
C:\Jersey\jersey-bundle-1.8.jar;C:\Jersey\jersey-archive-1.8\lib\asm-
3.1.jar;C:\Jersey\jersey-archive-1.8\lib\jsr311-api-1.1.1.jar
```

# Creating a web project

In this section we shall create a web project and add the JAX-RS project facet to the web project. Select **File | New | Other** and in the **New** wizard select **Web | Dynamic Web Project**. Click on **Next**. In the **New Dynamic Web Project** wizard specify a project name (**EclipseJAX-RS**) in the **Project name** field and configure a new target runtime for **Oracle WebLogic Server 12c (12.1.1)**. Click on the **Modify...** button under **Configuration**, as shown in the following screenshot:

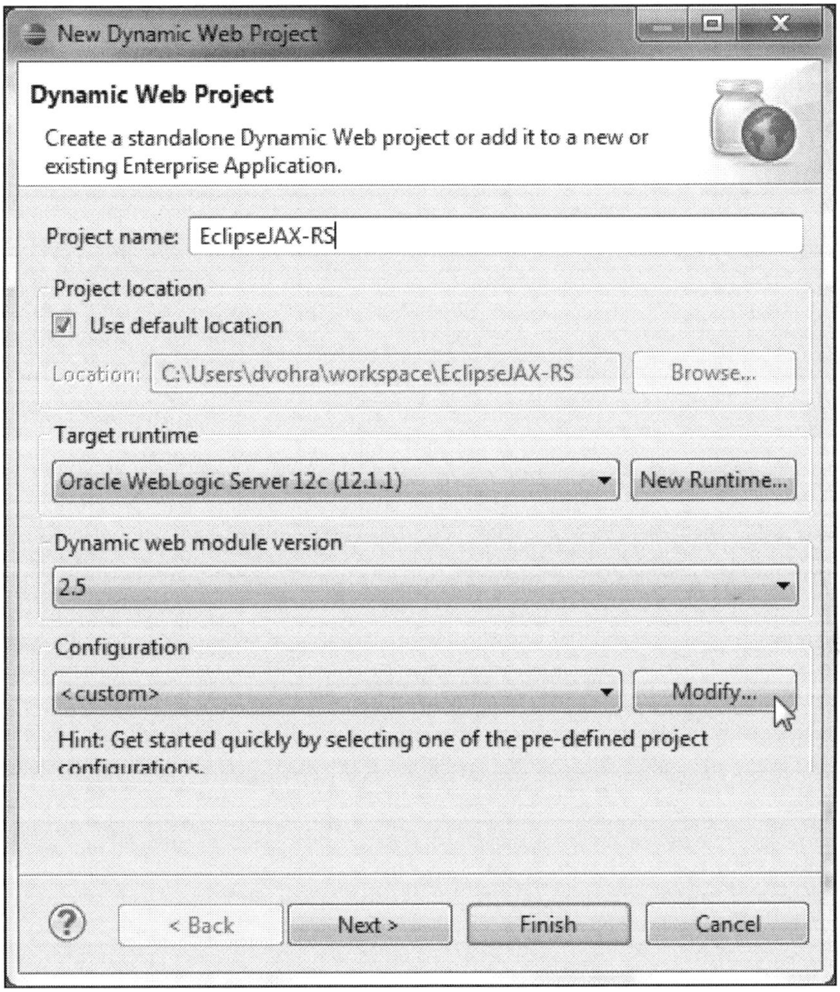

In the **Project Facets** window, select the **JAX-RS (REST Web Services)** project facet with **1.1** as **Version**. Click on **OK**, as follows:

Click on **Next** in the **New Dynamic Web Project** wizard, as follows:

Select the default Java settings for source folders on the build path (`src`) and default output folder (`build/classes`). Click on **Next**. Select the default **Web Module** settings for **Context root** (`EclipseJAX-RS`), **Content directory** (`WebContent`), and the **Generate web.xml deployment descriptor** checkbox, which is selected by default, and click on **Next**. In the **JAX-RS Capabilities** dialog box specify **JAX-RS servlet name** (`JAX-RS Servlet` by default), and specify **JAX-RS servlet class name** as `com.sun.jersey.spi.container.servlet.ServletContainer` (default), which is a Servlet for deploying root resource classes. Specify **URL mapping patterns** (`/jaxrs/*` by default). Configure a **JAX-RS Implementation Library**. Select **User Library** as **Type** and click on the **Manage...** button, as shown in the following screenshot:

In **User Libraries** click on **New...**. In **New User Library** specify **User library name** (`JAX-RS User Library`) and click on **OK**. A user library gets added. Click on **Add JARs...** to add Jersey JARs to the user library, as follows:

Add the Jersey JARs `C:/Jersey/jersey-bundle-1.8.jar`, `C:/Jersey/jersey-archive-1.8/lib/asm-3.1.jar`, and `C:/Jersey/jersey-archive-1.8/lib/jsr311-api-1.1.1.jar`. Click on **OK**, as follows:

The **Include library with this application** checkbox should be checked and the **Deploy** radio button under it should be selected to include and deploy **JAX-RS User Library** with the application to WebLogic Server. Click on **Finish** in **JAX-RS Capabilities**, as shown in the following screenshot:

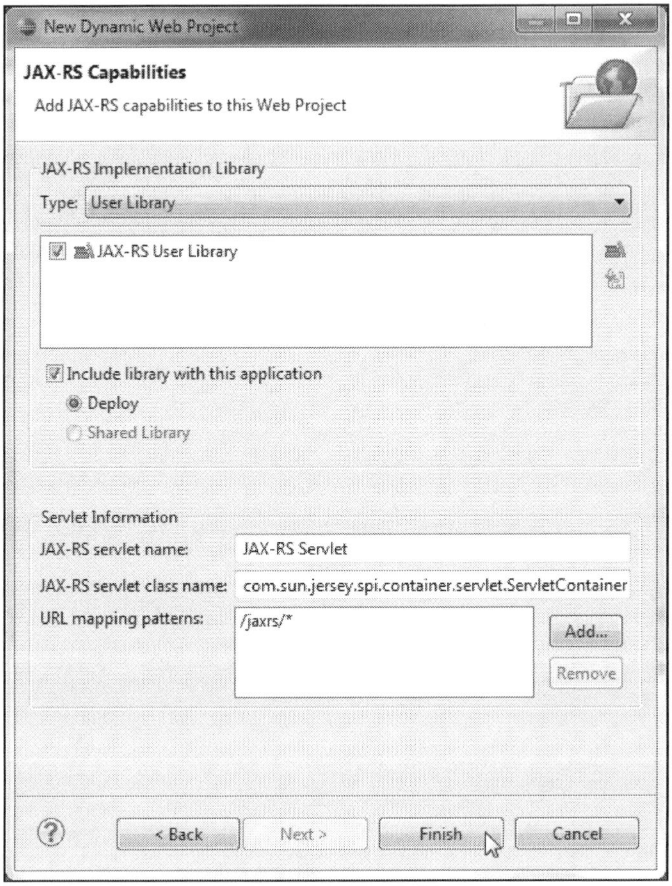

The **EclipseJAX-RS** web project gets created. The targeted runtimes get configured with the JAX-RS project facet. The JAX-RS user libraries get added to the project, as shown in the following screenshot:

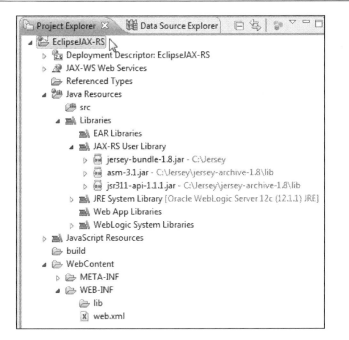

JAX-RS `Servlet` and the Servlet mapping get configured in **web.xml**, as follows:

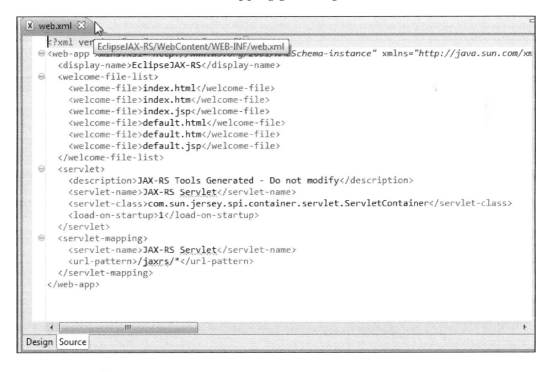

The `web.xml` file is listed, as follows:

```xml
<?xml version="1.0" encoding="UTF-8"?>
<web-app xmlns:xsi="http://www.w3.org/2001/XMLSchema-instance"
xmlns="http://java.sun.com/xml/ns/javaee" xmlns:web="http://java.sun.
com/xml/ns/javaee/web-app_2_5.xsd" xsi:schemaLocation="http://java.
sun.com/xml/ns/javaee http://java.sun.com/xml/ns/javaee/web-app_2_5.
xsd" id="WebApp_ID" version="2.5">
  <display-name>EclipseJAX-RS</display-name>
  <welcome-file-list>
    <welcome-file>index.html</welcome-file>
    <welcome-file>index.htm</welcome-file>
    <welcome-file>index.jsp</welcome-file>
    <welcome-file>default.html</welcome-file>
    <welcome-file>default.htm</welcome-file>
    <welcome-file>default.jsp</welcome-file>
  </welcome-file-list>
  <servlet>
    <description>JAX-RS Tools Generated - Do not modify</description>
    <servlet-name>JAX-RS Servlet</servlet-name>
    <servlet-class>com.sun.jersey.spi.container.servlet.
ServletContainer</servlet-class>
    <load-on-startup>1</load-on-startup>
  </servlet>
  <servlet-mapping>
    <servlet-name>JAX-RS Servlet</servlet-name>
    <url-pattern>/jaxrs/*</url-pattern>
  </servlet-mapping>
</web-app>
```

# Creating and running a resource class

Next, we shall create a RESTful web service resource using a root resource class. A **root resource class** is a POJO, annotated with the @PATH annotation and consisting of at least one method annotated with the @PATH annotation or request method designator such as @GET, @PUT, @POST, or @DELETE. We shall create a root resource class with some resource methods using the @GET request method designator. Select **File** | **New** | **Other** and in the **New** wizard select **Java** | **Class**. Click on **Finish**. In **New Java Class** specify **Source folder** (EclipseJAX-RS/src), specify **Package** (jaxrs), and specify a class name (HelloWorldResource) in the **Name** field. Click on **Finish**, as shown in the following screenshot:

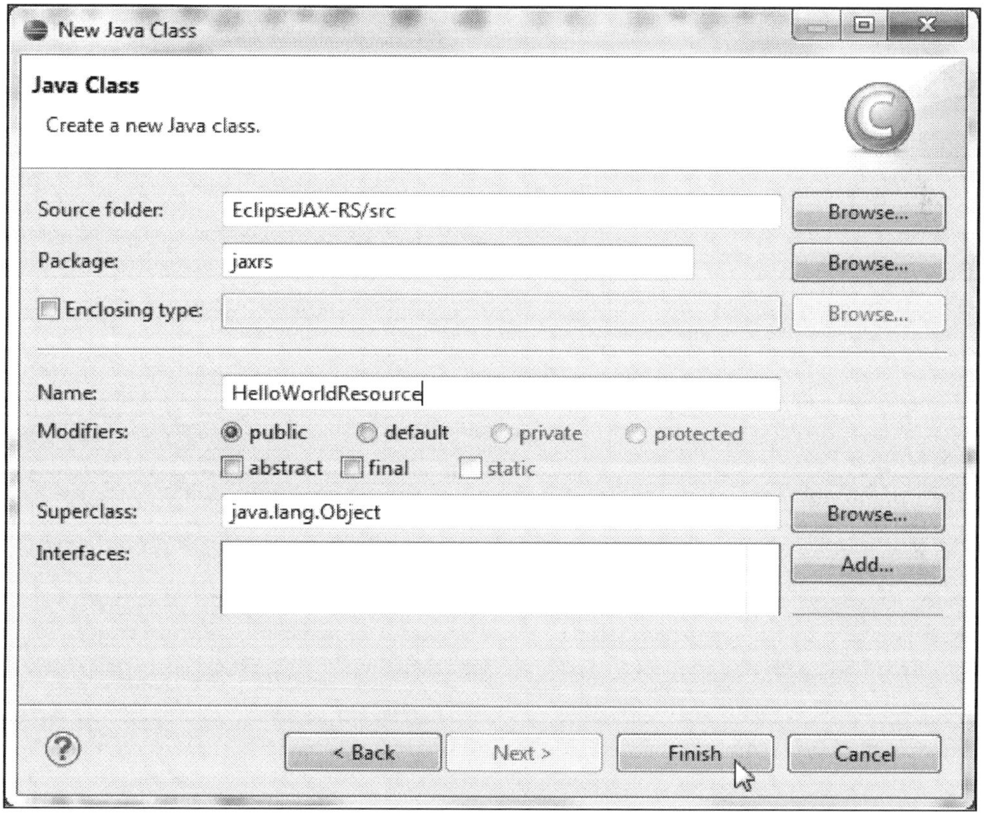

Annotate the Java class with the @PATH annotation. Specify the URI path on which the Java class shall be hosted as /helloworld:

```
@Path("/helloworld")
public class HelloWorldResource {
...
}
```

We shall add resource methods to produce three different MIME types. Add the getClichedMessage(), getXMLMessage(), and getHTMLMessage() methods (the method names are arbitrary) and annotate each of them with the @GET annotation, which indicates that the methods shall process HTTP GET requests from the client. Specify the return type for each of the methods as String, and annotate each of the methods with the @PRODUCES annotation and in that specify a different MIME type for each of the methods. Specify the MIME types—text/plain, text/xml, and text/html. We shall output a "Hello JAX-RS" method for which we will add a return statement in each of the resource methods in a format corresponding to the MIME type. The root resource class is listed next; some sections of the code listing have been commented out because we shall be testing the resource class using each of the resource methods separately. The resource method annotated with @Produces("application/xml") is included to demonstrate the requirement for the produced MIME type to match the acceptable MIME type:

```
package jaxrs;

import javax.ws.rs.GET;
import javax.ws.rs.Produces;
import javax.ws.rs.Path;
import javax.ws.rs.core.MediaType;


// The Java class will be hosted at the URI path "/helloworld"
@Path("/helloworld")
public class HelloWorldResource {
```

```
  // The Java method will process HTTP GET requests
  //
  // The Java method will produce content identified by the MIME Media
  // type "text/plain"
  @GET
  @Produces("text/plain")
  public String getClichedMessage() {
    // Return some cliched textual content
    return "Hello JAX-RS";
  }

  //@GET
  //@Produces("application/xml")
  //public String getXMLMessage() {
  //  return "<?xml version=\"1.0\"?>" + "<hello> Hello JAX-RS" + "</
hello>";
  //}

//   @GET
//   @Produces("text/xml")
//   public String getXMLMessage() {
//     return "<?xml version=\"1.0\"?>" + "<hello> Hello JAX-RS" + "</
hello>";
//   }

  //@GET
  //("text/html")
//public String getHTMLMessage() {
//   return "<html> " + "<title>" + "Hello JAX-RS" + "</title>"
  //      + "<body><h1>" + "Hello JAX-RS" + "</body></h1>" + "</html>
";
  //}

}
```

Next, we shall run the resource class producing different types of output. Comment out the methods not to be tested and keep one resource method uncommented for each of the test runs. First, test the `text/plain` MIME type as output. Right-click on the resource class and select **Run As | Run on Server**, as shown in the following screenshot:

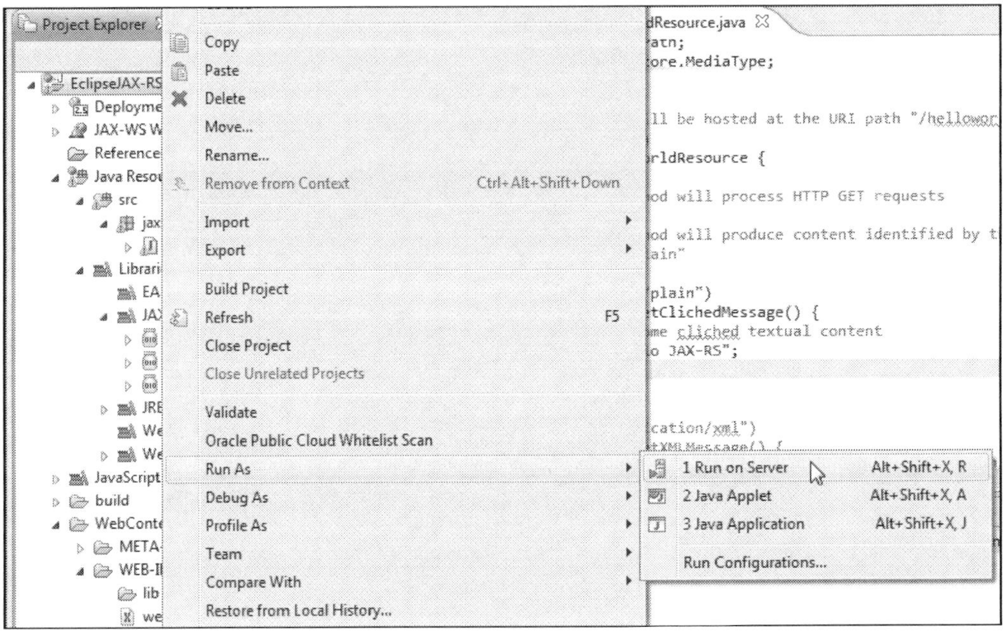

In the **Run On Server** window select the server to run the resource class. Click on **Next**:

In **Add and Remove** resources add the **EclipseJAX-RS** application to the **Configured** section using the **Add** button. Click on **Finish**, as follows:

On the WebLogic Server, the `com.sun.jersey.api.core.WebAppResourceConfig` class, which dynamically searches for root resource and provider classes in the web application resource paths `WEB-INF/lib` and `WEB-INF/classes`, gets initiated. The root resource class `jaxrs.HelloWorldResource` gets found. Jersey application Version 1.9 gets initiated, as follows:

The **EclipseJAX-RS** module gets deployed on the WebLogic Server and gets listed under **Deployments**, as shown in the following screenshot:

Invoke the RESTful web service resource identified with the URL `http://localhost:7001/EclipseJAX-RS/jaxrs/helloworld` in a web browser. In the URL `EclipseJAX-RS` is the context root and `jaxrs` is the servlet mapping for the JAX-RS servlet, and `/helloworld` is the URI path for the root resource class. As only one of the resource methods has been uncommented, the method gets invoked. A text message, **Hello JAX-RS,** gets displayed as the output, as shown in the following screenshot:

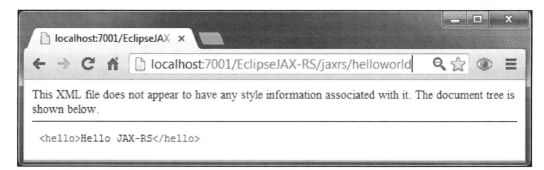

We had commented out all the resource methods other than the one that produces the `text/plain` MIME media type. If we had uncommented all the resource methods, the first resource method in the root resource class gets invoked. To include all resource methods and be able to invoke a specific resource method, the URI for the resource methods must be unique. A URI may be associated with a resource method using the `@PATH` annotation on the resource method. We have not annotated resource methods with `@PATH`. To test a different resource method, uncomment just that resource method or alternatively make the method the first in the resource class. Next, uncomment just the `getXMLMessage()` method annotated with `@Produces("text/xml")`. Run the application to display the output message **Hello JAX-RS** as `text/xml`:

Similarly, display the output message as the `text/html` MIME media type for which you need to uncomment just the `getHTMLMessage()` method annotated with `@Produces("text/html")`:

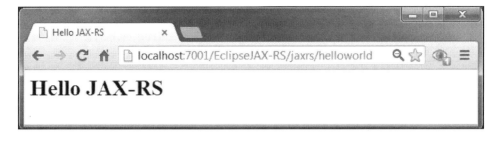

# Creating and running a test client

Jersey provides a client API to invoke a JAX-RS web service. In this section we shall create a REST client to test the JAX-RS web service. Create a Java class, `TestClient.java`. Select **File** | **New** | **Other**. Select **Java** | **Class** in the **New** wizard. In the **New Java Class** window specify a source folder (`EclipseJAX-RS/src` is the default) in the **Source folder** field, specify a package name (`jaxrs`) in the **Package** field, and specify a class name (`TestClient`) in the **Name** field. Click on **Next**, as shown in the following screenshot:

In `TestClient.java` we invoke the resource methods using the Jersey client API. The `com.sun.jersey.api.client.Client` class is the main class for creating resource instances. First, create a `ClientConfig` object, which represents the client configuration such as property names and features that may be used by the `Client` object, using the constructor for `DefaultClientConfig`. Create a `Client` instance from `ClientConfig` using the static method `create(ClientConfig)`. Create a `WebResource` object from the `Client` object using the `resource(URI)` method of a `Client` class. A `WebResource` object is built using the base URI for the JAX-RS web service. A `WebResource` object is an encapsulation of a web resource and is used to send requests to the web resource and receive responses from the web resource.

```
ClientConfig config = new DefaultClientConfig();
Client client = Client.create(config);
WebResource service = client.resource(getBaseURI());
```

The web service method response is obtained by invoking the `get()` method on a `WebResource` object with the `String.class` argument. Add paths to the base URI of the `WebResource` object using the `path()` method, which returns a new `WebResource` object. Add acceptable media types to the `WebResource` object using the `accept()` method and get a response by invoking the `get()` method. We shall test the `HelloWorldResource` class using three different types of media types—text, XML, and HTML.

To invoke the resource method that produces a `plain/text` MIME media type, specify the URI to the method using the `path()` method that may be invoked multiple times to build the resource URI path. Add `jaxrs` and `helloworld` to the URI path. Specify the acceptable media type as `TEXT_PLAIN` using the `accept()` method. As the return type of the resource methods is `String`, a resource method is invoked using `String.class` as an argument to the `get()` method, as follows:

```
System.out.println(service.path("jaxrs").path("helloworld").
accept(MediaType.TEXT_PLAIN).get(String.class));
```

Similarly, output the response as XML and HTML using the `MediaType.TEXT_XML` and `MediaType.TEXT_HTML` media types. Add a `getBaseURI()` method to return the base URI, which is built using `UriBuilder` and the URL `http://localhost:7001/EclipseJAX-RS`, as follows:

```
private static URI getBaseURI() {
    return UriBuilder.fromUri("http://localhost:7001/EclipseJAX-RS")
        .build();
}
```

The Jersey client API test class is listed, as follows:

```
package jaxrs;

import java.net.URI;

import javax.ws.rs.core.*;
import com.sun.jersey.api.client.*;
import com.sun.jersey.api.client.config.*;

public class TestClient {
  public static void main(String[] args) {
    ClientConfig config = new DefaultClientConfig();
    Client client = Client.create(config);
    WebResource service = client.resource(getBaseURI());


    System.out.println(service.path("jaxrs").path("helloworld").
accept(MediaType.TEXT_PLAIN).get(String.class));

  //  System.out.println(service.path("jaxrs").path("helloworld").
accept(MediaType.TEXT_XML).get(String.class));

  //  System.out.println(service.path("jaxrs").path("helloworld").
accept(MediaType.TEXT_HTML).get(String.class));

  }

  private static URI getBaseURI() {
    return UriBuilder.fromUri("http://localhost:7001/EclipseJAX-RS")
        .build();
  }

}
```

We shall run the client to test outputting each of the response media types such as text, HTML, and XML. The acceptable media type in the client class must match a MIME media type produced in the resource class. We shall test the client using one media type in a test run. First, in the TestClient class uncomment only the System. out statement that accepts the TEXT_PLAIN media type:

```
System.out.println(service.path("jaxrs").path("helloworld").
accept(MediaType.TEXT_PLAIN).get(String.class));
```

Also, in the `HelloWorldResource` class uncomment only the resource method that produces the `text/plain` media type:

```
@GET
  @Produces("text/plain")
  public String getClichedMessage() {
    // Return some cliched textual content
    return "Hello JAX-RS";
  }
```

Right-click on **TestClient.java** and select **Run As | Java Application**, as shown in the following screenshot:

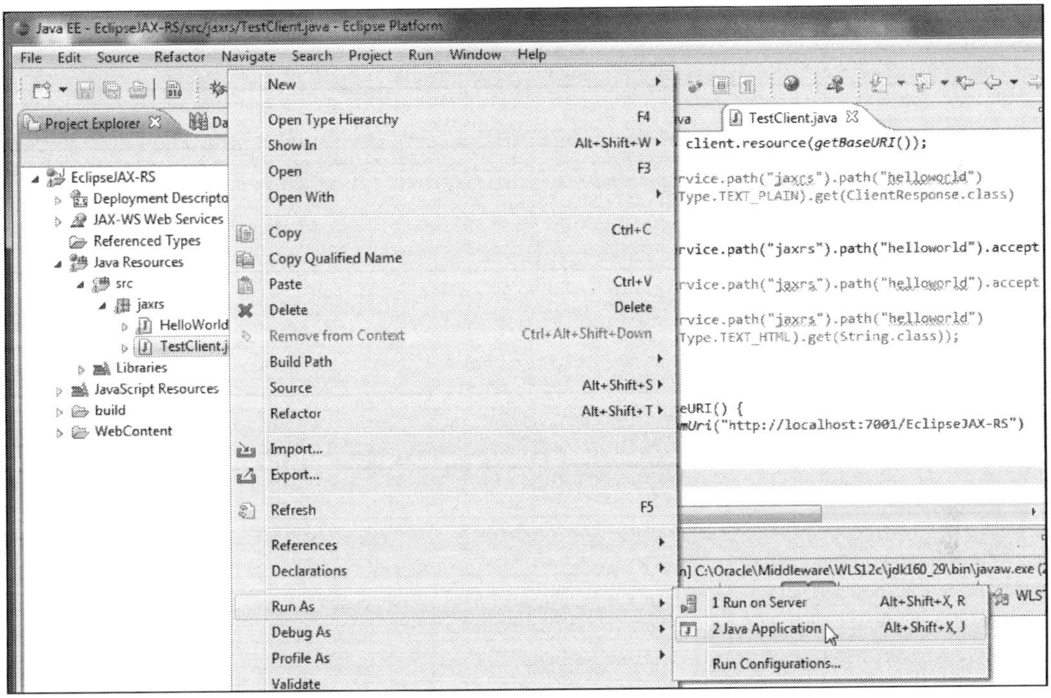

The text message **Hello JAX-RS** is returned from the JAX-RS web service and is displayed as the output, as shown in the following screenshot:

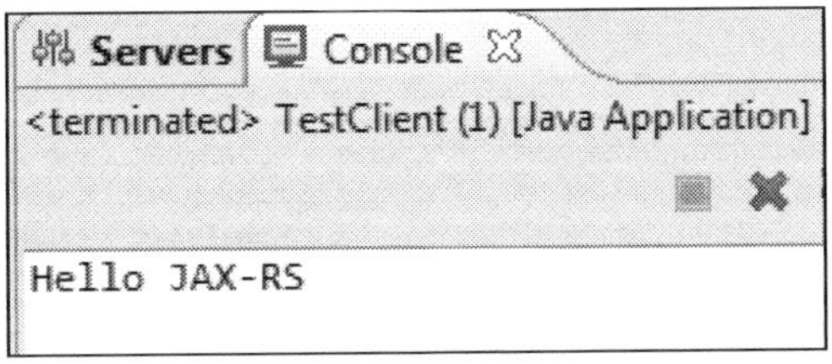

Next, produce and retrieve an HTML message. In the `HelloWorldResource` class uncomment only the resource method that produces the `text/html` media type:

```
@GET
  @Produces("text/html")
public String getHTMLMessage() {
    return "<html> " + "<title>" + "Hello JAX-RS" + "</title>"
        + "<body><h1>" + "Hello JAX-RS" + "</body></h1>" + "</html> ";
}
```

In the `TestClient` class uncomment only the `System.out` statement that accepts the `TEXT_HTML` media type:

```
System.out.println(service.path("jaxrs").path("helloworld").
accept(MediaType.TEXT_HTML).get(String.class));
```

Run the `TestClient.java` class as before to produce an HTML output:

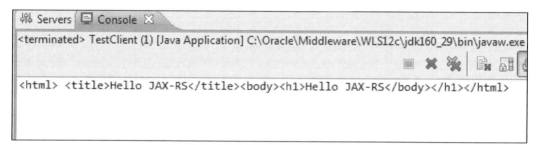

The acceptable media type must match a MIME media type produced by the resource class. If a produced MIME media type and the acceptable media type do not match, `com.sun.jersey.api.client.UniformInterfaceException` is generated. For example, set the acceptable media type to `MediaType.TEXT_XML` by uncommenting only the following `System.out` statement in the `TestClient` class:

```
System.out.println(service.path("jaxrs").path("helloworld").
accept(MediaType.TEXT_XML).get(String.class));
```

In `HelloWorldResource` uncomment only the resource method that produces the MIME media type `application/xml`, as follows:

```
@GET
   @Produces("application/xml")
   public String getXMLMessage() {
      return "<?xml version=\"1.0\"?>" + "<hello> Hello JAX-RS" + "</
hello>";
   }
```

Run `TestClient.java` as a Java application. `UniformInterfaceException` gets generated. A response status of **406** is output, which implies that "The resource identified by the request is only capable of generating response entities which have content characteristics not acceptable according to the accept headers sent in the request" (`http://www.w3.org/Protocols/rfc2616/rfc2616-sec10.html`).

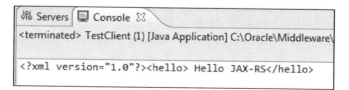

The error is removed by uncommenting the resource method that produces the MIME media type `text/xml`, as follows:

```
@GET
   @Produces("text/xml")
   public String getXMLMessage() {
      return "<?xml version=\"1.0\"?>" + "<hello> Hello JAX-RS" + "</
hello>";
   }
```

The `TestClient` class has the `System.out` statement that accepts the `TEXT_XML` media type uncommented. When `TestClient.java` is re-run, the `text/xml` message gets displayed as the output, as shown in the following screenshot:

```
Servers    Console
<terminated> TestClient (1) [Java Application] C:\Oracle\Middleware\

<?xml version="1.0"?><hello> Hello JAX-RS</hello>
```

We kept only some of the resource methods in the root resource class and only some of the System.out statements in the client uncommented to demonstrate producing and retrieving different media types. If all the resource methods are kept uncommented, the resource method that produces the MIME media type that matches the most acceptable media type, as specified by the client, gets invoked. Multiple MIME media types may be specified in a @Produces annotation. If more than one media type is equally acceptable, the one specified first gets selected. Next, we shall invoke all the resource methods from the client. Uncomment all the resource methods in the HelloWorldResource class and uncomment all the System. out statements that invoke the resource methods in the TestClient class. Start the WebLogic Server if not already started, right-click on **TestClient** in the **Project Explorer** tab, and select **Run As | Java Application**. All the resource methods get invoked, and the XML, HTML, and text messages get displayed as output, as shown in the following screenshot:

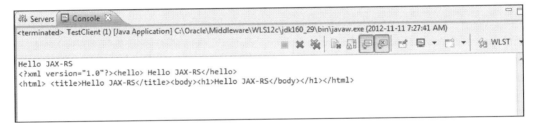

# Summary

In this chapter we discussed RESTful web services using **Java API for RESTful Web Services (JAX-RS)**, which are specified in the JSR 311 specification. We used the JAX-RS project facet for the RESTful web service. We created a root resource class, which is exposed as a URI path using the @PATH annotation. Subsequently, we created a Jersey client API to invoke the web service.

In the next chapter we will use the Spring project facet to create a Spring framework application in Oracle Enterprise Pack for Eclipse.

# 10
# Spring

Spring is a layered application development framework for Java that provides integration between different Java/Java EE components using a POJO-based programming model. The word "layered" implies that Spring Framework's functionality is grouped into layers consisting of modules. Spring's modular design makes it feasible to use only some of the modules for the required functionality. Spring provides the infrastructure to develop a Java/Java EE application. Spring Framework may be used on any kind of deployment platform such as a standalone application, a web (Servlet) container such as Tomcat, an application server such as Oracle WebLogic Server, or a cloud environment such as Amazon EC2. Spring supports commonly used web technologies such as AJAX and RESTful web services. Spring **Model View Controller (MVC)** provides a component model for developing scalable, testable, annotation-based web applications. Spring supports data access using all of the commonly used technologies/frameworks such as JDBC, JPA, Hibernate, and JDO. Spring is supported by a vast array of open source Spring projects that provide application-specific functionality, such as the Spring Web Services for document-driven web services or the Spring Batch project for batch applications. For a complete list of Spring projects refer to http://www.springsource.org/projects.

Spring Framework's layered architecture consists of 20 modules divided into the following seven layers:

- **Core Container**: The Core Container is based on the **Inversion of Control (IoC)** principle, more specifically the **Dependency Injection (DI)** design pattern. DI is the mechanism by which Spring bean objects define their own dependencies. The container injects the dependencies when it creates a bean, "inversion" implying that it is the bean that instantiates the dependencies. `BeanFactory` configures, instantiates, and assembles the dependencies among the objects. Developing a Spring application involves a lot of different classes, and the classes are able to be developed and unit tested independently and integrated with DI, providing loose coupling. The Context module in the Core Container provides a mechanism to access objects similar to a JNDI registry. The Context module supports Java EE features such as EJB and JMX and has `ApplicationContext` as the main interface.

- **Data Access/Integration**: The Data Access module consists of the JDBC, **Object-Relational Mapping (ORM)**, **Object/XML Mapping (OXM)**, JMS, and Transactions modules. The ORM module provides support for the commonly used ORM frameworks such as JPA, JDO, Hibernate, and iBatis. The OXM module supports Object/XML frameworks such as XMLBeans, Castor, and JAXB. The JMS module supports messaging and the Transactions module provides programmatic and transactional management.

- **Web**: The Web layer provides support for web-related features such as Spring MVC and portlets.

- **AOP**: The AOP module provides support for the AOP Alliance based aspect-oriented programming model. Spring is based on **aspect-oriented programming (AOP)**. AOP complements **object-oriented programming (OOP)** by providing an aspect as the unit of modularity in addition to the traditional OOP class. The aspect-oriented programming model provides decoupling of various functions (aspects) that span an application from the objects they effect using method interceptors and pointcuts. Some examples of aspects are logging and caching. We shall discuss AOP with an example in a latter section.

- **Aspects**: The Aspects module provides integration with AspectJ (`http://www.eclipse.org/aspectj/`), an aspect-oriented extension to Java.

- **Instrumentation**: The Instrumentation module provides support for class instrumentation and class-loader implementations.

- **Test**: The Test module provides testing of a Spring application with JUnit and TestNG.

A Spring bean may be any POJO such as a POJO web service or an EJB 3.0 proxy object. Spring implements the IoC principle (`http://en.wikipedia.org/wiki/Inversion_of_control`) via the DI (`http://en.wikipedia.org/wiki/Dependency_injection`) design pattern. Spring configuration may be specified using an XML configuration file and/or as an annotation-based configuration.

While it is not feasible to discuss all of Spring's features in a chapter, we shall explore some AOP-related features in Spring such as method interception and the schema-based aspect definition, as follows:

- **Method interception**: Method interception is a mechanism by which a method invocation is intercepted to output other information about the method call such as method name, class name, and performance statistics. Spring implements around advice (behavior customization) using method interception as recommended by AOP Alliance (`http://aopalliance.sourceforge.net/`). Around advice is "around" (before or after) a join point such as a method invocation. Around advice is the most useful kind of advice and may be used to shortcut the advised method invocation.

- **Schema-based aspect definition**: Schema-based aspect definitions are used to implement aspects and the advice contained in the aspects on join points, which are just method executions, as matched by pointcuts. We shall illustrate this with an example in a latter section.

In this chapter we will cover the following:

- Setting the environment
- Creating a web project with Spring facet
- Method interception
- Schema-based aspect definitions

# Setting the environment

We need to install **Oracle Enterprise Pack for Eclipse (OEPE)** and Oracle WebLogic Server. The Spring AOP relies on AspectJ. Download and extract `aspect-1.7.1.jar` from `http://www.eclipse.org/downloads/download.php?file=/tools/aspectj/aspectj-1.7.1.jar`. We also need to download the AspectJ dependency file, `cglib-2.2.jar` from `http://sourceforge.net/projects/cglib/files/cglib2/2.2.3/`, and CGLIB dependency file, `asm-3.3.jar` from `http://forge.ow2.org/project/download.php?group_id=23&file_id=17184`. After creating a web project as explained in the next section, add the following JAR files to the `CLASSPATH` variable in the `C:\Oracle\Middleware\user_projects\domains\base_domain\bin\startWebLogic` batch script (Spring Framework JAR files become available to be added after the Spring Framework library has been added to the Spring web project in Eclipse IDE, as discussed in the next section).

```
C:\aspectj1.7\lib\aspectjweaver.jar; C:\aspectj1.7\lib\aspectjtools.
jar; C:\aspectj1.7\lib\aspectjrt.jar; C:\aspectj1.7\lib\org.aspectj.
matcher.jar;C:\Spring\asm-3.3.jar;C:\Spring\cglib-2.2.jar;C:\
Users\dvohra\workspace\libraries\Spring Framework 2.5.6\spring-
framework-2.5.6\dist\spring.jar;C:\Users\dvohra\workspace\libraries\
Spring Framework 2.5.6\spring-framework-2.5.6\dist\lib\jakarta-
commons\commons-logging.jar;C:\Users\dvohra\workspace\libraries\Spring
Framework 2.5.6\spring-framework-2.5.6\dist\modules\spring-aop.jar;
```

# Creating a web project with Spring facet

First we need to create a web project in OEPE. Select **Web | Dynamic Web Project** in the **New** wizard. In **New Dynamic Web Project** specify a project name in the **Project name** field, and configure a target runtime for **Oracle WebLogic Server 12c (12.1.1)**. Click on **Modify...** under the **Configuration** section, as follows:

In **Project Facets** select the **Spring** project facet with **2.5** as **Version**. Click on **OK**:

Click on **Next** in **New Dynamic Web Project**. Select the default Java settings; source folder as `src` and output folder as `build/classes`. Click on **Next**. Specify **Context root** (`Spring`) and **Content directory** (`WebContent` by default), check the **Generate web.xml deployment descriptor** checkbox, and click on **Next**. Select **User Library** as **Type**, and click on the **Download Library** button, as shown in the following screenshot:

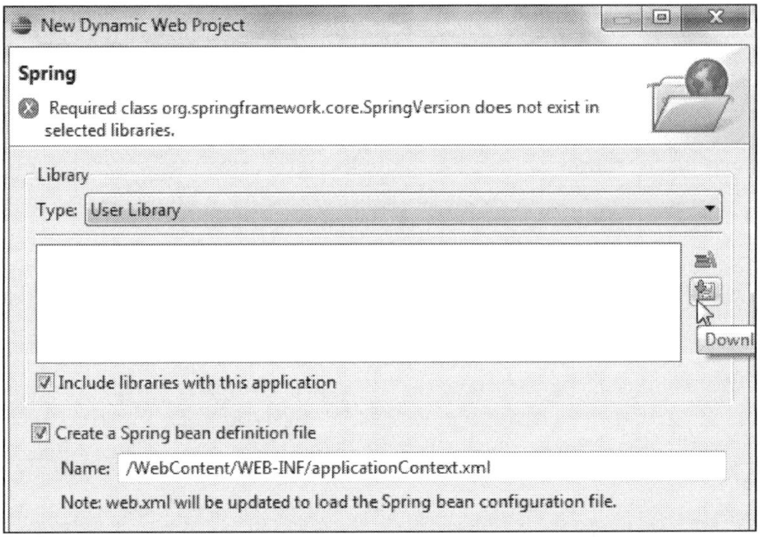

In **Download Library** select the **Spring Framework 2.5.6** library from **Oracle**. Click on **Next**, as follows:

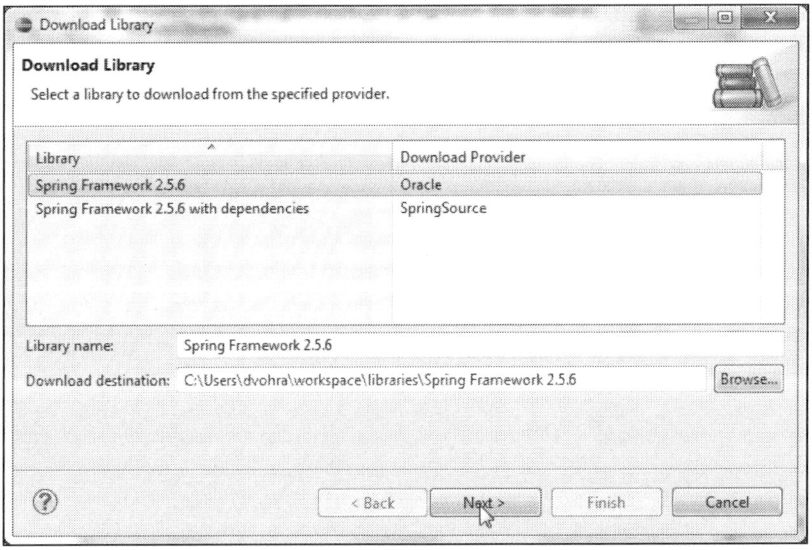

The library gets added. Click on **Finish** in the **Spring** dialog box, which has the library configuration, as follows:

A **Spring** web project gets created. The directory structure of the **Spring** project, which includes the **Spring Framework 2.5.6** library, is shown in the following screenshot:

The Spring bean definition file, **applicationContext.xml,** also gets created, as shown in the preceding screenshot. The SpringBean factory configuration may be specified either in the `beanDefinition.xml` file or the `WEB-INF/applicationContext.xml` file, the latter being more suitable for a web application. The method interception example is not a web application while the AspectJ example is a web application. For the method interception example, in this section we will use `beanDefinition.xml`, therefore delete the `applicationContext.xml` file. Right-click on the project node and select **Properties**. Select the **Java Build Path** node. The `spring.jar` file should be in the build path, as shown in the following screenshot:

# Method Interception

In this section we shall discuss the method interceptor mechanism provided by the Spring AOP framework.

# Creating a Spring bean class

First we need to create a Spring bean, which is an object managed, instantiated, and configured by Spring Framework. We shall create a JavaBean class for the Spring bean. The JavaBean object implements a journal catalog with properties representing the catalog's journal name, publisher, edition, title, and author. The bean class also provides accessor methods for the bean properties. We need to create an interface, `CatalogInterface`, for the bean class. Select the project node and select **File | New | Other**. In the **New** wizard select **Java | Interface** and click on **Next**. Specify a package name (`spring.catalog`) in the **Package** field and an interface name (`CatalogInterface`) in the **Name** field and click on **Finish**, as shown in the following screenshot:

A `spring.catalog.CatalogInterface` interface gets added to the `src` folder. The `CatalogInterface.java` interface is listed, as follows:

```
package spring.catalog;

public interface CatalogInterface {

    public void setJournal(String journal);

    public String getJournal();

    public void setPublisher(String publisher);

    public String getPublisher();

    public void setEdition(String edition);

    public String getEdition();

    public void setTitle(String title);

    public String getTitle();

    public void setAuthor(String author);

    public String getAuthor();

}
```

Next add the bean class `Catalog.java`, which implements the interface. Select **File | New** and select **Java | Class** in **New** and click on **Next**. In the **New Java Class** dialog box specify the package name (`spring.catalog`) in the **Package** field and the class name (`Catalog`) in the **Name** field, and select **spring.catalog.CatalogInterface** as the interface to implement. Click on **Finish**, as follows:

The `spring.catalog.Catalog.java` class gets added to the web project.

In the Spring bean class provide implementation for the accessor methods for the bean properties. Also add a test method, `getTestMessage()` that returns a `String` message. The `Catalog.java` class is listed, as follows:

```
package spring.catalog;

public class Catalog implements CatalogInterface {

  private String journal;
  private String publisher;
  private String edition;
  private String title;
  private String author;


public Catalog(){}
  public Catalog(String journal, String publisher, String edition,
      String title, String author) {

    this.journal = journal;
    this.publisher = publisher;
    this.edition = edition;
    this.title = title;
    this.author = author;
  }

  public String getAuthor() {

    return author;
  }

  public String getEdition() {

    return edition;
  }

  public String getJournal() {

    return journal;
  }

  public String getPublisher() {

    return publisher;
  }

  public String getTitle() {
```

```
      return title;
   }

   public void setAuthor(String author) {

      this.author = author;

   }

   public void setEdition(String edition) {

      this.edition = edition;

   }

   public void setJournal(String journal) {

      this.journal = journal;

   }

   public void setPublisher(String publisher) {

      this.publisher = publisher;

   }

   public void setTitle(String title) {

      this.title = title;

   }

   public String getTestMessage() {
      return "Spring Bean Test";
   }

}
```

# Creating a bean definition file

In this section we will create a Spring bean definition file, `beanDefinition.xml`, to configure the Spring bean, the `Catalog` JavaBean, with Spring Framework. The name of the bean definition file is arbitrary, but the bean definition file must conform the Spring XML Schema `http://www.springframework.org/schema/beans`. The root element of `beanDefinition.xml` is `beans` and each of the `bean` sub-elements represent a Spring bean. We shall register the following three beans with the bean configuration file:

- The Catalog JavaBean
- An interceptor bean
- A proxy bean

We shall discuss the three beans in more detail in latter sections. Select the project node in the **Project Explorer** tab to create a bean configuration file and select **File | New | Other**. In the **New** dialog box select **Spring Bean Configuration File** under **Spring** and click on **Next**, as shown in the following screenshot:

In the **New Spring Bean Definition file** dialog box select the project folder, specify beanDefinition.xml as **File name**, and click on **Next**, as shown in the following screenshot:

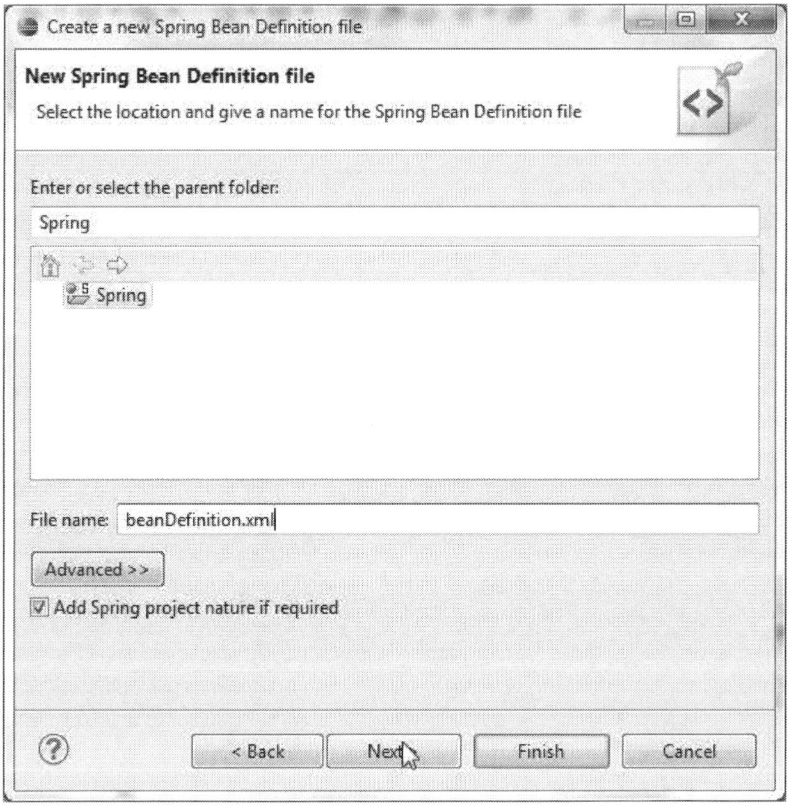

In the dialog box for selecting XSD namespaces select **http://www.springframework. org/schema/beans/spring-beans-2.5.xsd** and click on **Next**, as shown in the following screenshot:

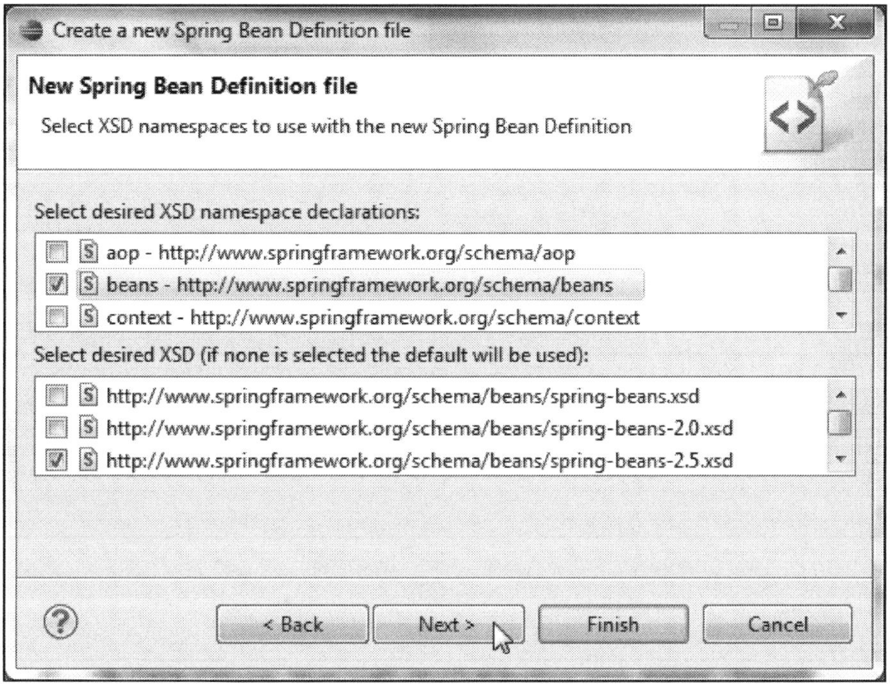

In the **Select Bean Config Sets to add the new Spring Bean definition to** dialog
box click on **Finish**. A Spring bean definition file, **beanDefinition.xml,** gets created,
as shown in the following screenshot. We need to add a <bean> element for each
of the beans to be registered with Spring Framework. Add a bracket (<) within the
element and in the pop-up window select **< > bean**, as follows:

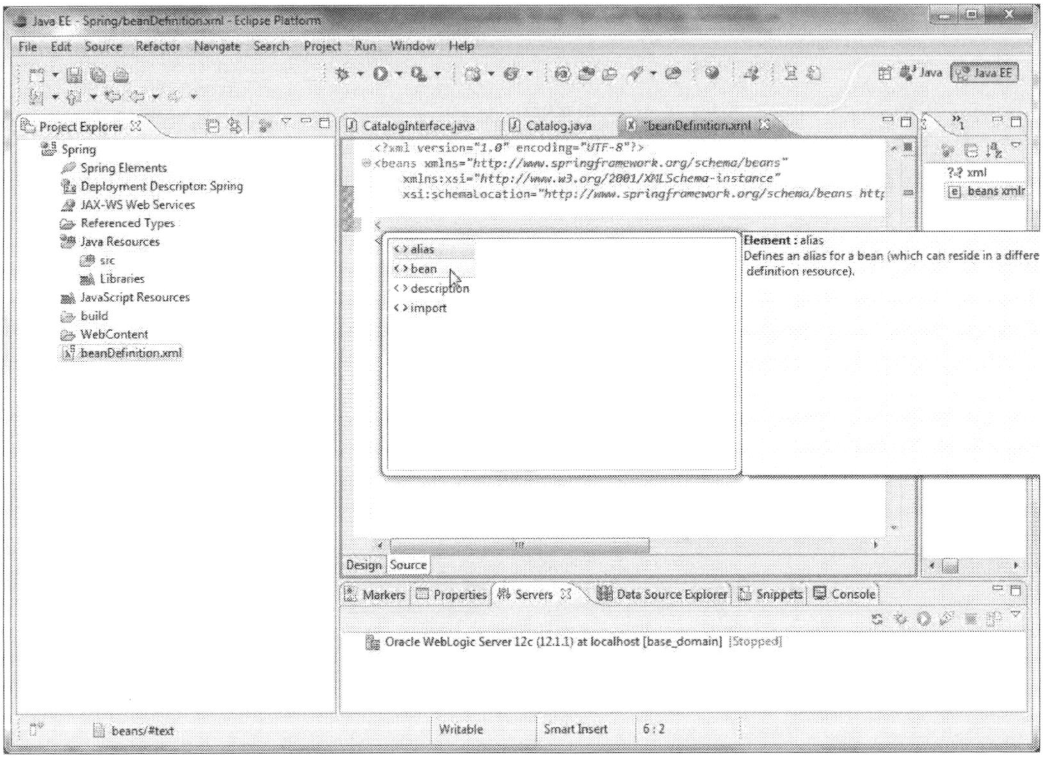

A element gets added, as shown in the following screenshot:

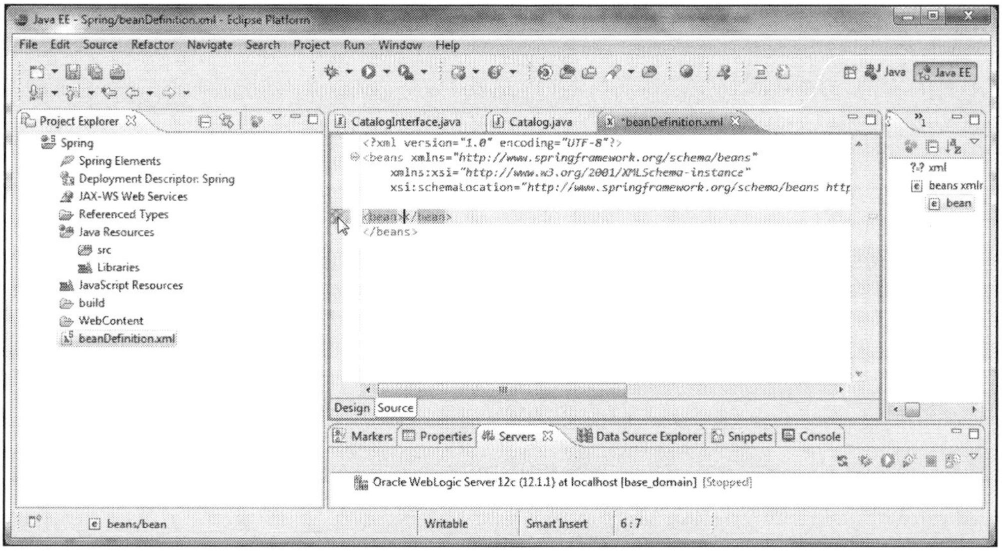

Next add an `id` attribute to the `<bean>` element. Select the **Design** tab, right-click on **bean**, and select **Add Attribute | id**, as shown in the following screenshot:

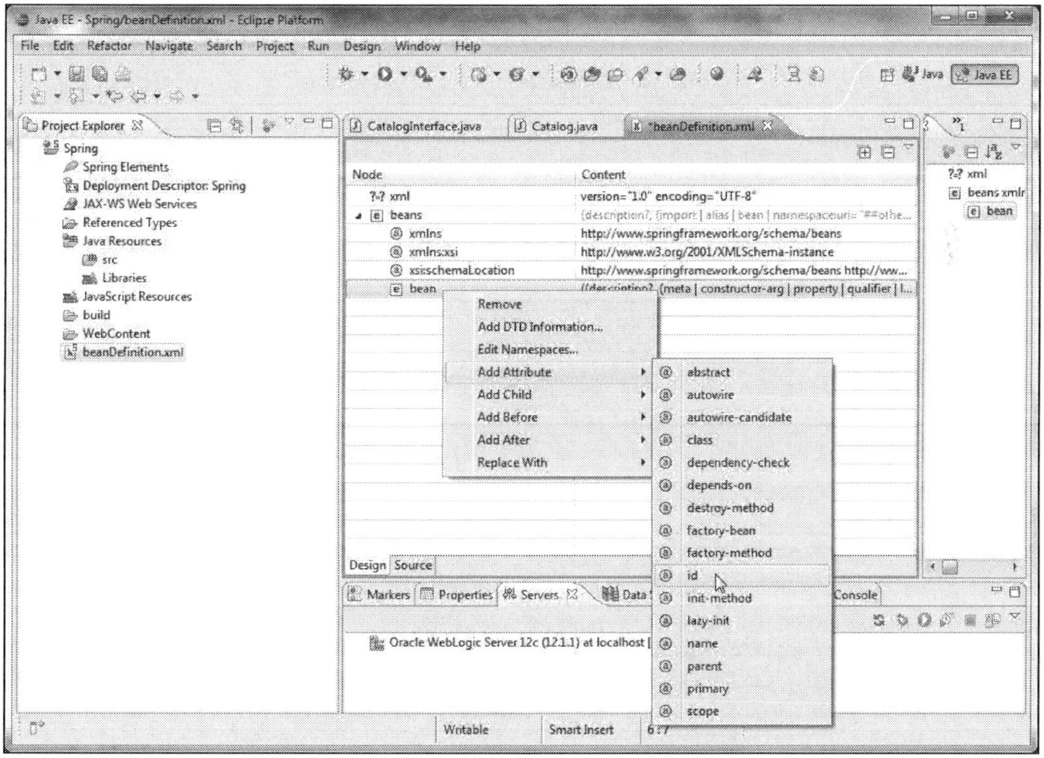

An **id** attribute gets added to the **bean** element. Specify `spring.catalog` as the **id** attribute's value, as follows:

| Node | Content |
|------|---------|
| ?-? xml | version="1.0" encoding="UTF-8" |
| ▲ [e] beans | (description?, (import \| alias \| bean \| namespace:uri="##othe... |
| ⓐ xmlns | http://www.springframework.org/schema/beans |
| ⓐ xmlns:xsi | http://www.w3.org/2001/XMLSchema-instance |
| ⓐ xsi:schemaLocation | http://www.springframework.org/schema/beans http://ww... |
| ▲ [e] bean | ((description?, (meta \| constructor-arg \| property \| qualifier \| l... |
| ⓐ id | spring.catalog |

Right-click on **bean** and select **Add Attribute | class**. Specify `spring.catalog.`
`Catalog` as the `catalog` attribute's value. Right-click on the **beans** element and select **Add Child | bean**, once each for the interceptor bean and the proxy bean. Similar to constructing the `bean` element for the `Catalog` class, construct `bean` elements for an interceptor bean and a proxy bean. The following table lists the beans to add:

| bean | id | class |
|------|-----|-------|
| Catalog JavaBean | `spring.catalog` | `spring.catalog.Catalog` |
| Interceptor bean | `interceptor` | `spring.catalog.CatalogInterceptor` |
| Proxy bean | `proxyBean` | `org.springframework.aop.framework.`<br>`ProxyFactoryBean` |

The bean definition file with the beans added is shown in the **Design** view, as follows:

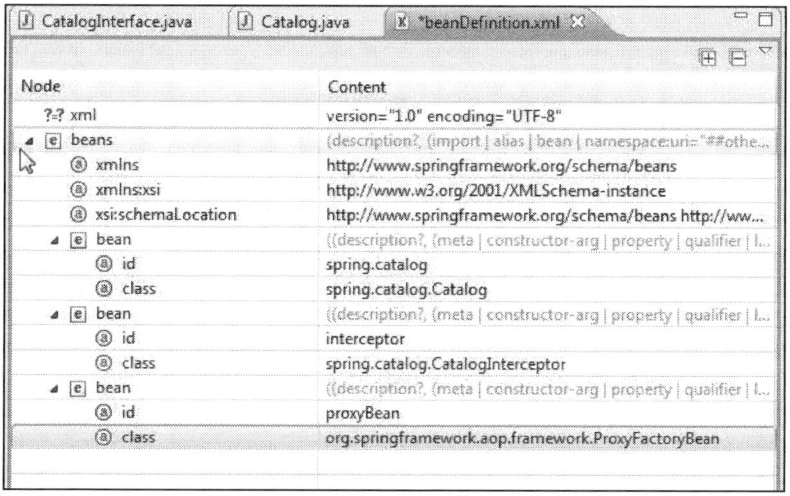

To add a property right-click on the bean with ID as **proxyBean** and select **Add Child | property**, as shown in the following screenshot:

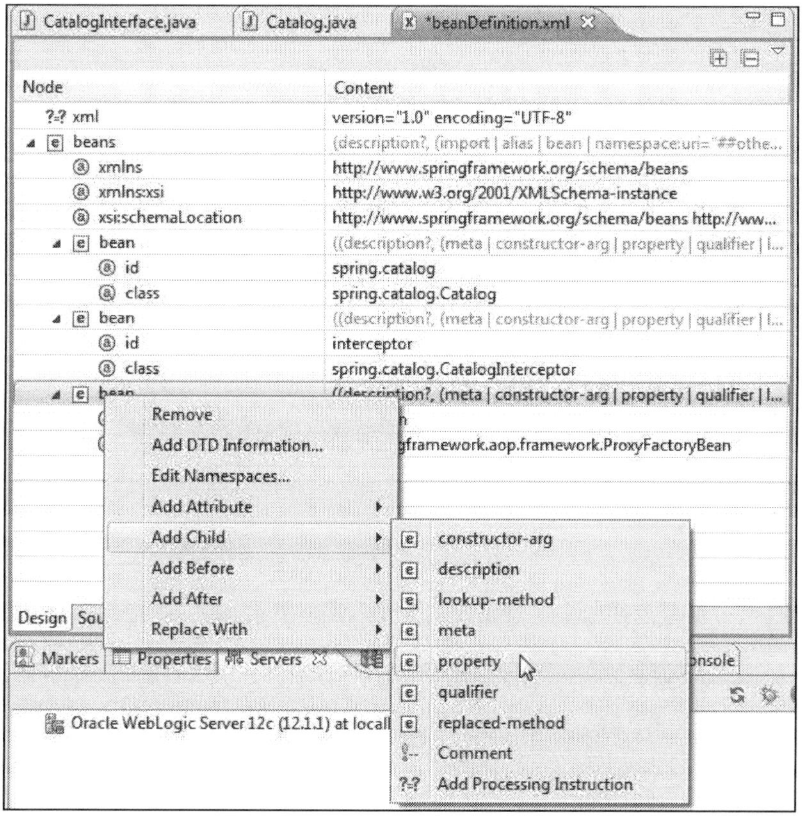

Specify `interceptorNames` as the property name. To add a `<list>` value right-click on property and select **Add Child | list**, as shown in the following screenshot:

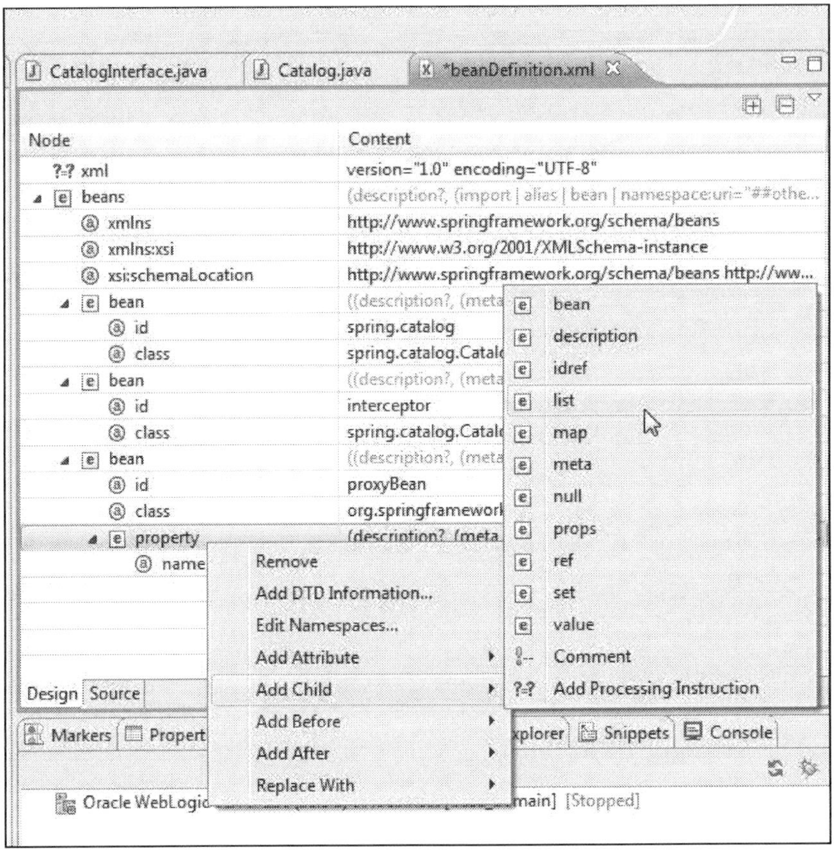

To add a `<value>` element to the `<list>` element right-click on list and select **Add Child | value**, as shown in the following screenshot:

| Node | Content |
|---|---|
| ?-? xml | version="1.0" encoding="UTF-8" |
| ▲ ⓔ beans | (description?, (import \| alias \| bean \| namespace:uri= "##othe... |
| ⓐ xmlns | http://www.springframework.org/schema/beans |
| ⓐ xmlns:xsi | http://www.w3.org/2001/XMLSchema-instance |
| ⓐ xsi:schemaLocation | http://www.springframework.org/schema/beans http://ww... |
| ▲ ⓔ bean | ((description?, (meta \| constructor-arg \| property \| qualifier \| l... |
| ⓐ id | spring.catalog |
| ⓐ class | spring.catalog.Catalog |
| ▲ ⓔ bean | ((description? ... |
| ⓐ id | interceptor |
| ⓐ class | spring.catalog |
| ▲ ⓔ bean | ((description? ... |
| ⓐ id | proxyBean |
| ⓐ class | org.springfra... |
| ▲ ⓔ property | (description?, ... |
| ⓐ name | interceptorNa... |
| ⓔ list | ((description? ... |

Context menu items:

| | |
|---|---|
| ⓔ | bean |
| ⓔ | description |
| ⓔ | idref |
| ⓔ | list |
| ⓔ | map |
| ⓔ | null |
| ⓔ | props |
| ⓔ | ref |
| ⓔ | set |
| ⓔ | value |
| ⌄⌄ | Comment |
| ?-? | Add Processing Instruction |

Right-click menu:

- Remove
- Add DTD Information...
- Edit Namespaces...
- Add Attribute ▸
- Add Child ▸
- Add Before ▸
- Add After ▸
- Replace With ▸

Design | Source

Markers

Oracle We ... ase_domain] [Stopped]

For the **interceptorName** property specify `interceptor` as the list value. Similarly, add the **proxyInterfaces** and **target** properties. Specify `spring.catalog.` `CatalogInterface` as the value for **proxyInterfaces**. The **target** property requires a **ref** sub-element. Right-click on property and select **Add Child | ref**, as shown in the following screenshot:

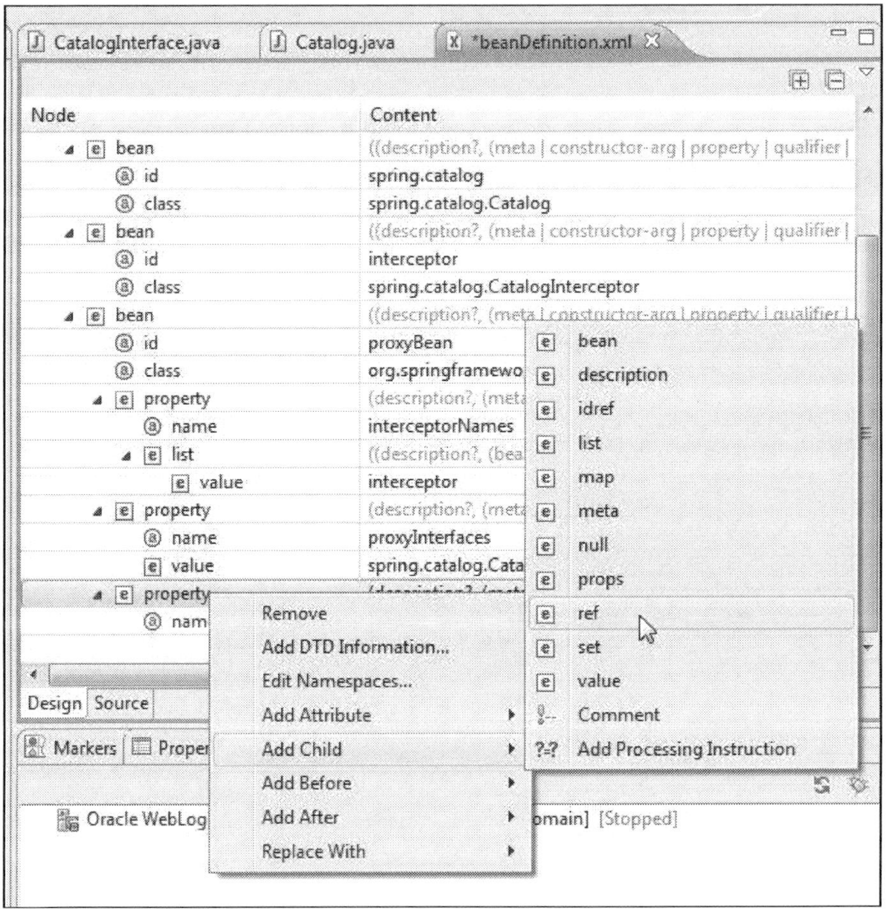

To the **ref** element we need to add the local attribute. Right-click on **ref** and select **Add Attribute | local**, as shown in the following screenshot:

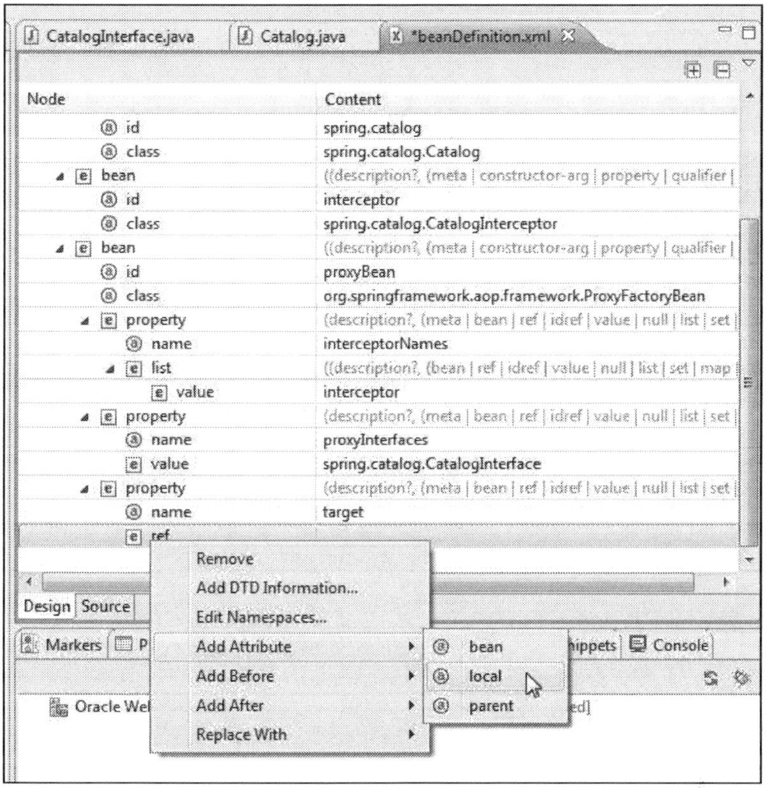

Specify `spring.catalog` as the value of the **ref** attribute. Add another property to **proxyBean** called **proxyTargetClass** and set its value to **true**. The properties of **proxyBean** are shown in the following screenshot:

To the bean for JavaBean `Catalog` add `constructor-arg` sub-elements for arguments to the constructor for the JavaBean. The constructor has parameters for journal, publisher, edition, title, and author, as follows:

```
<constructor-arg index="0" value="Oracle Magazine" />
<constructor-arg index="1" value="Oracle Publishing" />
<constructor-arg index="2" value="November-December 2010" />
<constructor-arg index="3" value="Agile Architecture" />
<constructor-arg index="4" value="Bob Rhubart" />
```

The bean properties' values may also be specified as `property/value`. The `property/value` alternative is essentially the same as `constructor-arg` and is recommended if the `property` value has a lot of characters to escape, which may be accomplished using a CDATA section; a CDATA section is only available in an element, and not in an attribute.

```
<property name="journal">
    <value>Oracle Magazine</value>
  </property>
  <property name="publisher">
    <value>Oracle Publishing</value>
  </property>
  <property name="edition">
    <value>November-December 2010</value>
  </property>
  <property name="title">
    <value>Agile Enterprise Architecture</value>
  </property>

  <property name="author">
    <value>Bob Rhubart</value>
</property>
```

The bean definition file is listed, as follows:

```
<?xml version="1.0" encoding="UTF-8"?>
<beans xmlns="http://www.springframework.org/schema/beans"
  xmlns:xsi="http://www.w3.org/2001/XMLSchema-instance"
xmlns:aop="http://www.springframework.org/schema/aop"
  xsi:schemaLocation="http://www.springframework.org/schema/beans
http://www.springframework.org/schema/beans/spring-beans-2.5.xsd
http://www.springframework.org/schema/aop http://www.springframework.
org/schema/aop/spring-aop-2.5.xsd">
  <bean id="spring.catalog" class="spring.catalog.Catalog">
    <constructor-arg index="0" value="Oracle Magazine" />
    <constructor-arg index="1" value="Oracle Publishing" />
    <constructor-arg index="2" value="November-December 2010" />
    <constructor-arg index="3" value="Agile Architecture" />
    <constructor-arg index="4" value="Bob Rhubart" />
  </bean>
  <bean id="interceptor" class="spring.catalog.CatalogInterceptor"></
bean>

  <bean id="proxyBean" class="org.springframework.aop.framework.
ProxyFactoryBean">
    <property name="proxyInterfaces">
      <value>spring.catalog.CatalogInterface</value>
    </property>
    <property name="interceptorNames">
      <list>
        <value>interceptor</value>
```

```
        </list>
      </property>

      <property name="target">
        <ref local="spring.catalog"></ref>
      </property>
      <property name="proxyTargetClass">
        <value>true</value>
      </property>
    </bean>
  </beans>
```

# Creating a method interceptor

The `org.aopalliance.intercept.MethodInterceptor` interface is used to intercept calls on an interface prior to the target. In order to modify the behavior of a method, the interceptor bean class should implement the interface and implement the `invoke(MethodInvocation)` method of the interface. Create an interceptor Java class, `CatalogInterceptor`, that implements the `MethodInterceptor` interface in the `spring.catalog` package. Select the **MethodInterceptor** interface with the **Add...** button, as shown in the following screenshot:

**CatalogInterceptor.java** gets added to the **Spring** project, as shown in the following screenshot:

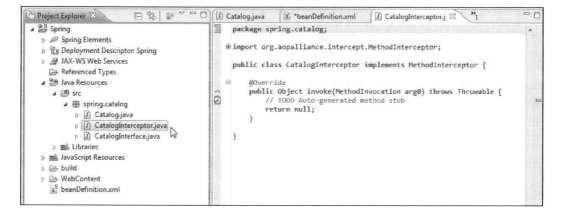

In the `invoke()` method we obtain the name of the intercepted method and the name of the class containing the intercepted method as output. The `CatalogInterceptor` method is listed, as follows:

```java
package spring.catalog;

import org.aopalliance.intercept.MethodInterceptor;
import org.aopalliance.intercept.MethodInvocation;

public class CatalogInterceptor implements MethodInterceptor {

  @Override
  public Object invoke(MethodInvocation inv) throws Throwable {

    System.out.println("Intercepted method - "
        + inv.getMethod().getDeclaringClass()

        + " - " + inv.getMethod().getName());

    return null;
}}
```

# Creating a Spring client

In this section we will create a Java client for the Spring bean and invoke the bean's method. We instantiate the Spring bean that represents the `spring.catalog.Catalog` JavaBean and invoke its method. Subsequently, we instantiate the proxy bean `proxyBean`, which is configured with an interceptor. We invoke the methods of the target class to demonstrate that the method interceptor intercepts the method calls and outputs the method name and the name of the containing class. Select **File | New** and in the **New** wizard select **Java | Class** to create a Spring client class, `SpringClient`, in the same package as the JavaBean and the interceptor class.

The `JavaClient` class gets added. Right-click on the project in the **Project Explorer** tab and select **Properties**. In **Properties** select **Java Build Path**. Add external JARs, **asm-3.3.jar** and **cglib-2.2.jar,** to the **Java Build Path** window, as shown in the following screenshot:

We will create two versions of the `SpringClient.java` class. In the first version we instantiate the `Catalog` JavaBean and invoke its methods without the method interceptor. Instantiate the `Catalog` bean using the `<constructor-arg >` elements or `property/value` in `beanDefinition.xml`, as discussed earlier. Add a `loadContext()` method to instantiate the Spring container. Create an `ApplicationContext` class in the `loadContext()` method from the `beanDefinition.xml` file using the constructor for `FileSystemXmlApplicationContext` that takes a bean definition XML file, as follows:

```
private void loadContext() {
    String filename = "beanDefinition.xml";
    context = new FileSystemXmlApplicationContext(filename);
}
```

In the `main` method create an instance of the `SpringClient` class and invoke the `loadContext` method, as follows:

```
SpringClient client = new SpringClient();
client.loadContext();
```

Instantiate the JavaBean with the `spring.catalog` ID using the `getBean` method:

```
Catalog catalog = (Catalog) context.getBean("spring.catalog");
```

Output the bean properties' values, as follows:

```
System.out.println(catalog.journal);
System.out.println(catalog.publisher);
System.out.println(catalog.edition);
System.out.println(catalog.title);
System.out.println(catalog.author);
```

Invoke the `getTestMessage()` method and output the returned message, as follows:

```
String test = catalog.getTestMessage();
    System.out.println(test);
```

The `SpringClient.java` class is listed, as follows:

```
package spring.catalog;

import org.springframework.context.ApplicationContext;
import org.springframework.context.support.
FileSystemXmlApplicationContext;


public class SpringClient {

  private static ApplicationContext context;

  /**
   * Load up the Spring container
   */

  private void loadContext() {
    String filename = "beanDefinition.xml";
    context = new FileSystemXmlApplicationContext(filename);
  }

  public static void main(String[] args) {

      SpringClient client = new SpringClient();
      client.loadContext();
      //getBean spring.catalog Interceptor method not invoked.
```

```
Catalog catalog = (Catalog) context.getBean("spring.catalog");

System.out.println(catalog.journal);
  System.out.println(catalog.publisher);
  System.out.println(catalog.edition);
  System.out.println(catalog.title);
  System.out.println(catalog.author);

String test = catalog.getTestMessage();
System.out.println(test);


  }
}
```

Right-click on the **SpringClient.java** application and select **Run As | Java Application**, as shown in the following screenshot:

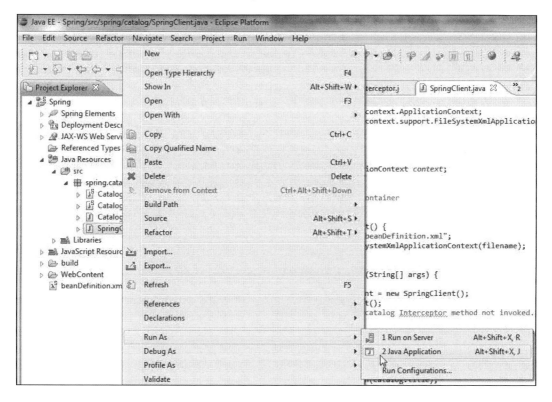

As the `Catalog` JavaBean is not configured with a method interceptor, the method calls do not get intercepted and the values returned by the accessor methods get output, as shown in the following screenshot:

```
Markers | Properties | Servers | Data Source Explorer | Snippets | Console ⅩⅩ
<terminated> SpringClient [Java Application] C:\Oracle\Middleware\jdk160_29\bin\javaw.exe (2012-09-29 1:01:42 PM)

29-Sep-2012 1:01:49 PM org.springframework.context.support.AbstractApplicationContext prepare
INFO: Refreshing org.springframework.context.support.FileSystemXmlApplicationContext@ecd7e: d
29-Sep-2012 1:01:49 PM org.springframework.beans.factory.xml.XmlBeanDefinitionReader loadBean
INFO: Loading XML bean definitions from file [C:\Users\dvohra\workspace\Spring\beanDefinition
29-Sep-2012 1:01:49 PM org.springframework.context.support.AbstractApplicationContext obtainF
INFO: Bean factory for application context [org.springframework.context.support.FileSystemXmL
29-Sep-2012 1:01:49 PM org.springframework.beans.factory.support.DefaultListableBeanFactory p
INFO: Pre-instantiating singletons in org.springframework.beans.factory.support.DefaultListab
Oracle Magazine
Oracle Publishing
November-December 2010
Agile Architecture
Bob Rhubart
Spring Bean Test
```

In the second version of the `SpringClient` application we shall instantiate the proxy bean that is configured with the interceptor method. We shall reference the proxy through the Spring container. Create a `XmlBeanFactory` object, as follows:

```
XmlBeanFactory beanFactory = new XmlBeanFactory(new ClassPathResource(
   "beanDefinition.xml"));
```

Instantiate the proxy bean with the `getBean` method, as follows:

```
Catalog catalog = (Catalog) beanFactory.getBean("proxyBean");
```

Invoke the `getTestMessage` method and output the value returned:

```
String test = catalog.getTestMessage();
   System.out.println(test);
```

Invoke the setter methods to set the values of the bean properties, as follows:

```
catalog.setJournal("Oracle Magazine");
catalog.setPublisher("Oracle Publishing");
catalog.setEdition("November-December 2010");
catalog.setTitle("Agile Enterprise Architecture");
catalog.setAuthor("Bob Rhubart");
```

Output the bean properties. `SpringClient.java` is listed, as follows:

```
package spring.catalog;

import org.springframework.beans.factory.xml.XmlBeanFactory;
import org.springframework.core.io.ClassPathResource;

public class SpringClient {

  public static void main(String[] args) {

    // reference the proxy through the Spring container

      //getBean proxyBean Interceptor method invoked.


  /** * Load up the Spring container
     */
  XmlBeanFactory beanFactory = new XmlBeanFactory(new ClassPathResource(
  "beanDefinition.xml"));


   //getBean proxyBean Interceptor method invoked.

    Catalog catalog = (Catalog) beanFactory.getBean("proxyBean");

    String test = catalog.getTestMessage();
    System.out.println(test);

catalog.setJournal("Oracle Magazine");
catalog.setPublisher("Oracle Publishing");
catalog.setEdition("November-December 2010");
catalog.setTitle("Agile Enterprise Architecture");
catalog.setAuthor("Bob Rhubart");
    System.out.println(catalog.journal);
      System.out.println(catalog.publisher);
      System.out.println(catalog.edition);
      System.out.println(catalog.title);
      System.out.println(catalog.author);


  }
}
```

Right-click on **SpringClient.java** and select **Run As | Java Application**. As the proxy bean is configured with the interceptor method, the method invocations get intercepted. The invoke method of the `CatalogInterceptor` class gets invoked. The method name and the name of the containing class are obtained as output. The bean properties' values do not get output as the method invocations are intercepted:

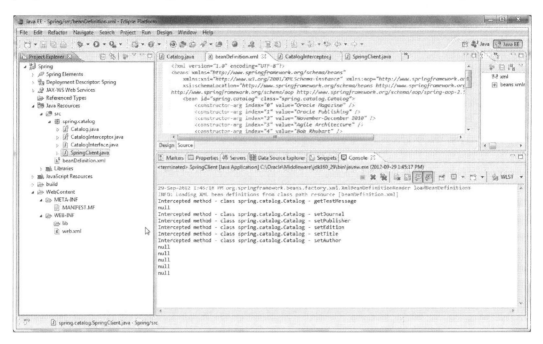

# Schema-based aspect definitions

Spring Framework supports aspect-oriented programming in which modularity is provided via an aspect. An **aspect** is just a function such as logging or caching. Spring implements AOP with schema-based aspect definitions using the `aop` namespace. Alternatively, AOP may be implemented declaratively using the `@Aspect` annotation from AspectJ. We use the `aop` namespace to implement Spring AOP in this section.

We develop a web application consisting of a JSF page for user input, and `applicationContext.xml` to create `BeanFactory` and `ApplicationContext`. Some of the `aop` namespace tags are discussed in the following table and explained with a demonstration in a latter section:

| Tag | Description |
| --- | --- |
| aop:aspectj-autoproxy | Enables @AspectJ aspects in Spring with autoproxying beans. |
| aop:config | All aspects and advisors must be declared within aop:config. |
| aop:pointcut | Declares a pointcut. |
| aop:aspect | Declares an aspect. |
| aop:after-returning | Declares advice that runs after matched method execution completes normally. |
| aop:after-throwing | Declares advice that runs after matched method execution exits by throwing an exception. |
| aop:advisor | Declares an advisor. |
| aop:before | Declares advice that runs before matched method execution. |
| aop:after | Declares advice that runs no matter how the matched method execution exits. |

Create a web project, `SpringJSF`, for the Spring AOP similar to the Spring project that we created for the method interceptor example. Add the **Spring** project facet to the web project. Also add the **JSF** project facet. The subsequent sections apply to the `SpringJSF` project.

# Creating a Spring and JSF faceted web project

Select **Web | Dynamic Web Project** in the **New** wizard. In **New Dynamic Web Project** specify SpringJSF as **Project name**, and configure a target runtime for **Oracle WebLogic Server 12c (12.1.1)**. Click on **Next**. Select the default Java settings; source folder as src and output folder as build/classes. Click on **Next**. Specify **Context root** (SpringJSF) and **Content directory**, check the **Generate web.xml deployment descriptor** checkbox, and click on **Finish**. A **SpringJSF** project gets created. Right-click on the **SpringJSF** project and select **Project Properties**. In **Properties** for **SpringJSF** select the **JavaServer Faces 1.2** and **Spring 2.5** project facets. Click on the **Further configuration available...** button:

| Project Facets | | |
|---|---|---|
| Configuration: `<custom>` | | |
| **Project Facet** | **Version** | |
| ☐   Apache XMLBeans | | |
| ☐   Axis2 Web Services | | |
| ☐   CXF 2.x Web Services | 1.0 | |
| ☑   Dynamic Web Module | 2.5 | ▾ |
| ☑   Java | 1.6 | ▾ |
| ☐   Java Annotation Processing Support | 5.0 | |
| ☑   JavaScript | 1.0 | |
| ☑   JavaServer Faces | 1.2 | ▾ |
| ☐   JAX-RS (REST Web Services) | 1.1 | ▾ |
| ☐   JAXB | 2.1 | ▾ |
| ☐   JPA | 2.0 | ▾ |
| ☐   JSTL | 1.2 | ▾ |
| ☐   Oracle Coherence | 3.7.1 | ▾ |
| ☐   Oracle WebLogic SCA | 12.1.1 | |
| ☐   Oracle WebLogic Scripting Tools (WLST) Support | 12.1.1 | ▾ |
| ☐   Oracle WebLogic Web App Extensions | 12.1.1 | ▾ |
| ☐   Oracle WebLogic Web Service Clients | 2.1 | |
| ☐   Oracle WebLogic Web Services | 2.1 | |
| ☑   Spring | 2.5 | ▾ |
| ☐   Struts | 1.3 | ▾ |
| ☐   Trinidad | 1.2 | ▾ |
| ☐   WebDoclet (XDoclet) | 1.2.3 | ▾ |

ⓘ   Further configuration available...

In **JSF Capabilites** select **User Library** as **Type** under **JSF Implementation Library** and click on the **Download Library** button, as shown in the following screenshot:

Select the **JSF 1.2 (Mojarra JSF API Implementation 1.2_15-b01-FCS)** library to download and click on **Next**, as follows:

The JSF 1.2 library gets added to the faceted project. Select the **JSF 1.2 (Mojarra JSF API Implementation 1.2_15-b01-FCS)** and **Spring Framework 2.5.6** libraries. Check the **Include libraries with this application** checkbox. Check the **Configure JSF servlet in deployment descriptor** checkbox. Click on **Next**, as shown in the following screenshot:

Next configure the project to use Spring Framework. Select the **Spring Framework 2.5.6** library if not already selected. Check the **Create a Spring bean definition file** checkbox. Click on **OK**, as shown in the following screenshot:

In **Project Facets** the Spring and JavaServer Faces project facets are shown configured. Click on Apply. Click on OK.

A Spring and JSF faceted web project gets created. The JSF and Spring libraries are shown added to the project:

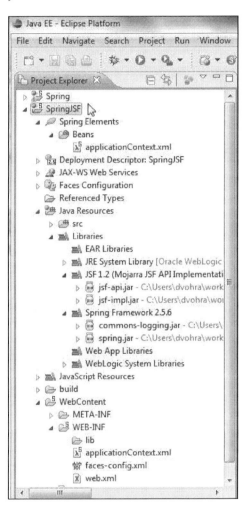

The Spring AOP framework requires the AspectJ library in the classpath. Add the AspectJ library and dependencies shown in the following screenshot to the **Java Build Path** window:

**Java Build Path**

| Source | Projects | Libraries | Order and Export |

JARs and class folders on the build path:

- ▷ asm-3.3.jar - C:\Spring
- ▷ aspectjrt.jar - C:\aspectj1.7\lib
- ▷ aspectjtools.jar - C:\aspectj1.7\lib
- ▷ aspectjweaver.jar - C:\aspectj1.7\lib
- ▷ cglib-2.2.jar - C:\Spring
- ▷ org.aspectj.matcher.jar - C:\aspectj1.7\lib
- ▷ EAR Libraries
- ▷ JRE System Library [Oracle WebLogic Server 12c (12.1.1) JRE]
- ▷ JSF 1.2 (Mojarra JSF API Implementation 1.2_15-b01-FCS)
- ▲ Spring Framework 2.5.6
    - Access rules: No rules defined
    - Native library location: (None)
    - Publish/export dependency: /WEB-INF/lib
    - ▷ commons-logging.jar - C:\Users\dvohra\workspace\libraries\Spring Framework 2.5.6\spring-framework-2.5.6\dist\
    - ▷ spring.jar - C:\Users\dvohra\workspace\libraries\Spring Framework 2.5.6\spring-framework-2.5.6\dist
- ▷ Web App Libraries
- ▷ WebLogic System Libraries

# Creating a bean class

In this section we will create a JavaBean that we configure as a Spring bean and use in a pointcut expression. Create a Java class, `Catalog.java`, by selecting **Java | Class** in the **New** wizard.

To the `Catalog.java` JavaBean add properties for journal, publisher, edition, title, and author. Also add accessor methods for the JavaBean properties. The getter accessor methods should return the initial values for the bean properties. As we require `StringBuffer` for the `after-returning-advice` pointcut expression and not a string, we used the `StringBuffer` constructor. To return a value from the getter methods, the `Catalog` JavaBean's properties may alternatively be instantiated using `property/value` or `constructor-arg` in `applicationContext.xml`.

The JavaBean class, `Catalog.java`, is listed, as follows:

```
package spring.catalog;

public class Catalog {

  private String journal;
  private String publisher;
  private String edition;
  private String title;
  priavte String author;

  public Catalog() {
  }

  public Catalog(String journal, String publisher, String edition,
      String title, String author) {

    this.journal = journal;
    this.publisher = publisher;
    this.edition = edition;
    this.title = title;
    this.author = author;
  }

  public java.lang.StringBuffer getAuthor() {

    return new StringBuffer("Bob Rhubart");
  }

  public java.lang.StringBuffer getEdition() {



    return new StringBuffer("November-December 2010");
  }

  public java.lang.StringBuffer getJournal() {

    return new StringBuffer("Oracle Magazine");
  }

  public java.lang.StringBuffer getPublisher() {
```

```
        return new StringBuffer("Oracle Publishing");
    }

    public java.lang.StringBuffer getTitle() {

        return new StringBuffer("Agile Enterprise Architecture");
    }

    public void setAuthor(String author) {

      this.author = author;

    }

    public void setEdition(String edition) {

      this.edition = edition;

    }

    public void setJournal(String journal) {

      this.journal = journal;

    }

    public void setPublisher(String publisher) {

      this.publisher = publisher;

    }

    public void setTitle(String title) {

      this.title = title;

    }

}
```

# Creating an AOP JavaBean

In this section we create a JavaBean that we configure with Spring Framework in `applicationContext.xml` as a Spring AOP aspect. Select **File | New** and in the **New** wizard select **Java | Class**. Create a Java class, `CatalogAOP.java`, in the same package as the `Catalog.java` JavaBean.

The pointcut expression is used to match join points and the advice is the action taken by the aspect. The aspect's pointcut expression and the aspect's advice type are configured in `applicationContext.xml` in the next section. We configure the `aop:after-returning` advice for each of the getter methods in the `Catalog` Spring bean which returns values for bean properties as `SpringBuffer`. In the advice we invoke the setter methods of the Spring aspect bean, `CatalogAOP.java`, with the values returned by the getter methods of the `Catalog` JavaBean as arguments. The Spring AOP framework invokes the setter methods of the Spring aspect bean, `CatalogAOP`, dynamically after returning from the getter methods of the `Catalog` Spring bean. In the setter methods in the aspect bean we first output the bean property values returned by the `Catalog` bean prepended by the method name and subsequently modify the bean property values by adding labels to precede the bean properties. For example, the `setTitle(String title)` method modifies the `Catalog` JavaBean's `title` property by prepending it with `"Title: "`, as follows:

```
public void setTitle(StringBuffer title) {
    System.out.println("setTitle method invoked" + title);
    title.insert(0, "Title: ");
}
```

The `CatalogAOP.java` Spring AOP aspect is listed, as follows:

```
package spring.catalog;

public class CatalogAOP {

    private String journal;
    private String publisher;
    private String edition;
    private String title;
    private String author;

    public CatalogAOP() {
    }
```

```java
public CatalogAOP(String journal, String publisher, String edition,
    String title, String author) {

  this.journal = journal;
  this.publisher = publisher;
  this.edition = edition;
  this.title = title;
  this.author = author;
}

public String getAuthor() {

  return author;
}

public String getEdition() {

  return edition;
}

public String getJournal() {

  return journal;
}

public String getPublisher() {

  return publisher;
}

public String getTitle() {

  return title;
}



public void setEdition(StringBuffer edition) {
  System.out.println("setEdition method invoked" + edition);
  //edition.insert(0, "Edition: ");

}
```

```
     public void setJournal(StringBuffer journal) {
       System.out.println("setJournal method invoked" + journal);
       //journal.insert(0, "Journal: ");
     }

     public void setPublisher(StringBuffer publisher) {
       System.out.println("setPublisher method invoked" + publisher);
//     publisher.insert(0, "Publisher: ");


     }

     public void setTitle(StringBuffer title) {
       System.out.println("setTitle method invoked" + title);
//     title.insert(0, "Title: ");


     }
     public void setAuthor(StringBuffer author) {
       System.out.println("setAuthor method invoked" + author);
       //author.insert(0, "Author: ");
     }
   }
```

# Creating an applicationContext.xml configuration file

The Spring AOP including the pointcuts, aspects, and advice are configured in the Spring configuration file, WEB-INF/applicationContext.xml. For using the Spring AOP framework we need to enable AspectJ support. To enable the AspectJ support add the aop:aspectj-autoproxy element. Add < and select the **aop:aspectj-autoproxy** element from the pop-up window. First configure a Spring bean for the CatalogAOP JavaBean, which we subsequently configure as an aspect.

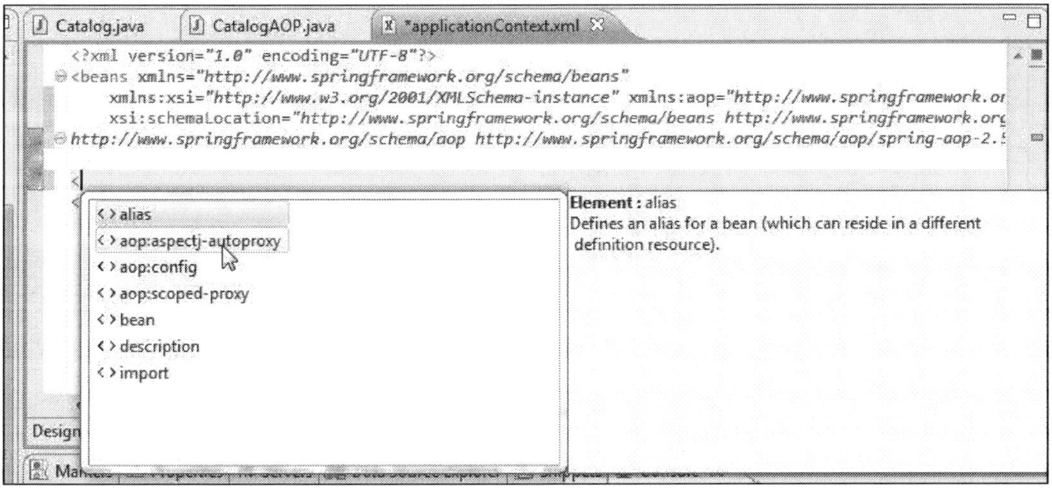

All aspects and advisors are declared within the `aop:config` element. Add a `<` character to add the `aop:config` element to the Spring configuration file and select the **aop:config** element from the pop-up window, as shown in the following screenshot:

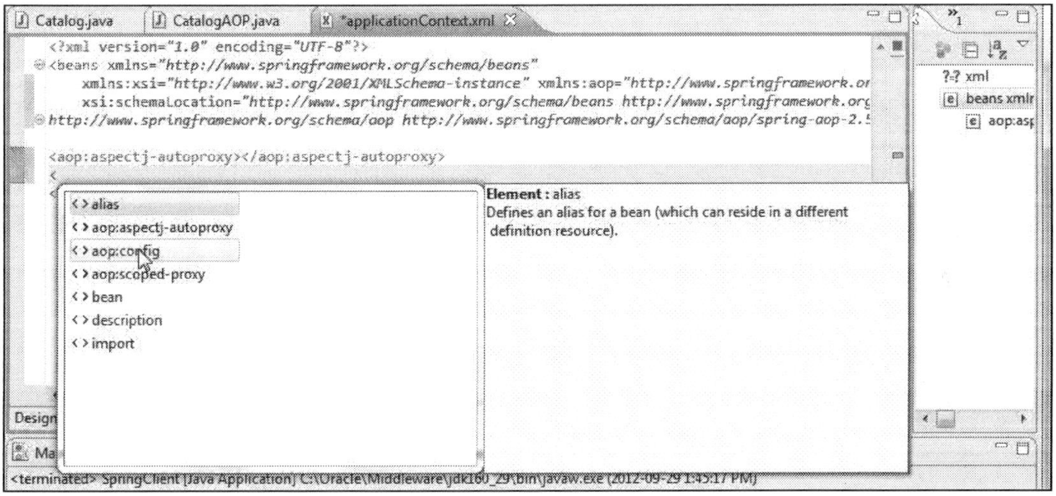

If the `target` object does not use any interfaces, Spring AOP uses CGLIB to create the proxy for the `target` object. Right-click on **aop:config** and **Add Attribute** and select **proxy-target-class** to specify the use of CGLIB to set the `proxy-target-class` attribute of `aop:config` to `true`.

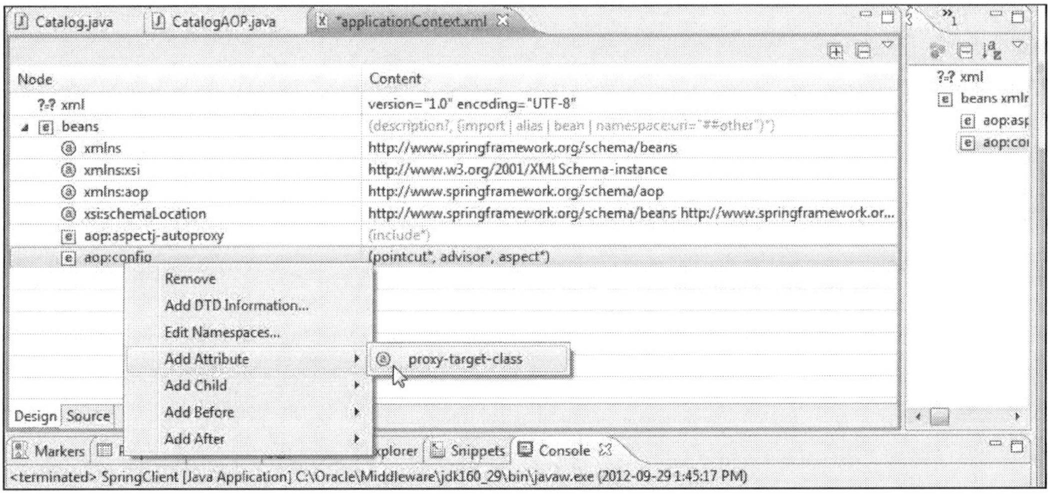

A pointcut is used to match join points. A join point in Spring AOP is a method execution. Next add a pointcut definition to the `aop:config` element; a pointcut definition within `aop:config` may be used for several aspects and advisors. We shall use the "bean" **pointcut designator (PCD)** to specify the `Catalog` Spring bean for matching join points. Right-click on **aop:config** and select **Add Child | pointcut**, as shown in the following screenshot:

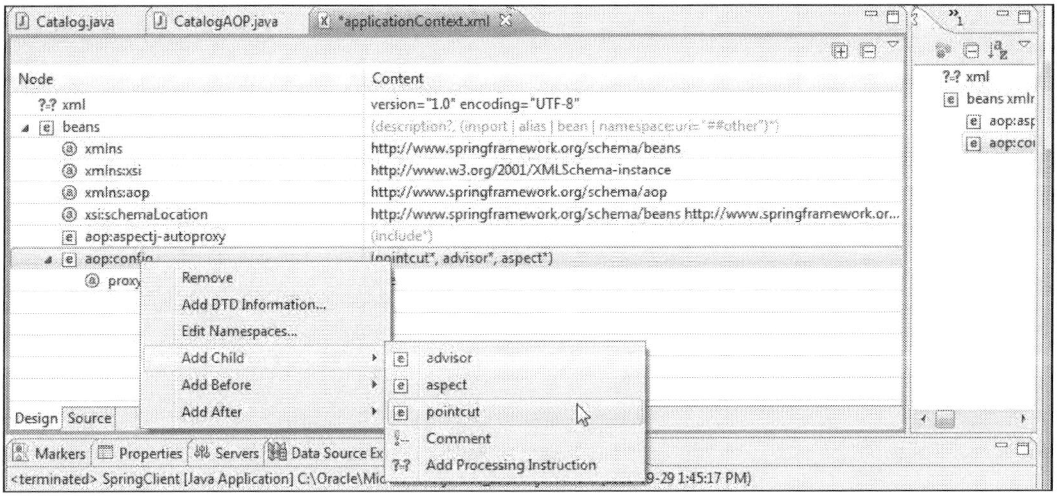

Specify the value of the **expression** attribute as **bean(CatalogBean)** and **catalogBeanPc** as **id**, as shown in the following screenshot:

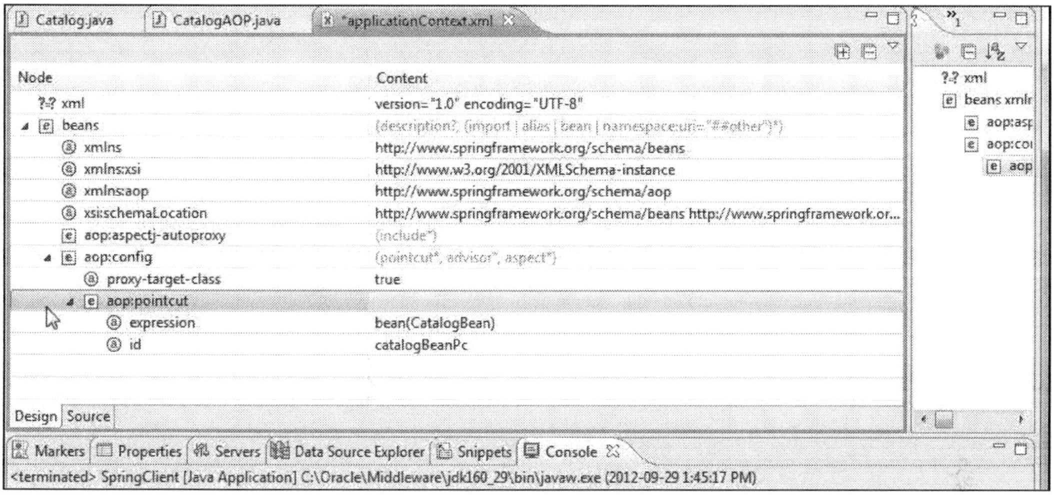

Next add an aspect. Right-click on **aop:config** and select **Add Child | aspect**, as follows:

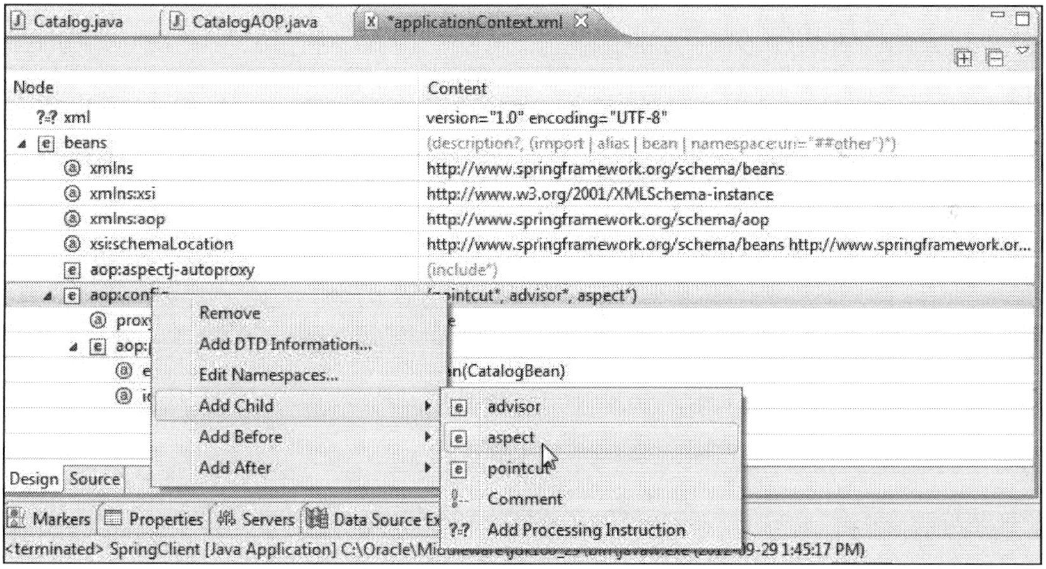

To the `aop:aspect` element add a `ref` attribute to refer to the `catalogBeanAOP`
Spring bean, which is the aspect Spring bean. Right-click on **aop:aspect** and select
**Add Attribute | ref**, as shown in the following screenshot:

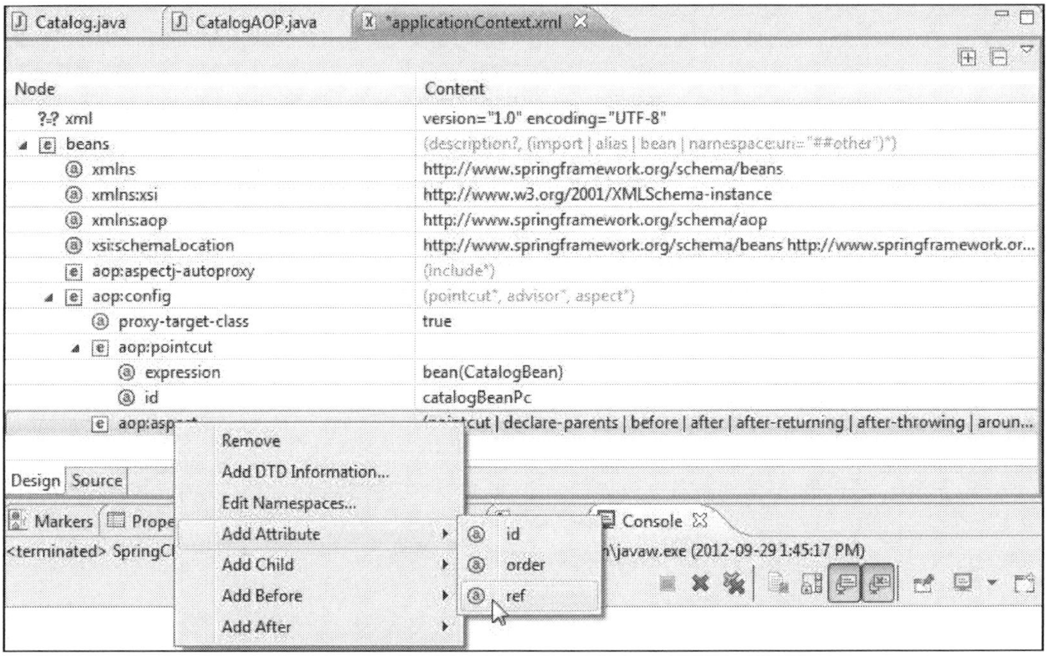

The **catalogBeanAOP** Spring bean gets configured as an aspect, as follows:

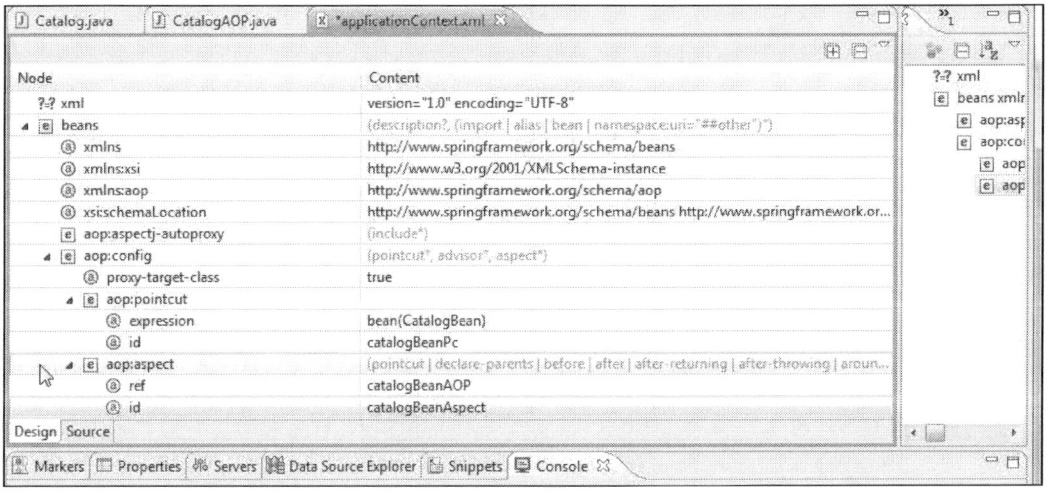

Next we shall configure the `after-returning` advice for each of the getter methods of the `catalogBean` Spring bean, which has the bean class as the `Catalog` JavaBean. Right-click on **aop:aspect** and select **Add Child | after-returning**. After-returning advice is the advice to be run when a method returns without throwing an exception.

To the `after-returning` element add the attributes discussed in the following table, which is just the advice for one join point:

| Attribute | Value | Description |
|-----------|-------|-------------|
| pointcut | execution(java.lang.StringBuffer getJournal(..)) | This specifies the pointcut expression to match a join point, which is the method call to getJournal that returns StringBuffer. |
| method | setJournal | This is the method of the aspect to invoke. |
| returning | journal | This is the advice method parameter to which the return value of the getJournal method is passed as an argument. The type of the returned value should match the parameter type. |
| arg-names | journal | This specifies argument names for the advice method. |

Similarly, add the after-returning advice for other join points (method executions are the only type of join points supported by Spring). The Spring configuration file with the after-returning advice for all the join points is listed, as follows:

```xml
<?xml version="1.0" encoding="UTF-8"?>
<beans xmlns="http://www.springframework.org/schema/beans"
  xmlns:xsi="http://www.w3.org/2001/XMLSchema-instance"
xmlns:aop="http://www.springframework.org/schema/aop"
  xsi:schemaLocation="http://www.springframework.org/schema/beans
http://www.springframework.org/schema/beans/spring-beans-2.5.xsd
http://www.springframework.org/schema/aop http://www.springframework.
org/schema/aop/spring-aop-2.5.xsd">
  <bean id="catalogBean" class="spring.catalog.Catalog">
    <!--
      <property name="journal"> <value>Oracle Magazine</value> </
property>
```

```xml
        <property name="publisher"> <value>Oracle Publishing</value>
        </property> <property name="edition"> <value>November-December
        2010</value> </property> <property name="title"> <value>Agile
        Enterprise Architecture</value> </property> <property
name="author">
        <value>Bob Rhubart</value> </property>


    <constructor-arg index="0" value="Oracle Magazine" />
    <constructor-arg index="1" value="Oracle Publishing" />
    <constructor-arg index="2" value="November-December 2010" />
    <constructor-arg index="3" value="Agile Enterprise Architecture"
/>
    <constructor-arg index="4" value="Bob Rhubart" />-->
  </bean>


  <bean id="catalogBeanAOP" class="spring.catalog.CatalogAOP"/>


  <aop:aspectj-autoproxy />
  <aop:config proxy-target-class="true">
    <aop:pointcut expression="bean(catalogBean)" id="catalogBeanPc"></
aop:pointcut>
    <aop:aspect ref="catalogBeanAOP" id="catalogBeanAspect">
      <aop:after-returning pointcut="execution(java.lang.StringBuffer
getJournal(..))"
        method="setJournal" returning="journal" arg-names="journal" />
      <aop:after-returning pointcut="execution(java.lang.StringBuffer
getPublisher(..))"
        method="setPublisher" returning="publisher" arg-
names="publisher" />
      <aop:after-returning pointcut="execution(java.lang.StringBuffer
getEdition(..))"
        method="setEdition" returning="edition" arg-names="edition" />
      <aop:after-returning pointcut="execution(java.lang.StringBuffer
getTitle(..))"
        method="setTitle" returning="title" arg-names="title" />
      <aop:after-returning pointcut="execution(java.lang.StringBuffer
getAuthor(..))"
        method="setAuthor" returning="author" arg-names="author" />
    </aop:aspect>

  </aop:config>
</beans>
```

The Spring configuration file in the **Design** view is shown in the following screenshot:

| Node | Content |
|---|---|
| ?-? xml | version="1.0" encoding="UTF-8" |
| ▲ [e] beans | {description?, (import \| alias \| bean \| namespace:uri="##other")*} |
|     @ xmlns | http://www.springframework.org/schema/beans |
|     @ xmlns:xsi | http://www.w3.org/2001/XMLSchema-instance |
|     @ xmlns:aop | http://www.springframework.org/schema/aop |
|     @ xsi:schemaLocation | http://www.springframework.org/schema/beans http://www.springframework.or... |
| ▷ [e] bean | {(description?, (meta \| constructor-arg \| property \| qualifier \| lookup-method \| repl... |
| ▷ [e] bean | {(description?, (meta \| constructor-arg \| property \| qualifier \| lookup-method \| repl... |
|   [e] aop:aspectj-autoproxy | {include*} |
| ▲ [e] aop:config | {pointcut*, advisor*, aspect*} |
|     @ proxy-target-class | true |
|   ▷ [e] aop:pointcut | |
|   ▲ [e] aop:aspect | {pointcut \| declare-parents \| before \| after \| after-returning \| after-throwing \| aroun... |
|     @ ref | catalogBeanAOP |
|     @ id | catalogBeanAspect |
|     ▲ [e] aop:after-returning | |
|       @ pointcut | execution(java.lang.StringBuffer getJournal(..)) |
|       @ method | setJournal |
|       @ returning | journal |
|       @ arg-names | journal |
|    ▷ [e] aop:after-returning | |
|    ▷ [e] aop:after-returning | |
|    ▷ [e] aop:after-returning | |
|    ▷ [e] aop:after-returning | |

Design | Source

# Creating a JSF page

In this section we create a JSF page to output the `catalogBean` Spring bean's
(`Catalog.java` JavaBean) properties. We demonstrate the effect of the aspect
Spring bean `catalogAOPBean` on the `catalogBean` Spring bean's properties' values.
Select **File** | **New**. In the **New** wizard select **Web** | **JSP** and click on **Next**. Select the
**WebContent** folder under **SpringJSF**, specify `catalog.jsp` as **File name,** and click
on **Next**. Select **New JavaServer Faces (JSF) Page (html)** as **JSP Template**. Click on
**Finish**, as follows:

A JSP, `catalog.jsp`, gets added to the `SpringJSF` project. In the `catalog.jsp` output the values for the `catalogBean` properties using the `h:outputText` element. `catalog.jsp` is listed as follows:

```xml
<?xml version="1.0" encoding="ISO-8859-1" ?>
<jsp:root xmlns:jsp="http://java.sun.com/JSP/Page" xmlns:f="http://
java.sun.com/jsf/core" xmlns:h="http://java.sun.com/jsf/html"
version="2.0">
    <jsp:output omit-xml-declaration="true" doctype-root-
element="HTML" doctype-system="http://www.w3.org/TR/html4/loose.dtd"
doctype-public="-//W3C//DTD HTML 4.01 Transitional//EN"/>
    <jsp:directive.page language="java"
        contentType="text/html; charset=ISO-8859-1"
pageEncoding="ISO-8859-1" />
```

```
<f:view>
    <html>
      <head>
        <meta http-equiv="Content-Type"
              content="text/html; charset=ISO-8859-1"/>
        <title>Catalog</title>
      </head>
      <body>
        <h:form><table>

          <tr><td> <h:outputText value="#{catalogBean.journal}"/></
td></tr>
           <tr><td><h:outputText value="#{catalogBean.publisher}"/></
td></tr>
          <tr><td> <h:outputText value="#{catalogBean.edition}"/></
td></tr>
           <tr><td><h:outputText value="#{catalogBean.title}"/></td></
tr>
           <tr><td><h:outputText value="#{catalogBean.author}"/></
td></tr>

        </table></h:form>
      </body>
    </html>
  </f:view>

</jsp:root>
```

To `faces-config.xml`, add the following application element so that EL expressions also recognize Spring beans as managed beans:

```
<application><el-resolver>org.springframework.web.jsf.
el.SpringBeanFacesELResolver</el-resolver></application>
```

The modified **faces-config.xml** file is shown in the following screenshot:

# Running the JSF page

In this section we shall run `catalog.jsp` to demonstrate the effect of the aspect on the `catalogBean` Spring bean's properties. Start the WebLogic Server, or the server gets started when the application is run. In the first run comment out the modifications, which prepend labels to the Spring bean's properties in the `CatalogAOP` JavaBean's setter methods, as follows:

```
//edition.insert(0, "Edition: ");
//journal.insert(0, "Journal: ");
//publisher.insert(0, "Publisher: ");
//title.insert(0, "Title: ");
//author.insert(0, "Author: ");
```

Right-click on **catalog.jsp** and select **Run As | Run on Server**, as shown in the following screenshot:

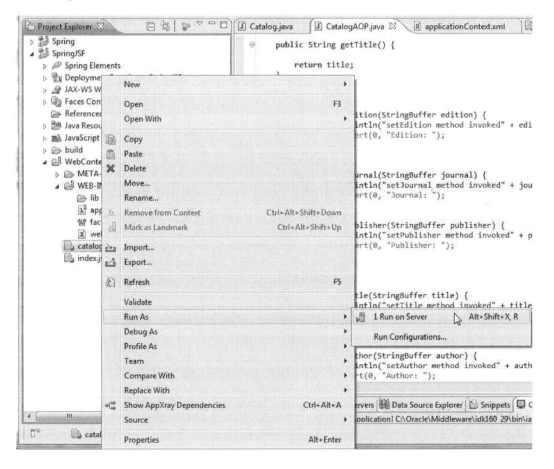

Start the WebLogic Server if not already started and click on **Finish**. The **SpringJSF** application gets deployed to the WebLogic Server. The server output shows (shown in the console in the next illustration) that the setter methods of the Spring AOP aspect bean get invoked and the `catalogBean` Spring bean's properties' values get output. Next run `catalog.jsp` with the URL `http://localhost:7001/SpringJSF/faces/catalog.jsp`. The `catalogBean` Spring bean's properties' values get output, as follows:

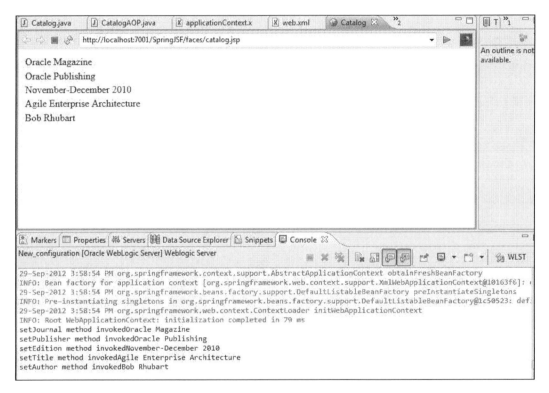

In the second run uncomment the modifications to the `catalogBean` Spring bean's properties' values in the aspect Spring bean, `catalogAOPBean`. The aspect gets applied and the `catalogBean` Spring bean's properties get modified, as shown in the output.

```
CatalogAOP.java    Catalog    Catalog ⌧                          Task List ⌧

      http://localhost:7001/SpringJSF/faces/catalog.jsp
                                                                 Find          All   Activate...
Journal: Oracle Magazine
Publisher: Oracle Publishing
Edition: November-December 2010
Title: Agile Enterprise Architecture
Author: Bob Rhubart                                              Outline ⌧

                                                                 An outline is not available.



Problems  @ Javadoc  Declaration  Servers  Console ⌧
New_configuration [Oracle WebLogic Server] Weblogic Server                                    WLST
<1-Oct-2012 12:33:37 o'clock PM PDT> <Notice> <Server> <BEA-002613> <Channel "Default[9]" is now listening on 127.0.0.1:7001 for
<1-Oct-2012 12:33:37 o'clock PM PDT> <Notice> <Server> <BEA-002613> <Channel "Default[10]" is now listening on 0:0:0:0:0:0:0:1:70
<1-Oct-2012 12:33:37 o'clock PM PDT> <Notice> <Server> <BEA-002613> <Channel "Default" is now listening on 2001:0:4137:9e76:808:1
<1-Oct-2012 12:33:37 o'clock PM PDT> <Notice> <Server> <BEA-002613> <Channel "Default[5]" is now listening on fe80:0:0:0:808:1eae
<1-Oct-2012 12:33:37 o'clock PM PDT> <Notice> <WebLogicServer> <BEA-000331> <Started the WebLogic Server Administration Server "A
<1-Oct-2012 12:33:37 o'clock PM PDT> <Warning> <Server> <BEA-002611> <The hostname "dvohra-PC", maps to multiple IP addresses: 19
<1-Oct-2012 12:33:38 o'clock PM PDT> <Notice> <WebLogicServer> <BEA-000365> <Server state changed to RUNNING.>
<1-Oct-2012 12:33:38 o'clock PM PDT> <Notice> <WebLogicServer> <BEA-000360> <The server started in RUNNING mode.>
<1-Oct-2012 12:33:39 o'clock PM PDT> <Warning> <Log Management> <BEA-170011> <The LogBroadcaster on this server failed to broadca
setJournal method invokedOracle Magazine
setPublisher method invokedOracle Publishing
setEdition method invokedNovember-December 2010
setTitle method invokedAgile Enterprise Architecture
setAuthor method invokedBob Rhubart
```

# Summary

In this chapter we created a Spring Framework application using the Spring project facet. We discussed method interception with a method interceptor and a Spring client. We also learned about **aspect-oriented programming** (AOP) in combination with JSF. We discussed creating a Spring bean, a bean definition file, and an AOP JavaBean.

In the book we learned how to use some of the Java EE technologies in Eclipse 3.7 using project facets provided in Oracle Enterprise Pack for Eclipse 12*c*. If another version of Eclipse or Oracle Enterprise Pack for Eclipse is used, some of the features supported may be slightly different and some of the procedures to develop Java EE applications may be slightly different.

# Index

Article entity
  about 28, 46
  creating 46
Article entity class 46
aspect 374
AspectJ 342
aspect-oriented programming (AOP) 342
Aspects module 342
association
  cascade value, setting for 31-33
Association Tables 28
asynchronous 253
Asynchronous JavaScript and XML. *See*
      AJAX
autocompletion 253

# B

band element 116
BasicTemplate.xhtml 204
bean class
  creating 381
bean definition file
  creating 353-365, 386-394
beanDefinition.xml file 348, 353
bindings file
  generating 302-304
build file
  creating 306-312
build script
  creating 65-67
  running 68-70
build.xml file
  about 64, 65, 275, 306
  property elements, adding 307, 308

# C

caching 374
cascade 31
cascade value
  setting, for association 31-33
cascading 31
Catalog entity
  about 28, 30, 38
  creating 38, 39

Catalog entity class 40
CatalogExcelReport.jsp file 121, 125
CatalogInterceptor class 374
CatalogInterceptor method 367
CatalogInterface 348
Catalog.java 144, 200, 226
catalog.jsp file 62, 63
catalog.jsp page 164
CatalogPDFReport.jsp file 121
CatalogType object 86
catalog.xml file 104
client class
  creating 304-306
columnFooter element 116
columnHeader element 116
commons-beanutils-1.8.3-bin.zip file 111
commons-beanutils-1.8.3.jar file 111
commons-beanutils-bean-collections-
      1.8.3.jar file 111
commons-beanutils-core-1.8.3.jar file 111
commons-digester-2.1.jar file 111
commons-logging-1.1.1-bin file 111
commons-logging-1.1.1.jar file 111
complexType element 85
components
  adding, to JSF page 151-164
config.jar file 121
configuration file
  creating 114-121
config.xml file 114, 121
Core Container 342
CoreDocument class 235
CoreInputText class 226
createJournalType() method 92
createMarshaller() method 92
createNamedQuery method 52
createStatement() method 271, 272
createTestData method 52, 61
createValueExpression() method 143, 193

# D

Data Access module 342
database table
  creating 134

PreparedStatement object 230
processRequest() method 266
processResponse() method 266
project facet 136
propOrder element 100
put method 122
PUT method 317

# Q

queryString element 115

# R

readyState property 264
remote business interface 57
removeEdition method 39
report design
  creating 122
reportFont element 115
report title
  setting 122
ReportTitle parameter 116, 122
Representational State Transfer. *See* REST
RequestContext object 220
resource class
  creating 327-334
  running 327-334
ResourceServlet 214, 220
REST 317
RESTful
  principles 318
RESTful web service 317, 341
ResultSetDataModel object 144, 149
ResultSetDatModel object 144
ResultSet object 144, 149
root resource class 327

# S

schema-based aspect definitions
  about 343, 374, 375
  AOP JavaBean, creating 384
  bean class, creating 381
  bean definition file, creating 386-394
  JSF faceted web project, creating 376-380
  Spring faceted web project,
    creating 376-380

Section entity
  about 28, 44
  creating 44
Section entity class 44
send() method 264
server
  web service, running on 291-294
servlet
  about 258
  creating 258-261
servlet-class element 261
servlet-mapping element 261
servlet-name element 261
session bean class 53
session bean facade
  about 49
  creating 49-51
  EntityManager, creating 51
  getter methods, specifying 52
  remote business interface 57
  session bean class 53
  test data, creating 52, 53
setBorder() method 193
setCellPadding() method 193
setHeader() method 143
setJournal method 52
setParameter method 53
setValueExpression() method 193
setValue method 143
setValue() method 144
setVar() method 193
setWrappedData() method 144, 194
SOAP 283
Spring
  about 341
  URL, for projects 341
Spring bean class
  creating 348, 350
Spring client
  creating 368-374
Spring facet
  web project, creating with 344-348
Spring faceted web project
  creating 376-380
staticText element 116

## T

tables
  creating, in Oracle database  15, 16
  entity beans, creating from  26, 27
templating  171
test client
  creating  60, 61, 334-340
  running  334-340
test data
  creating  52, 53
testData method  60
Test module  343
textField element  116
textFieldExpression element  116
title element  116
Tomcat  341
tr:commandButton tag  241
tr:commandLink tag  238
tr:document element  241
tr:document tag  235
tr:form element  241
tr:form tag  236
tr:group element  241
Trinidad
  about  213
  configuring, in OEPE 12c  214
  managed bean, creating  223-234
  UIs, creating  222
Trinidad application
  running  248-252
Trinidad components
  adding, to application  235-248
Trinidad project
  creating, in OEPE 12c  215-222
Trinidad UIs
  creating  222
tr:inputText tag  241
tr:outputText component  252
tr:panelFormLayout  235
tr:panelFormLayout element  241

## U

UIComponent instances  171
ui:component tag  172
ui:composition tag  172, 206
ui:decorate tag  172
ui:define tag  172, 206
ui:fragment tag  172
ui:include tag  173
ui:insert tag  173, 206
ui:param tag  173
UIXForm class  236
url-pattern element  261
user interface (UI)  133

## V

validateCatalogId() function  263
ValueExpression object  143
variable element  116
view declaration language (VDL)  171

## W

web application
  creating  121, 122
  creating, for AJAX  256, 257
  deploying  126-131, 277, 278
  Excel report, creating  124-126
  JDBC connection, creating  123
  packaging  126-131, 274, 275
  PDF report, generating  123
  report design, creating  122
  report title, setting  122
  running  131, 132, 279-282
Web layer  342
WebLogic
  web service, creating  288-290
WebLogic web service
  creating  288-290
weblogic-webservices.xml file  298
web project
  creating  319-326
  creating, in Eclipse  134-137
  creating, with Spring facet  344-348
  JAX-RS project facet, adding to  319-326

**Thank you for buying**
# Java EE Development with Eclipse

## About Packt Publishing

Packt, pronounced 'packed', published its first book "*Mastering phpMyAdmin for Effective MySQL Management*" in April 2004 and subsequently continued to specialize in publishing highly focused books on specific technologies and solutions.

Our books and publications share the experiences of your fellow IT professionals in adapting and customizing today's systems, applications, and frameworks. Our solution based books give you the knowledge and power to customize the software and technologies you're using to get the job done. Packt books are more specific and less general than the IT books you have seen in the past. Our unique business model allows us to bring you more focused information, giving you more of what you need to know, and less of what you don't.

Packt is a modern, yet unique publishing company, which focuses on producing quality, cutting-edge books for communities of developers, administrators, and newbies alike. For more information, please visit our website: www.packtpub.com.

## About Packt Open Source

In 2010, Packt launched two new brands, Packt Open Source and Packt Enterprise, in order to continue its focus on specialization. This book is part of the Packt Open Source brand, home to books published on software built around Open Source licences, and offering information to anybody from advanced developers to budding web designers. The Open Source brand also runs Packt's Open Source Royalty Scheme, by which Packt gives a royalty to each Open Source project about whose software a book is sold.

## Writing for Packt

We welcome all inquiries from people who are interested in authoring. Book proposals should be sent to author@packtpub.com. If your book idea is still at an early stage and you would like to discuss it first before writing a formal book proposal, contact us; one of our commissioning editors will get in touch with you.

We're not just looking for published authors; if you have strong technical skills but no writing experience, our experienced editors can help you develop a writing career, or simply get some additional reward for your expertise.

# [PACKT] open source✤
## PUBLISHING    community experience distilled

## Java EE 6 Development with NetBeans 7

ISBN: 978-1-849512-70-1          Paperback: 392 pages

Develop professional enterprise Java EE applications quickly and easily with this popular IDE

1. Use features of the popular NetBeans IDE to accelerate development of Java EE applications

2. Develop JavaServer Pages (JSPs) to display both static and dynamic content in a web browser

3. Covers the latest versions of major Java EE APIs such as JSF 2.0, EJB 3.1, and JPA 2.0, and new additions to Java EE such as CDI and JAX-RS

## Java EE 6 with GlassFish 3 Application Server

ISBN: 978-1-849510-36-3          Paperback: 488 pages

A practical guide to install and configure the GlassFish 3 Application Server and develop Java EE 6 applications to be deployed to this server

1. Install and configure the GlassFish 3 Application Server and develop Java EE 6 applications to be deployed to this server

2. Specialize in all major Java EE 6 APIs, including new additions to the specification such as CDI and JAX-RS

3. Use GlassFish v3 application server and gain enterprise reliability and performance with less complexity

Please check **www.PacktPub.com** for information on our titles